The Foreign Policy of the Third Reich

For Erika

The Foreign Policy
of the Third Reich

Klaus Hildebrand

translated by Anthony Fothergill

University of California Press
Berkeley and Los Angeles

University of California Press
Berkeley and Los Angeles

First published in the German Federal Republic as Deutsche
Aussenpolitik 1933-1945 by Verlag W. Kohlhammer,
Stuttgart, 1970
ISBN: 0-520-01965-2 cloth-bound
0-520-02528-8 paper-bound

Library of Congress Catalog Card Number: 79-149942

Printed in the United States of America

3 4 5 6 7 8 9 0

Contents

Contents

Preface

It takes some courage to attempt, at this point in time, a brief general assessment of the foreign policy of Nazi Germany. This is true even if one deliberately avoids providing a complete chronicle of the events of 1933 to 1945 and remains instead within the framework of an interpretative essay. If such an undertaking nevertheless seems worthwhile, indeed necessary, it is to counteract the danger of an 'atomisation' of history at a time when specialist monographs abound, by focusing attention once again, however tentatively, on the central political issues and personalities of the period.

But for the guidance provided by the studies of Andreas Hillgruber on the foreign policy of the Third Reich, it would certainly have been impossible for me to approach this subject. It was he who established the existence of Hitler's *Stufenplan*, the plan, that is, to expand German power in carefully calculated stages, first by restoring the Reich to the status of a Great Power after the defeat of 1918; second to further Germany's rise to a position of pre-eminence in central Europe; then to secure continental hegemony and gain 'Lebensraum' in the East by subjugating the Soviet Union; and finally to lead this 'Greater Germanic Reich of the German Nation' on the road to overseas global expansion. Hillgruber's discoveries provided the encouragement and the point of departure for my efforts to relate the intentions and actions of Hitler and the other German politicians and military leaders to the domestic conditions of the National Socialist era and to recent German history in general. My aim was to arrive at an interpretation of the phenomenon of National Socialism which would reflect the continuity and discontinuity in German history from the Kaiser's Reich to the 'Third Reich', by means of an analysis of the inter-relationship between domestic factors and foreign policy from 1933 to 1945. Professor Hillgruber (University of Cologne) was in fact kind enough to read my manuscript and provide many constructive criticisms. I am deeply indebted to him on both counts.

I am also most grateful for the help of two friends, Dr Volker Berghahn (University of East Anglia), with whom I discussed at length all the problems dealt with in this book and who also read through the manuscript with great care and attention, and Dr John Röhl (University of Sussex) who, after making many helpful suggestions about the original German text, expertly and selflessly supervised the English edition.

An invaluable aid to my work was provided by the study of Professor Hans-Adolf Jacobsen (University of Bonn), which attempts to show the structural basis underlying the formulation of Nazi foreign policy.

Dr Jost Dülffer (University of Cologne), Professor Werner Link (University of Kassel), Professor Michael Stürmer (University of Kassel) and Professor Hans-Ulrich Wehler (University of Bielefeld) were all willing to read my sketches on German foreign policy and make detailed and useful comments. It goes without saying both that I am sincerely grateful to all those who helped me and that the responsibility for the final result remains entirely my own.

The manuscript for the first German edition, which appeared in 1971, was completed in 1969. It has not been possible properly to integrate into the English edition the results of research published after 1969. However such works, the most important of which is General L. Weinberg's *The Foreign Policy of Hitler's Germany. Diplomatic Revolution in Europe, 1933–36*, by no means invalidate either the conclusions or the basic purpose of this book, which is to provide a synthesis between a structural analysis and a more traditional account of the historical events of 1933–45, in the hope that such a general interpretation of German foreign policy in the 'Epoch of Fascism' might point the way to further research on the history of the Prussian–German Reich from Bismarck to Hitler.

Bielefeld, January 1973   K.H.

Introduction
Continuity or Change in German Foreign Policy since Bismarck

The thesis of the primacy of foreign policy has been sharply disputed in postwar German historical writing.[1] It is now almost commonplace to insist that due regard be paid to the interdependence of domestic and foreign policies and that this is the crucial characteristic of modern historiography. Not least because of such theoretical considerations, a book on the foreign policy of the Third Reich requires justification in terms of theme and some initial reflection on method. This study attempts to sketch the main outline of German foreign policy from 1933 to 1945 and to summarise the state of research. Further, there are new ideas to be presented concerning the planning and aims of foreign policy, and the realisation and failure of these aims in the 1930s and 1940s. In so doing I hope to fill a gap in the otherwise extensive literature on the Third Reich, its Führer, Adolf Hitler, and the National Socialist movement.[2] However, I do not intend to offer a comprehensive history of diplomatic relations between the great powers. Such an account might seem to be a complete history of the Second World War and the years prior to it, but in fact it would merely be a descriptive exercise, which might gather the facts but would not explain them. And it is precisely explanation which seems to be what is needed today in connection with all research into Hitler's dictatorship in order that we may understand the phenomenon of Adolf Hitler, which we may 'reasonably regard as the most acute problem' facing the historian today.[3]

One way of reaching this goal, which at the same time allows us better to understand our present historical position, is to see foreign policy in the Third Reich as the climax of the Imperialist Age in world history.[4] This was the outcome of a European political system dominated by the principles of 'balance of power or hegemony',[5] and the culmination, or rather ruination, of the national history of Prussia–Germany.[6]

In the best traditions of German historical scholarship[7] thorough examination has been made over the decades of sources under the influence of a belief in the 'primacy of foreign policy'. This bias exists not least of all because the leading politicians from Bismarck to Hitler largely judged foreign policy to be the domain of the true statesman. We know[8] today how dependent a function foreign activities may perform and how they are sometimes made to serve domestic intentions quite directly. It is precisely for this reason that a look at the foreign policy of the Third Reich would seem useful—it will enable us not only to inquire into Hitler's 'ultimate aims', the planning of his party and the ideas of those conservatives who, first willingly, then with increasing reluctance supported him, but also to get down to the problem of locating the position of the National Socialist system and its Führer in the history of the Prussian–German state.

Taking as limits those dates normally adopted in reference books on modern history, our study will thus be concerned with the period 1933–45,[9] without attributing to these dates any importance other than as a conventional means of orientation.

Certainly, in the consciousness of many of those who experienced it, 1945 has gone down as a turning point in world history. The capitulation of the German Reich clearly ushered in the period of supremacy of the USA and USSR. From differing motivations[10] these two powers had already intervened in the political arena of the 1930s, even if this was not directly obvious to the majority of contemporaries, and Hitler had included both in the ranks of his opponents. It is true that Great Britain, one of the victors of the Second World War, remained at the head of a seemingly powerful Commonwealth.[11] What was clear, however, was that the events of the war had helped to accelerate the process of Britain's political and economic decline which had begun a long time earlier.[12] At the turning point of 1945 both the defeated Germany, the two parts of which very soon rose again to become middle-ranking powers, as well as the victorious Britain, which at the same time declined to a medium power, represented the waning of the age of European supremacy in the world.

In contrast, spurred into action through the course of the Second World War, the revolutionary liberation movements in the countries of the colonial and semi-colonial world intensified their efforts to gain emancipation. Soon, both the new super-powers which superseded the European system of power politics had to pay regard to the wishes and ideas of the Third World.[13, 14]

This sharp gulf, represented by the watershed year of 1945, the effect of which extended right into the life of the private individual, should not trap us into overlooking the fact that strong elements of continuity have survived that date. Above all, the 'new morality' in international politics,[15] so strongly demanded, indeed so hopefully awaited, has up to the present day quite clearly been unable to influence the course of world history decisively. In 1945, when the atom bomb was dropped on the territory of the Asian ally of the Third Reich, ushering in the nuclear age, the belief prevailed that war could not be regarded for much longer as a political weapon which might be used to force certain aims upon members of the international community. But hardly any consequences were ever drawn from this insight and neither was war banned. Instead, states now in possession of the most terrifying modern weapons continue to think in categories[16] which in principle have been familiar in European politics since the days of Henry II of England (1133–89), Philippe Auguste II of France (1165–1223) and Charles V of Spain (1500–58). In the shadow of the Cold War, the origins of which may be traced back into the war years, and American nuclear policy, the political leadership in the Federal Republic of Germany was getting itself established. These statesmen too thought (and to a considerable degree still continue to think) in political categories of a specifically German nature which remained determining factors from the days of Bismarck to the Third Reich. In the following pages we will come to analyse these categories. At the same time, however, we should not overlook the fact that the Federal Republic of Germany, playing only the role of a middle-

3

ranking power, will never again be able to intervene in world politics as decisively as was the case with the German Reich in the preceding epochs of European and world history. As a starting point for our study we should fix in our minds firstly that in 1945 the German Reich ceased to exist as an autonomous factor in foreign affairs, and secondly that in sharp contrast to the aftermath of the 1914–18 war, the successor states of the Reich found themselves reduced to the ranks of second- or third-rate powers. Finally, this date surely represents the end of the Prussian–German Great Power created by Bismarck in the 1860s through swiftly executed armed conflicts and in alliance with the bourgeoisie.[17]

The discussion about continuity or discontinuity in the foreign policy of the Prussian–German state seems still more problematic if we take a glance at the year 1933. In 1968 there appeared in West Germany an extensive and extremely well-informed study written by the political scientist Hans-Adolf Jacobsen,[18] based on a body of documentary material which could hardly be improved upon. This work seeks to give plausibility to the thesis that 1933 marked the beginning of a fresh chapter in the history of German foreign policy which was a new and typically National Socialist one. Hitler's 'revolutionary' methods, his activities in foreign affairs involving fifth columns, his foreign policy planning founded on a racist ideology, the agitation of the most varied groups within the state-party of the Third Reich and their not inconsiderable influence on the foreign policy decision-making process—all these elements, together with a policy which in its aims knew no limits, led Jacobsen to register 1933 as a break in the history of German foreign policy. In the meantime his bold theory has met with some opposition. With equally weighty arguments Andreas Hillgruber, for example, lays the accent on continuity in German foreign policy from 1866/71 to 1945 which characterises the 'road from Bismarck to Hitler'.[19] A task largely occupying us in our study will therefore be to follow this controversy, not only from the perspective of contemporaries, but also from a relatively secure retrospective point of view, and to achieve some clarification of the issue. It will therefore be impossible to avoid making use at times of the methods of historical comparison: political situations, aims and strategies of foreign policy employed in the Third Reich will be compared with those of preceding epochs. It will also be necessary to determine the differences and similarities by means of questions such as the following: Who determined the principles of foreign policy before and after 1933? Which interests decisively influenced decisions on foreign policy before and after 30 January 1933? Had German society, which formed the framework for the foreign policies which were pursued both before and after the 'seizure of power' in 1933, basically changed after this date? Which aims of foreign policy were envisaged before and after Hitler's take-over of power? In which ways did different German governments attempt to realise these aims? Were thoroughly familiar political paths followed, or was the attempt made to achieve the goals by adopting strategies of a predominantly adventurous and revolutionary kind? What ultimate status was attributed to the role of foreign policy within the society of the Bismarck era, of Wilhelmine Germany, the Weimar Republic and Hitler's Reich?

In order to be able to answer all these questions, it would seem helpful to paint in the historical background by reviewing the course of foreign policy of the Prussian–German state, without which it would be impossible to understand the events of the years 1933–45. Our purpose here is not to trace a line 'from Luther to Hitler' and to brand particularly the Prussian kings with their militarism and their policy of expansion as predecessors of Hitler.[20] It would seem more fruitful to restrict ourselves to a more certain area of research and attempt to explain briefly in the context of the history of the Prussian–German state those historical presuppositions to which German foreign policy in the 1930s and '40s saw itself subject.

In its precarious situation as a new Great Power, Prussia–Germany was faced with the alternative either of maintaining its position of semi-hegemony, in effect guaranteed only by Britain's goodwill, or of rising to the position of a world power. This option remained a vital issue for German foreign policy right up to and including the years of the Third Reich.[21] Shortly after the founding of the German Imperial Reich, the exposed position of this new member of the European political system was clearly revealed in the so-called 'war-in-sight crisis' in 1875. In reaction to this event, three strategies were developed under the Bismarckian Reich as possible options of foreign policy. Andreas Hillgruber[22] has summarised these alternatives systematically, and we will reiterate them here together with supplementary considerations because we will encounter them again in a more or less clear form when we look at foreign policy under the Third Reich.

Firstly, Bismarck considered the possibility of solving future crises in foreign policy which might confront the Prussian–German state by means of a so-called strategy of compensation. Borrowing the methods adopted by cabinets over the previous centuries of exchanging land and haggling over territory, Bismarck thought he would either manage to come to a settlement with France by agreeing to a partition of Belgium, or he would achieve peaceful coexistence with Russia (whose increasing size seemed far more threatening to the Chancellor) by contemplating a partition of south-eastern Europe (including, if the worst came to the worst, the Habsburg monarchy).

The second foreign political strategy discussed in the Bismarck era, and one which continually re-emerges in later periods of German history, was the concept of a preventive war, an idea which was aired within the General Staff and supported primarily by the ageing von Moltke. This strategy was to be employed in an international situation regarded as favourable to Germany, when, by means of a lightning military attack, a potential or probable enemy of the Reich could be defeated in order to gain room for diplomatic activities. Bismarck himself hardly ever supported such a solution, which to him seemed far too risky. For in view of the unstable domestic situation within the Prussian–German Reich, he preferred to know that the Army stood securely behind him and the Crown in the event of any future civil strife, and he rejected, therefore, the idea of risking the very existence of the Army in a war endangering the whole of the prevailing European social and political order.

Finally, it is necessary to mention the third choice, actually practised by Bismarck. It was a strategy later taken up by Bethmann Hollweg and, with differing premises, also by representatives of Weimar revisionist diplomacy like Stresemann. Bismarck's starting point was his assumption and pursuance of a policy which he regarded as defensive, its object being to guarantee the European status quo, to whose fundamental continuance, in his view, the social order in Prussia–Germany was bound. Starting from such a premise, he attempted 'to export overseas'[23] the international tensions within the European political system; he sought to stir up partly contrived conflicts on the periphery to divert and channel surplus and explosive energy away from the European continent. In Europe, the Reich was to continue to exist in principle within the frontiers created between 1866 and 1871—even if for economic reasons 'plans for Central Europe' were discussed.[24] At the same time, in the course of so-called 'secondary integration' (Sauer), the Reich extended its power overseas in an imperialistic way. In this way Europe was to remain protected from the war which to Bismarck's understanding—and here he differed in view from some of the officers of the General Staff—threatened to devour and destroy the social order in Europe and the Reich. The policy of overseas expansion, on the other hand, consciously launched by the founder of the Reich, supported this endeavour in two ways. First it satisfied the need to acquire sources for raw materials and new export outlets, necessities springing from the existing political and social order and the desire to preserve it. In addition, it helped simply by meeting the need, latent in the minds primarily of the middle class in Germany, for a 'new and dynamic' policy.

A fourth fundamental possibility open to German foreign policy,[25] and one which we will continually meet in the discussions of conservatives in the Third Reich, can be recognised in the policy of world power which was being debated already in the Bismarckian era and which found practical expression in the politics of the Wilhelmine Reich. It is not our task here to decide whether, as Fritz Fischer believes, the political aim of striving to become a world power unleashed the forces causing the First World War, or whether his opponents are right, who similarly acknowledge the postulate that Germany strove for world hegemony, but who nevertheless do not regard the policies of the German government in 1914 as having led to the war; they, Fischer's opponents, rather speak of war aims as those goals which Germany envisaged only after the outbreak of hostilities, which aimed at the establishment of Germany as a world power.[26] As far as we are concerned, what seems decisive here is that, in accordance with the Brest–Litovsk war aims programme (1917–18)[27] realised under pressure from the 3rd High Command and particularly Ludendorff, broad tracts of land lying directly adjacent to the Reich in the East and belonging to the newly established revolutionary Russian state, were conquered and placed under German control. In effect, these areas were to create for Germany the nucleus of a position as a world power—for the subsequent extension of the Reich overseas was also a settled matter[28] in the minds of the German imperialists who dictated the 'forgotten peace'[29] of Brest–Litovsk. The plan to achieve world power in two stages, first by creating the continental foundation and then by expanding overseas, which can already be clearly traced in the discussion on war aims during the First World War, finds its precursors in the Wilhelmine Reich[30] and the era of Bismarck. Besides basic power-political considerations, no small role was played by socioeconomic requirements in determining that, on the one hand, a central European solution in the form of an 'economic empire' was pressed for and, on the other (or as an alternative), that overseas colonial aims were kept in view. However, as a starting-point for our consideration of the shaping of Hitler's ideas and his 'programme', the importance of the peace of Brest–Litovsk can hardly be exaggerated when we bear in mind at the same time that the 'Eastern solution' of Brest–Litovsk was achieved in the year which saw the end of the war. With the involvement of the USA the war really acquired global dimensions[31] and for the first time in the history of the once homogeneous European political system, the Russian Revolution made quite plain the existence of social tensions on an international scale.[32] In Germany, total war found expression in the 'Hindenburg Programme'. The European nations were already becoming familiar with prisoner resettlement operations and the service obligations of the home population.[33] In the Western democracies, the political landscape was dominated by charismatic leaders. In Germany, there arose the Deutsche Vaterlandspartei (German Fatherland Party), an organised popular movement with a membership soon numbering more than a million, which had departed from the legitimist monarchical make-up of the Reich; demagogues like Admiral von Tirpitz[34] emerged to lead them. Indeed, in the south-east European theatre of the war, the Bulgarian allies of the Central Powers were already employing methods against the enemy Serbs which, under the name of Auschwitz, were later to shock the whole world.[35]

In view of the sense of triumph prevailing after the Brest–Litovsk peace treaty, and the fact that German troops were still standing deep in enemy territory, the German population, almost to a man, received the German collapse of November 1918 with feelings of incomprehension and deep humiliation. Only through the legend of the 'stab in the back'[36] did they believe they could explain the defeat. However, considering the situation from a historical perspective, in spite of the limitations of the Versailles Treaty, which were felt to be unbearable, German foreign policy in and after 1919 had a greater choice of possibilities open to it than it had hitherto had in Wilhelmine Germany or the era of Bismarck. For, backed up by an economy in structural working order, politicians responsible for foreign affairs in the Weimar Republic were for the first time able to shift and tack relatively freely between England and Russia, and could develop strategies which were meant to bring about a revision of the dictated peace of Versailles and Germany's rejoining the international community of Great Powers.[37] By employing an economic lever Stresemann, for example, adopting a government policy reminiscent of Bismarck's and showing links with the Wilhelmine traditions of Rathenau and Bethmann Hollweg,[38] attempted to win European influence and even gain an indirect economic supremacy for Germany in Europe.[39] At the same time, however, von Seeckt, Chief of the General Staff, was speculating on restoring 'the splendour and glory' of the dead monarchy by means of rearmament and armed conflict.[40] While views were being discussed everywhere on the respective chances of a direct military and an indirect economic option open to German foreign policy, a mass movement of the middle class who had been impoverished by the war and inflation, set about gaining electoral votes in the Weimar Republic. They believed they would be able to achieve this aim largely by demanding a 'stronger' foreign policy and hoped to offer their supporters not only economic but above all psychological recovery from the defeat suffered in the world war. This they wanted to do by means of foreign political alternatives to those policies of the 'parties within the system'.

Our study will first seek to examine which foreign policy ideas were represented within this movement on the nationalist right wing. Then in our analysis of foreign policy after 1933 we will go on to trace which ideas of this 'brown movement' were realised and which—significantly —were dropped. As was initially pointed out, our main purpose here is not to give a complete account of every event and occurrence in the field of foreign affairs in the manner of a chronicler.[41] From time to time, the telescope may well assist us in grasping the broad picture, so that we may then be able in other places to use the microscope when the process of decision-making has to be diagnosed and examined in full detail. It is not our intention to reduce German foreign policy solely to a matter of the decisions and activities of Hitler alone. Rather, the alternative options will be examined which were developed independently of, even in opposition to, Hitler by the Foreign Office (including von Ribbentrop, its Minister), by the Wehrmacht, above all in this respect by the navy under the Admiral of the Fleet, Raeder, as well as by the economic community (which itself included several groups with different interests). Even if these alternatives were never put into practice and were thus fruitless, they nevertheless belong to that totality of historical reality which alone can be called 'the truth'. To put it another way, and at the same time to extend the question in its practical implications, we must try to establish within the area of foreign affairs the nature of the connection between Hitler and the society which sustained him and at whose head he ruled and made decisions on foreign policy. Did he act in accordance with, and on behalf of social forces within the Germany of that time? Or does he confront us as a world-conquering dictator without a mandate or agreement from his society? And further: were there economic forces which have to be understood in terms of, and in connection with Hitler's Programme of power politics?

From such considerations it then follows—and this should have become clear by now—that we cannot write a purely political history, abstracted from social and economic preconditions. We cannot place such an emphasis on personalities as George Hallgarten has done for the Age of Imperialism. Nor can foreign policy be explained in purely economic terms, as Hans-Ulrich Wehler has tried to do so brilliantly for Bismarck's colonial politics—though here such an approach was clearly better suited to the subject-matter and was more feasible than in our case.[42] In the case of Nazi foreign policy, however, a further factor must be taken into consideration besides the themes of power politics and economic policy. This element which spans and relates both the other factors and which deserves attention as one of the motivating forces behind the foreign policy of the Third Reich is the ideology[43] based on racist dogma. Within the triangle formed by power politics, economics and ideology, it is valuable to analyse the foreign policy of the Third Reich against the background of the history of the Prussian–German nation and in the light of the central question of continuity or change.[44] In this way we may discover the explanation for the course and collapse of German politics. How does the ideological factor relate to the ideas of economic and power politics and their realisation in German foreign policy? Did the ideology, communicated to the public arena as propaganda, support the power politics in war and peace as contemporaries believed? Or did the ideology raise essentially irrational barriers, against which the realisation of a policy based on rational political deliberation had to founder. If this hypothesis were acknowledged as correct, we would have to ask whether this diagnosis of a power politics upset by dogma appears as a novelty in the history of Germany and consequently whether it is appropriate to judge 1933 as a break in the road from Bismarck to Hitler. Or did this phenomenon have its precedents in German history between 1866/71 and 1945 which would allow us, on the other hand, to talk of a continuity in German foreign policy from Bismarck's Reich to Hitler's?

1. Attitudes on Foreign Policy within the NSDAP before the 'Seizure of Power'

To win the electoral support of the middle classes, themselves eager for a nationalist restoration, one of the favourite methods adopted by the National Socialist movement was violently to criticise and denounce the foreign policy of the Weimar Cabinets.[1] But if we ask which ideas on foreign policy were represented within the Nazi Party (NSDAP—Nationalsozialistiche Deutsche Arbeiterpartei) in the 1920s—that is after the refounding of the party on 27 February 1925 up until the 'seizure of power' in January 1933—then we must first clarify the following issues.

It is one of the legends of the Press and history to imagine that the Nazi Party had a monolithic structure[2] and to conclude from this that even in the 1920s the Nazi Party spoke with *one* voice on foreign policy. At first sight the opposite seems to be true. As in all other areas of political life, the 'Führer Party' in the Weimar Republic shows itself as being an authoritarian-led anarchy in the field of foreign affairs too.[3] An apparent variety of opinions characterises foreign policy thinking within the Nazi Party. It is precisely this feature which constitutes the premise for a principle which ultimately became binding—the principle of understanding and regarding the decisions made by the Führer as a valid maxim of political conduct. It would certainly be going too far to regard this connection between apparent anarchy and actual leadership as a planned strategy on the part of the Führer, be it of an ingenious or devilish kind, depending on one's political colour. Yet it can hardly be overlooked that Hitler reaped the necessary profit both from the unavoidable differences inherently arising in a mass movement so varied and motley as the Nazi Party and from the feudings of his paladins. This advantage allowed him to rule relatively unhindered with increasing absolutism[4] later, in the 1930s. The infighting around him was the necessary precondition for Hitler to establish and guard his position as leader. Deciding the outcome of the various feuds thus lay increasingly in Hitler's hands.[5] He could make decisions and lead with supreme power because his lieutenants distrusted one another and never found themselves able to ally against him. For quite early on, it was the very myth of Hitler's leadership which gave birth to the movement and kept it alive. In the 1920s and '30s an out-and-out striving for power and the safeguarding of his very existence—'all or nothing'—were inseparable goals for Hitler. Both elements thrived on the food of permanent conflict and later found their logical outcome in the gamble in foreign policy over 'world power or downfall'. These consequences, however, were not so obvious to contemporary observers in the Weimar Republic as they are to us today in retrospect. Rather, to contemporaries, there appeared to be four different positions on foreign policy within the Hitler movement. First there were the so-called Wilhelmine Imperialists. Diametrically opposed to them were the revolutionary 'Socialists' within the Nazi Party. Towards the end of the Weimar Republic, a third group, the Agrarian Radicals, gathered around Darré, came on to the scene more and more. They apparently pursued the same aims in foreign policy as the fourth factor, Hitler, who in the field of foreign affairs also was supported willingly and in full faith by the essentially unthinking masses in the party and the electorate. The latter hoped to find release from the 'Versailles humiliation' and the social misery through the Führer's Programme. What is clear is that all these factions within the movement sought to gain influence in the shaping of Hitler's plans. But what will become evident when we come to consider Hitler's foreign policy during its implementation is that Hitler formulated and carried out his Programme while depending on the existing social order and even in a sense supposedly relying on its service, even if he did so unintentionally. We will have to forgo presenting in full detail here the various opinions on foreign policy within the Nazi Party during the so-called early phase of the movement from 1919–23, as this exercise alone would fill a book.[6] The points on foreign policy included in the National Socialist Party's Twenty-Five Point Programme, announced on 24 February 1920, must also be passed over. For the various positions on foreign policy actually adopted by different groups in the party appear more interesting than the compromise formula, that picture of vague wishes and conceptions, which is presented to us in that party programme.

To start with the right wing of the Nazi Party, we should first ask what were the ideas on foreign policy of the Wilhelmine Imperialists. Belonging to this faction of the party were representatives of that old group, largely made up of officers who had gained their most formative impressions during the years of the Wilhelmine Reich. Representing this wing within the Nazi Party were such men as Franz Xavier Ritter von Epp,[7] later to become Reich Governor in Bavaria and Colonial Minister designate in the 1940s, and General von Liebert,[8] well known from the Wilhelmine Reich as an enthusiastic supporter of colonialism and as a reactionary on the domestic front. They all dreamt of a restoration of the once mighty Hohenzollern Reich. They regarded it as desirable to regain as strong and supreme a position as possible for Germany on the continent of Europe. This they saw as the precondition for overseas expansion to win back Germany's lost colonies and to re-establish the frontiers of 1914. In the eyes of these representatives of 'Conservative Germany', but also in his own view, the most prominent member of the Nazi Party to belong to this foreign political grouping within the party was Hermann Göring. These adherents of a foreign policy aiming to restore the Reich understood both in continental as well as overseas terms, found support in large sections of the nationalist middle classes and in political pressure groups like the Pan-German League, the German Navy League and the colonial societies. Measured against the background of Weimar revisionist politics and the gamut of political opinion represented there, neither this faction nor its foreign aims seem to be extraordinarily original or typically National Socialist. Rather, in many aspects, they resemble the foreign policy maxims of the other parties of the centre and the right wing, like the DVP (German People's Party) and the

DNVP (German National People's Party). Men such as von Epp and von Liebert, representatives of imperialism in foreign policy and of reaction in domestic affairs, took the characteristic path from the extreme national right wing in Wilhelmine Germany to the Nazi Party in the Weimar Republic. What differentiated them from the official line of revisionist politics was the methods by which they hoped to achieve their goals. Whereas according to official policy the intention was to negotiate, they planned to rearm and fight. Whereas Stresemann skilfully used economic methods to achieve his aim, they persisted in thinking in military terms. In doing so, they found themselves in harmony with the chief representative of the armed forces, General von Seekt, Chief of the Supreme Command.

Only much later, after the takeover of power, did such men as Hjalmar Schacht,[9] Heinrich Schnee and Kurt Weigelt[10] join this conservative wing of Wilhelmine Imperialists. During the 1920s these men were still trying to accomplish their revisionist aims by essentially peaceful economic means, working through the parties supporting the Republic. Later, however, it was within the Nazi Party but in opposition to Hitler that they hoped to achieve their aims, which, compared to Hitler's Programme, were of a conservative imperialistic kind. In so doing, they became more and more closely allied to the Wilhelmine Imperialists.

In contrast to the conservative wing of the 'brown movement', the revolutionary 'socialists' within the party represented a completely different conception of foreign policy. We know from recent research[11] that the main group here was the working party of the North-west German Gauleiters, under the leadership of the Strasser brothers, Gregor and Otto, who stood in opposition to the Munich Party Centre. They demanded a socialism with nationalist leanings, but, unlike Hitler in this respect, had absolutely no intention of sacrificing the social or socialist demands in favour of the nationalist slogans. They planned to fulfil that magic formula of the combat veterans, that synthesis of socialism and nationalism[12] which Oswald Spengler had propagated in his essay on Prussian socialism[13] written in the third year of the First World War. The foreign aims of the Strasser group played an important and decisive role in this plan. Nevertheless, anybody regarding the numerous statements of prominent representatives of the 'North-western working party' and the various drafts concerning the field of foreign affairs would find cause for surprise. In some places there is talk of an 'alliance of the oppressed peoples of the world', among which was to be counted the German Reich. Yet there are other instances where the demand is made for a Central African Empire as an area for economic expansion for this same Reich. This striking contradiction can be explained, however, as soon as we look more searchingly into the dispute over the foreign political direction of the party, waged between the Strasser group and the Munich party leadership under Hitler. For it was in the altercation over Hitler's domestic and foreign aims that the socialist revolutionaries finally formulated their 'Fourteen theses on the German Revolution' in the summer of 1929, which clearly shows them in sharp contrast to all the other factions and their respective ideas on foreign policy. A decisive indication of this development can perhaps be found in the fact that the attitude of the 'socialists' round the Strasser brothers changed from one demanding an African Empire to a position rejecting any form of colonial or imperialist oppression. Furthermore, in 1929, they demanded an alliance of the subjugated peoples of the colonial and semi-colonial world, including a Germany exploited by the Versailles Treaty and the 'Western plutocracies'. But this development, which at first sight seems quite sensational, quickly reveals itself on closer examination to have had tactical causes. For the ideas which these leading figures, like the Strassers and Count Ernst zu Reventlow,[14] were now announcing in 1929 as their official programme—that the peoples exploited by imperialism should revolt against the capitalist democracies—were views which they had been supporting in principle since the mid-1920s.

But how could this demand for a colonial empire in Central Africa have come about, which was announced in such a decisive programme as that of the North German Strasser faction[15] against Hitler in November 1926? The group of the North German Gauleiters was concerned about the 'faulty development' of the Nazi Party—which was how they judged the history of this movement still in its infancy. Thus they determined to liberate Hitler from those influences, presumed to be harmful, which surrounded him in Munich and tie him down to the Twenty-five Point programme of 1920 again, which they regarded as the basis of the Nazi Party general policy. The third of the 25 points, however, affirmed that 'we demand territory and land (colonies) . . .' Although it was not at all clear within the party whether this meant the acquisition of land in the eastern region of the continent of Europe, or whether it meant overseas possessions in Africa, the Strasser brothers nevertheless understood this demand to express the wish of the party for a colonial empire. In order to adhere to the mutually formulated party line, indeed, in an effort to commit the errant Hitler to this original party programme and thereby to lead him back along the 'correct' path, the Strasser group, *par raison* but *contre coeur*, was forced to adopt the colonial demands too. They defined these in terms of the familiar wish for a Central African empire, such as had been discussed in Germany since the 1880s and which was well known to the German people since the 1914–18 discussions on war aims.[16] They soon recognised their mistake, however, and realised that Hitler would neither allow himself to be tied down to a mere paper programme nor did he have the slightest intention of compromising with his socialist opponents on their wishes concerning social, economic and foreign policy. Although the latter wished to win Hitler back onto their side, they never planned to overthrow him. From this moment in their conflict with Hitler, began the foreign policy programme which they were to maintain as binding right up to the split with the Nazi Party in July 1930 and subsequently, when they were in active and illegal opposition.

As a powerful state, the Reich should find sufficient territory for its people in Central Europe, but it should completely abstain from activities on the colonial level. Indeed, in their publicised support for the Indian people's fight for liberation, which continuously occupied the so-called Kampf Verlag newspapers of the North-west German working group, the difference between their foreign policy and that of Hitler becomes more than evident. Here we find enthusiasm for the uprising of the oppressed, and a hatred directed against Britain, regarded as the common enemy of coloured Indians and white Germans, as well as a bias towards the East and Russia, with whose cooperation they hoped to be able to assert themselves against the Western 'plutocracies'. On Hitler's side, on the other hand, we find an admiration for the British in their fight for the 'bastions of the white man' overseas and the desire to come to an understanding with Britain, so as to be able to overrun Soviet Russia. Together with their ideas on social policy, these differences in foreign policy contributed in no

17

small part to the socialists' final rupture with the Nazi Party in 1930.[17]

But soon there was another group within the movement, by now already powerful, who took over the role of opposition against those conservatives perpetually living in the past. This wing, round Richard Walther Darré,[18] the leader of German farmers, was not committed, however, to the notion of class but rather to a racial dogma, and thus they developed a different position on foreign policy from that of the Wilhelmine Imperialists. Governed by the 'blood and soil' ideology, the men round Darré contested right up to the mid-1930s the conservatives' imperialist plans for colonies, which they regarded as an indiscriminating 'pan-world policy', endangering 'racial purity'. The lot of the German people did not lie, they argued, in the acquisition of overseas colonies, which were well known and infamous for 'the squandering of German blood', but in the conquest and settlement of land in the east of the continent. If we trace these racially-steeped ideas of Darré's radicals back to their power-political roots, we discover that they were induced by their ideology of 'blood and soil' into seeking a union with Britain, in order to be able to conquer the land in Eastern Europe considered necessary for the settlement of farmers and the racial preservation of the people. Until these plans could be carried out, they were prepared to cover any demands made for raw materials from any overseas colony which might be acquired, but in principle they renounced every form of imperialism outside the European continent.

A fleeting glance at the ideas of these extremist agrarians united around Darré might mislead us into equating Hitler's central ideas on conquests in the East with these foreign political reflections of the Darré group—to which single concept Hitler's Programme has for far too long been commonly reduced.[19] A more exact examination shows, however, that Hitler's 'programme' is just as distinguishable from the policies of the Artamanen as from the Wilhelmine-tinged imperialism of the conservatives.

But so far as contemporary observers were concerned in their estimation of the Nazi Party and its foreign political conceptions, the following crucial conclusion can already be drawn at this point. Hardly any other party in the Weimar democracy offered such a wide choice of almost fundamentally different positions on foreign policy as the 'totalitarian' party of the Führer. By means of this offer, the party pretended to be just what each person at the time happened to be wanting, in order to win over the individual while remaining quite free from any kind of binding obligation.

Just what did the Programme of this man look like, who had developed more and more strongly from being the 'drummer'[20] of the nationalist right wing to becoming the Führer of the National Socialist movement?[21] In our analysis of the Führer's Programme, we will consciously limit ourselves to the years from 1924/25 onwards. By this time the formative stage of Hitler's ideas in the field of foreign affairs had come to a temporary close[22] and he was developing the essence of his conceptions in *Mein Kampf*—to take them up again and expand them in the so-called *Second Book* in 1928.[23] We intend to limit ourselves to these years because Hitler's remarks on foreign policy between the years 1919–23 seem far more conventional and indeed resemble those 'indiscriminate pan-world aspirations' of the Wilhelmine policies of the conservatives in Germany and within the Nazi Party, which he attacked so strongly in *Mein Kampf*. The Hitler of those years was still in fact dreaming of restoring the splendour and glory of the Hohenzollern monarchy within its pre-war frontiers. He yearned for the lost German colonies and still regarded Britain as one of the unquestionable enemies of the Reich. Only gradually did various motives and causes, different encounters and influences,[24] lead Hitler on to that path, signposted by anti-Bolshevism, anti-semitism and the conquest of *Lebensraum* (living space), to his Programme founded on racism and power politics. In general, the influence attributed to the White Russian emigrés in Munich and the *Protocols of the Elders of Zion* as motive for his anti-Bolshevism and anti-semitism are seen as having as much importance as the meetings with Dietrich Eckart and Alfred Rosenberg. The circle round the Munich geopolitician Professor Karl Haushofer, with whom Hitler came into contact through his later deputy, Rudolf Hess, seems to be responsible for the idea of *Lebensraum*[25] and its adoption in Hitler's Programme. It is common to attribute the change in Hitler's evaluation of Britain to the British attitude to the Ruhr occupation in 1923, so markedly different from that of France and Belgium, when, perhaps for the first time, Britain clearly applied the policy of appeasement and showed a 'friendly' attitude towards the Reich.

How all these factors influenced one another and interplayed in a complex finally evolving into Hitler's Programme,[26] indeed, whether it was considerations of racist ideology or of pure power politics which decisively influenced Hitler—all this requires further exhaustive examination. What can be clearly established, however, is that Hitler's 'programme' at the time, based on reconciliation with Britain and primarily directed towards expansion in the East, need by no means be regarded as peculiar or unique,[27] particularly since the roots of such ideas can be discovered in Wilhelmine and Bismarckian politics,[28] although now, admittedly, they were being taken up consistently and were being formulated into a programme.

What does seem spectacular in contrast to the demands of the other parties who pursued policies orientated towards revision, was what can be seen superficially as Hitler's 'renunciation of claims' on the South Tyrol and colonies—'renunciations' which in future were meant to prove advantageous within the framework of his Programme and which thus can hardly be regarded as anything more than temporary in this respect. For it was precisely this renunciation of claims on the former overseas possessions of the Reich and the naval installations connected with them that was to be the price paid for the British 'friendship' which Hitler thereby intended to purchase.[29] In alliance with Great Britain, or with her neutrality assured, Hitler planned afterwards to win mastery over the Continent. France was to be 'destroyed'[30] and Russia, 'the refuge of Bolshevism and Jewry', was to be smashed, in order to find the *Lebensraum*[31] regarded as necessary for the German people in the broad territories of the East. This central intention was meant to be achieved by means of a nexus of alliances brought about between Germany, Britain and Italy[32]—similarly wooed to friendship by the renunciation of the South Tyrol; and it was this goal which Hitler saw as his life-work. The forces motivating his ideas, however (racist dogma and shrewd power-political calculation), caused him to take into consideration further aims extending beyond this state of affairs into a visionary future, goals which were to be held in reserve as tasks for future generations. For reading his 'programme' as he presented it in *Mein Kampf*, the undeniable logic of Hitler's calculating power politics would alone lead us to the following question: when Germany, the master of Europe, had come to dominate the Continent completely (including the conquered territories in the East), would not the alliance with Britain become dispensable?[33] Hitler did believe that the 'friendship' between the Reich and Great Britain would for a long time[34] remain the basis of the political programme planned by him. Then, however, Germany would expand overseas from its continental base in order to support and enlarge its position as a world power through colonial possessions.[35] By this time, the Reich would be confronting the United States as a new and powerful enemy, to whom Germany, standing at the head of Europe, would have to 'show a bold front' in confrontation abroad and on the high seas.[36] These considerations of Hitler, stemming from the shrewd scheming of traditional power politics, were supplemented by a further factor which arose from the racist dogma in his ideas. During that long period of time when Germany, in 'friendship' with Britain, would hold supremacy on the Continent, the German Nation would be developing racially into the most superior people in the history of the world. This being so, the path to the mastery of the world could no longer be disputed.[37]

The interplay of racial and power-political motives reveals in principle three phases in Hitler's Programme. The first step, which presupposed the renunciation of colonial claims and the British alliance bought by this, was to subjugate continental Europe and Soviet Russia, thereby creating in Europe the nucleus for the position of world supremacy. Hitler saw this aim as his central task. Britain would certainly agree with his views on the Bolshevik menace and depart from her otherwise binding principle of the balance of power, and would accept Hitler's plan of waiving any claim to overseas colonies in exchange for a 'free hand' in the East. Britain would regard this as an agreement advantageous to British policy. As the second step Hitler then envisaged—either in alliance with Britain or in the face of British opposition—extending his efforts overseas and he set his sights on the consequent conflict with the United States, which could be conceived as a struggle between Europe and America for world supremacy. In accordance with his racist dogma of biologically breeding the German people to become a superior, Germanic élite, this power-political struggle for world supremacy, then, would quite certainly end in a German victory and with it German mastery of the whole globe.[38] All the power-political dynamism would thereby come to its end, and from then on there would no longer be a world to be conquered, only a conquered world. The racial supremacy of the German people, however, should then guarantee the permanence of this state of affairs: like a god, the new human being[39] would protect the world domination of the Germanic blood from all change. Thus world history would have fulfilled its racial purpose and, in culmination, the dynamic historical process was to fuse into the biologically static equilibrium of Utopia.

Despite this vision, which clearly and strongly influenced Hitler's thoughts, it is nevertheless worthwhile to pay regard to a characteristic difference between his notions and those of the radicals around Darré and the ideas of Alfred Rosenberg, who was his adviser on foreign affairs at the time. Neither the renunciation of claims to an overseas-based position of world power, nor the alliance with Britain bought by this renunciation, was regarded by Hitler as an eternal, 'natural' and radically motivated precondition for German politics. Rather, he attributed to these elements of his Programme a role of greater power-political and functional importance. Someone like Rosenberg, for example, in his 'Future Roads for German Foreign Policy'[40] regarded the fundamental principle of a separation of spheres of interest in the world between the land power, Germany, and the sea power, Britain, as a permanent factor. Hitler, on the other hand, was well aware of the inherent logic of power politics which would determine the course of world history for a long time to come, and he saw the British alliance far more from the point of view of a medium-term aim. He even talked of how the present sacrifice of overseas claims would help to make all the more certain the fulfilment of those goals of continental acquisitions which he regarded as the necessary precondition for an extension of power beyond the frontiers of Europe.

Today we know that Hitler's calculations on supremacy and world power concealed a decisive mistake. Britain, the vital key to German foreign policy and its expansionist challenges ever since the days of Bismarck and Wilhelm II and Tirpitz[41] right up to Hitler's time, did not behave 'according to plan'. Thus Hitler was forced, if we accept his view, to make the crucial alteration in his Programme, which in the latter half of the 1930s and the war years so compromised his original plan, spaced out in phases over a long period of time. This compromise was such that, in terms of his plan, we can already see well beyond the first, continental, stage on the road to world domination and can recognise the second, overseas, Atlantic stage. In fact ultimately, in July 1941, even the distant aim of the struggle for world supremacy seems to have been within reach.

Everyone, above all the foreign statesmen whom Hitler regarded as enemies, could have been familiar with the core of Hitler's Programme as published in *Mein Kampf*. Even Stalin, the leading statesman in that nation which Hitler had selected as his chief victim, was thoroughly acquainted with Hitler's thoughts after having studied the Programme carefully, when Hitler came to power in 1933.[42] How would the statesmen of Europe react to Hitler's foreign policy? Indeed, would Hitler be able to implement his Programme at all within the coalition 'Government of National Concentration'?

2. Traditional Demands for Territorial Revision as the Prelude to the Expansionist Strategy of the Third Reich (1933–35)

In January 1933 the coalition 'Government of National Concentration', a political cartel made up of German Nationalists and the National Socialists,[1] ostensibly set about rescuing Germany from the economic misery and the 'national humiliation' which was held to be responsible for it. For some time it was the domestic political issues which dominated the scene in Germany. *Gleichschaltung* (the imposition of political conformity), the Reichstag fire, the persecution of socialists, the Jewish boycott and the hunting down of communists—all these issues made the strongest impression in the first months, indeed in the whole initial phase of the National Socialist régime, during the period of so-called consolidation. Hitler and his conservative 'guards' in the Cabinet of 30 January divided the power between them. For that reason, during this period of 'partial fascism' up to 1936–37,[2] the Führer ought to be understood not only as an active leader but also as one dependent on his society and its representatives in the economy, the armed forces and the bureaucracy. Within Germany, the events on the domestic front were for the time being occupying the limelight; the internationalist left wing judged Hitler largely as the outrider heralding the conservative reaction,[3] one who would soon have done his duty and would then be sent home. But abroad meanwhile, the reaction of foreign countries and the expectations they held *vis-à-vis* the foreign political intentions of the new government of Chancellor Hitler varied considerably.

Relatively early on, by 1931, after the spectacular electoral success of the National Socialists the previous September, representatives of the public media in England—the country which was the central link in Hitler's intended alliance system—were already beginning to become interested in the aims of the foreign policy of the Nazi movement and its Führer. There was one problem in particular which preoccupied the British journalists when they came to interview Hitler in the 'Brown House' in Munich in 1931. Would the Führer of the National Socialist Party, as Chancellor of a German government, re-adopt those Wilhelmine naval, colonial and world-power policies which still remained all too fresh in the memories of the British? As already explained in *Mein Kampf* in 1925, Hitler elucidated again to the British his 'Basic Plan' for an Anglo-German partnership, and for British supremacy at sea, in return for which they would guarantee Germany a free hand in the East.[4] But now, in January 1933, Hitler stood at the head of a Conservative–National Socialist coalition cabinet. How would London react now? Despite there being the political programme *Mein Kampf*[5]—which admittedly had not yet appeared in English translation—there was probably hardly anybody who could make a safe judgment on the future course which the foreign policy of the 'coalition government' would take.[6] Even Vansittart,[7] the German expert and Under Secretary of State for the Foreign Office, went quite astray in the general judgment he made of Hitler's Programme in the otherwise most clear-sighted analysis he gave on 7 April 1934.[8]

As with the responsible politicians in Westminster, the view likewise prevailed on the Quai d'Orsay in Paris that, in spite of the complete dislike they had for the new men in Berlin, they should first of all wait to see which policy the Hitler Cabinet would in fact adopt.[9] Besides that, France felt itself to be unassailable behind the Maginot line. In accordance with a psychological need for peace shown by the French people, who were largely without power to act owing to social conflicts, French statesmen thought both militarily and politically in defensive terms.[10] This mood and policy was to a large extent influenced by the disappointing outcome of the Ruhr Occupation in 1923. For on that occasion, the United States had intervened and forced France into withdrawing, thus preventing her from achieving a political and military or economic supremacy over the continent of Europe.[11] At that time Britain, applying the policy of appeasement which was to influence the Westminster position more and more, also stepped in on the side of the Germans. As a result of the American policy of stabilisation which was of great benefit to Germany, the economic influence of France in Europe fell into strong decline, until indeed by 1925 she found herself reduced to a position of a certain inferiority.[12]

The third partner in the concert of Europe, who as a major power was supposed to play a decisive role in Hitler's 'new course', was Mussolini's fascist Italy, which for a long time was to continue looking down its nose haughtily at its ideological junior partner. Hitler's aim of a 'Berlin–Rome axis' was for the time being nothing more than a distant vision, for in Rome the Duce was keeping a watchful and jealous eye on the Austrian Republic and its continued existence.[13] For the economic dependence of Austria on the German Reich had only been prevented by the decision of a very small majority in the International Court of Justice at the Hague in 1931.[14]

The two great powers on the flanks, however—Stalinist Russia and an America racked by the Depression—hardly seemed of interest to Europe, nor, on the surface, did Russia and America seem very interested in the fate of Europe.[15] In Moscow, optimists thought that the fascist spell of the Hitler régime was merely the prelude to the transition into the communist mastery of Germany, while the pessimists forecast that Hitler's fascism would soon be followed by the openly reactionary dictatorship of von Papen, Hugenberg and Schacht.[16] Yet neither of these groups was ultimately in the right. For gradually, Adolf Hitler, 'the bailiff of Capitalism' won so much power that he was able to rise to become the master of his former 'stirrup boys'.[17] In distant America, at precisely the same time that Hitler was moving into the Chancellor's palace, Franklin D. Roosevelt was winning the election fight for President. The American capitalist system had run into a grave structural and economic crisis, and Roosevelt was largely occupied in restoring a new lease of life to it through his 'medicine' of the New Deal. Hitler and his Cabinet were likewise preoccupied with settling the economic crisis which was already on the wane in Germany. In the course of the 'fascist experiment' at finally overcoming the crisis, they regarded it as imperative to give top priority to rearmament.[18]

In the characteristic interplay of domestic and foreign policy is revealed the key to the foremost goals of the 'Government of National Concentration'. For all members of the Hitler Cabinet relied on the demand for rearmament. The officers under the Reichswehr Minister, von Blomberg, were foremost in advocating German rearmament—both for the traditional reasons of wishing to restore the political power of the Reich, and also for personal and professional reasons. The political desire for a strong Reich and considerations of economic benefits led men like von Neurath and Hugenberg to vote in favour of this idea. For ever since the 'Great Depression' of 1873–96,[19] it was well known in all western industrial countries, including the USA, that overseas expansion and military production were valuable and proven means of overcoming economic difficulties.[20] But the Reich would only be able to achieve overseas expansion and power on the Continent when it had built itself a strong army.[21] To create and arm such a force meant to overcome the economic crisis at the same time. Since socio-economic necessities thus played such an integral role in his concept, Hitler ultimately regarded rearmament as the most important precondition for his expansionist Programme.[22] Besides the army and the bureaucracy, the third decisive force in the conservative camp, the economic community with the mining and iron and steel industries as probably its most influential sector, also profited from the armament boom introduced immediately after the 'seizure of power'. This was particularly the case as Hitler, through the tool of the Deutsche Arbeitsfront (German Labour Front),[23] succeeded in raising the falling profits of the conservative partners in his régime by temporarily freezing wages at the level current during the time of the world economic crisis.

It already became clear in the first months after 30 January 1933 that the essentially traditional device of reforming and rearming an effective army was to serve Hitler in two ways. It would enable him to consolidate his position on the domestic front and at the same time it would satisfy the precondition for him to fulfil his expansionist aims. For the time being, indeed for a good part of the 1930s, Hitler's Programme was in principle to be in complete harmony both with the policy of the conservative Foreign Office—which for other countries embodied the calming continuity of the moderate Weimar government diplomacy of revision—and at the same time the demands of the Pan-German extremists of the Hugenberg mould.

Already in the first few days after the 'seizure of power', it became clear that Hitler was adhering to the aims drawn up in his Programme. In an address to the most senior officers of the Reichswehr, he expounded views thoroughly in line with his Programme set down in *Mein Kampf*.[24] Hitler said the most important aim was to gain political power. This would then serve either to fight for new export possibilities or, 'and probably better', to conquer new *Lebensraum* in the East, which would then be 'ruthlessly Germanised'. In connection with this, he described the present period of German rearmament as a dangerous phase of German policy. For it would now become clear whether France possessed statesmen who would be in a position to prevent this or whether they would permit it to happen. The typical attitude of Hitler in later years seems already to be apparent here, when he tests how far it would be possible to defy the Western powers. It indicates a basic characteristic of Hitler's policies: to hazard the political and military risk, while always leaving open the possibility of an immediate climb-down in the event of genuine resistance.[25] To complement these statements which are completely in line with the traditional power-political aspects of his Programme, we should take note of Hitler's corresponding statement of his plans to Admiral Raeder.[26] The Führer explained to the head of the German navy that he desired peace with Great Britain, Italy and Japan[27] and would therefore need the fleet only for continental purposes.

Thus, directly after 30 January 1933, Hitler set about bringing his plan into effect. He sought to do this under the shelter of the conservative policies of revision and in temporary agreement with both the Reichswehr and the German Foreign Office, which, under von Neurath, had in fact been trying for years to bring about a better understanding with the British—even if from motives different from Hitler's. In association with this disguised and secretly pursued policy,[28] the 'diplomacy by Press interview'[29] which Hitler skilfully and intensively engaged in during the first years of his rule also helped his activities in two respects. Firstly, the new Chancellor's declarations of peace deceived foreigners over the ultimately warlike intentions of his Programme. Secondly, as for example his conversations with Ward

Price,[30] the special correspondent of the pro-German Rothermere Press, indicate, it gave Hitler the welcome opportunity of presenting to the British—either directly or in a roundabout way—his offer of an alliance. In so doing, Hitler was steering a dangerous course between a domestic Scylla and a foreign political Charybdis. For he could not risk duping the conservative allies in his régime by declaring all too willingly that he would renounce overseas and military claims. These renunciations though were admittedly the familiar concessions to be made by the Reich to bring about the British alliance and in return the concession of a 'free political hand' for the Reich in the East. This position in turn—*vis-à-vis* his conservative allies—aggravated his desire to present in all urgency his plans for an Anglo-German alliance to London. For he could easily acquire the reputation among those in responsible positions in Downing Street, the Foreign Office and in Fleet Street of trying to re-introduce the Wilhelmine politics of world power, and it was precisely this impression which he was at such pains to avoid. Indeed on the domestic front Hitler did have to pay regard to the conservatives and their more or less clearly articulated revisionist demands. Yet despite this he gave far clearer expression to the chief element in his conception of an alliance system—his idea of reconciliation with Great Britain and the renunciation of German claims to world power—than the conservatives in the Reich thought good, particularly those who were organised in the colonial leagues.[31]

If at this stage we pause for one moment in our account, we can establish the following points. In the demand for rearmament Hitler's policy of planned expansionism was in harmony with the revisionist aims of the conservatives united round von Neurath, von Blomberg and Schacht. Rearmament was desired on the one hand to overcome the lasting economic crisis and on the other so that the aims of political revision or military expansion could be kept in sight. To this end and with ever greater disregard for the so-called turning point of the National Socialist 'revolution', Hitler conspicuously and significantly did not make use of the political devices of National Socialist institutions like Rosenberg's office, for example, which pursued policy on its own account.[32] Just as in the economic field he subordinated the established party ideas to the wishes of the capitalist leaders of the economy, so, in the area of military affairs, he decided in favour of the armed forces against the SA. Similarly, in the sector of foreign politics, he came out against the plans and methods of the National Socialist revolution in favour of power politics, which were pursued under the wing of the Foreign Office and which were temporarily linked to its policies.

In the course of a foreign policy pursued in such a traditional way, it was naturally of inestimable value to the National Socialist régime that Franz von Papen, one of the conservative ministers in Hitler's Cabinet, in concert with Eugenio Pacelli, the long-standing Papal Nuncio in Germany, succeeded in persuading the Vatican to sign the Concordat in July 1933.[33] By this time the 'Government of National Concentration' under Chancellor Hitler had gained the reputation of international credibility which the Führer needed in order to continue successfully. It probably hardly occurred to him that perhaps one or more SA leader felt himself to have been betrayed to the 'Roman priests' by his Führer. For Hitler had understood that his Programme, which would only acquire a new and revolutionary quality in the visionary future, stood the chance of being fulfilled only if it pursued those traditional aims necessary for the continued existence of German society.[34] He recognised that he had to follow the well-trodden path of power politics, though in so doing he considerably increased the normal tempo and did not shy at seemingly insurmountable obstacles. However, the fact that Hitler did not overshoot the mark, but in fact always thought first about consolidating his domestic position before seeking to make an offensive on the foreign political front, can perhaps be demonstrated by the occasion when Hugenberg, the Reich's Minister for Economic Affairs, appeared at the London Conference on World Economy in June 1933.[35] A German delegation under the leadership of von Neurath, the German Foreign Minister, was also present at the international conference, before which Hugenberg expressed himself in a sensational way which afterwards gave rise to heavy controversy. After a strong invective against Bolshevik Russia, the text of his speech, which was distributed among conference members, culminated in the demand that the German Reich should be granted overseas colonies to satisfy its demand for raw materials and that, in addition to this, possibilities of colonising territory in Eastern Europe would have to be accorded. Very soon it was being rumoured in international circles that this was one of Hitler's attempts to sound out international reaction to the German claims for revision. Today, we can assert with certainty that Hugenberg announced these demands without Hitler's direct authority and in a way running fundamentally counter to the thoughts expressed in his Programme, even if the German delegation and the Berlin Cabinet were in agreement. For nobody—not even the Führer—had contradicted Hugenberg and his plans in the preceding days and weeks. It was quite clearly Hitler's intention to avoid conflicts with the leader of the competing German Nationalists in the Cabinet. Now though, the chance was offered at home for Hitler to let his conservative partners stumble over an obstacle in the area of foreign policy, and thus finally bring about their downfall. Hitler seized this opportunity immediately. The Foreign Minister, von Neurath, had dissociated himself already from Hugenberg's sensational statements in the normal diplomatic manner.

Two trends in the conservatives' revisionist policy—differing tactically, though quite compatible in principle—thus become quickly apparent. On the one hand we can recognise the moderate governmental revisionism of the German Foreign Office and, on the other, the extremist version of Pan-Germanism, an equally familiar part of the German political scene since the turn of the century. But it was precisely because Hugenberg thought he knew and understood the wishes of the broad mass of the population and the aims of his Cabinet colleagues that he decided to present these to the world as the demands of the new nationalist government. Just as in the summer of 1911, in connection with the Second Morocco Crisis, the Foreign Office and the Pan-German League (as previously agreed, admittedly) impetuously pursued their different tactics only to come into conflict eventually with one another, each feeling itself betrayed by the other,[36] so now the storm burst between the moderate and extremist camps within the German revisionist movement. Hugenberg demanded satisfaction of the Foreign Minister and the Cabinet for the repudiation he suffered as a result of von Neurath's rebuttal. Just at this moment though, Hitler intervened in the quarrel on the side of his conservative 'watchmen' and achieved a convincing victory. Without in the least involving himself in the matter itself, which he regarded as closed, Hitler demanded that in future Hugenberg should engage four National Socialist State Secretaries in the departments in the Reich and in Prussia supervised by him.[37] In the meantime, however, the Economics Minister had already decided to resign and obviously only used this personal humiliation as inducement to leave the government. The German National 'Front',[38] which was already in a state of dissolution, thus lost its leading figure. Hitler, however, by way of foreign policy, had achieved a decisive victory on the home front; with it a further step towards 'undivided power' was now behind him.[39]

From the foreign political point of view, it may well be apparent to an observer looking back on this incident involving the impatient extremist Hugenberg and the cautious Hitler, that contemporaries in Britain at times seemed to be more in fear of the conservative 'Prussians' than of the obliging 'Austrian' Hitler.[40] It is true, of course, that the Führer did seek an agreement with Great Britain. But it was hardly the solution which the British were imagining at the time—the resumption of Germany's rightful place in the multilateral League of Nations—but rather a bilateral alliance between the two countries in accordance with his Programme. From this point of view, the decision of the Reich to leave the League of Nations and the Disarmament Conference of October 1933 appears to be thoroughly consistent. This step as much fulfilled Hitler's need for a bilateral agreement with England as it did the wish of the armed forces and the War Minister for rearmament. For von Blomberg was deeply involved in putting through the decision to withdraw from the International Disarmament Conference in opposition to the representative of the Foreign Office, Nadolny.[41] The next startling step of the Berlin government, the signing of the Non-Aggression Pact with Poland on 26 January 1934,[42] was also in accordance with this need to pursue a bilateral power policy outside the League of Nations which was so encumbered by the stigma of Versailles.

What motivated Hitler and German policy to turn towards a Poland which had been so heavily attacked by Germany during the 1920s?[43] Not only the general isolation of Germany in 1933–34, but also the 'plans for a preventive war'[44] against Germany contemplated by the Polish Chief of State, Marshal Pilsudski, shortly after the 'seizure of power', may well have contributed towards bringing about this improbable change in German policy. Pilsudski, in his turn, was persuaded into making a 'settlement' with Hitler not least of all because his proposals had met with such little support in France. His suggestion had been to overrun National Socialist Germany—this new factor threatening both France and Poland—by means of a 'policing action' resembling Cabinet politics of past centuries. The Quai d'Orsay was clearly ignoring all Polish feelers: in the East, Stalin's Russia was threatening Poland; and thus Poland, feeling itself threatened, and an isolated German Reich now came to a 'settlement'. In view of Hitler's basic blueprint and the emerging situation in foreign politics, the implications of this agreement between the dictatorships in Berlin and Warsaw became quite clear. It could serve as a possible spearhead against the Soviet Union or—if we bear in mind Hitler's speech addressed to the senior officers of the Reichswehr one month after signing the Non-Aggression Pact[45]—it could leave German lines temporarily free in the East, while in anticipation of British neutrality Germany could deal 'swift and decisive blows, first to the West and then to the East'. Thus new *Lebensraum* in the East would be gained and hegemony on the Continent would be achieved. By the signing of the Non-Aggression Pact, and in the hope that Britain would come to terms, Hitler would then be able to 'destroy France' completely in accordance with the Programme developed in *Mein Kampf*. But this step was merely to serve the purpose of subsequently turning to the East, be it in order to attack the Soviet Union with the aid of Poland— as we learn from the offer Göring made to Pilsudski in 1935 and from the discussions in 1939[46]—or be it to wage war first against Poland and then Russia.

The preparations towards the accomplishment of the first stage of Hitler's *Stufenplan*, the acquisition of hegemony on the Continent and the conquest of *Lebensraum* in the East, were now becoming evident. And it was not the revolutionary methods of National Socialist politics but rather traditional political measures and alliances which significantly determined the shape of Hitler's ideas and the steps he took.[47] Meanwhile measures were being adopted in the Reich against the Jewish population which corresponded to the racist ideas of National Socialism and which, under certain circumstances, might prevent the very approach by Britain so much sought after by Hitler. This fact already points to a later phase of events when Hitler's Programme foundered and the ideology and power politics ran into a conflict which could hardly be resolved. Yet the Führer still believed that he could convince the British statesmen and public even of the racist ideas laid down in his Programme. Or he thought he might be able to use the 'Jewish question' as a possible bargaining pledge against an obstructive Britain. But in the clash between power-political considerations and racist ideas, which as yet had not clearly emerged, there was one decisive factor: Great Britain herself completely disregarded the racist policy of the Germans in the formulation of her foreign policy. For a long time in the 1930s Great Britain, wooed in the traditional way by Hitler, paid primary attention to the foreign policy of the 'strategist' Hitler. While Britain did indeed abhor the racial policies of the Third Reich, she nevertheless regarded it generally as a matter of internal concern for the Germans. Perhaps this attitude can explain why, for example, the German Foreign Office could represent completely conscientiously the policy of Hitler as an attempt at revision and why, for example, the British Ambassador Sir Eric Phipps described the act of reconciliation between the Reich and Poland as a statesmanlike achievement for Hitler.[48]

The Führer seemed to have made a correct calculation. For officially Hitler excelled himself on the international stage with his good conduct. He agreed to Mussolini's suggestion of a four-power pact although he condemned it in practice. Thereby, he cleverly passed the blame of being an ill-doer onto France, who insisted on the Versailles decisions as well as on the binding implications of this treaty.[49] This was certainly another step in Hitler's aim of persuading Great Britain into the reconciliatory attitude of appeasement and of causing her to disown the French. It was not least of all this attitude of the British which led Hitler to work untiringly at laying the foundation-stone for his nexus of alliances and thereby win over the British. In Berlin, he presented his idea of reconciliation to the Lord Privy Seal, Anthony Eden,[50] and it was the idea of this alliance which led him to make Sir Eric Phipps the offer in November 1934[51] of limiting the size of the German fleet to one third of the British fleet. In order to be able to carry out his plan in stages, Hitler actually intended paying in naval and colonial currency. In so doing, he was able to count on an overwhelmingly broad consensus in almost all groups of the population during this initial stage in his foreign policy; above all, he could be sure of the support of the conservative groups within the ruling classes. For his rearmament programme was greeted with just as much support as the reoccupation of the Saarland was in January 1935 and the announcement of re-militarisation in March of the same year. Hitler very skilfully camouflaged the act of reintroducing military sovereignty from Britain and the world by claiming that the conclusion of the Franco–Soviet Pact in May 1935[52] had fundamentally changed the situation in Europe. This claim gave him the opportunity to adopt, without great danger, a course which had been under consideration for a long time. Slowly Benito Mussolini[53] also started making approaches to the German Reich—swinging into Hitler's camp completely when the Duce, under the influence of a group of Germanophiles led by his son-in-law Ciano, came to believe that the aim of 'restoring the Roman Empire' could best be achieved if Italy were on the side of the Reich. In contrast, the delivery of German raw materials to Italy during the Abyssinian Campaign (3 November 1935—7 July 1936), carried out against the decisions of the League of Nations, seems only of secondary importance in the change of heart in Rome's policy.[54] At all events, this act on Hitler's part was a test case for him to see how Great Britain, as the decisive power in the League of Nations, would behave were the Reich to oppose decisions made in Geneva.

Great Britain's reaction, or rather the lack of it, must have strengthened Hitler in his belief that London would eventually also be prepared to come to an agreement. Supported by the diplomats in the German Foreign Office, the officers in the Reichswehr and the representatives in the economic community, and carried forward on a wave of enthusiastic consent from the German bourgeoisie, and in part also the working class, Hitler seemed to have succeeded by the spring of 1935 in having satisfied the needs for revision integral to his programme of expansion. He seemed to have created the decisive conditions necessary for the announcement of further revisionist aims or for him to carry out the first stage of his Programme step by step. Germany had recovered its 'military standing' and was rearming on land and in the air at a rapid pace.[55] Italy was on the point of moving onto the side of the Reich. The agreement with Poland offered the opportunity of making revisions or expansionist movements in the West and, in addition to that, provided the precondition for a united Polish–German action against the USSR. Now the sole outstanding problem was to win over Britain, the keystone in Hitler's Programme—just as she had always been for the foreign policy of the Reich ever since the days of Bismarck. Hitler was offered the chance of direct talks when the British Foreign Minister, Sir John Simon, accompanied by Eden, visited Berlin in

March 1935.⁵⁶ Would the Führer now succeed in drawing Great Britain over to the side of the German Reich?

Primarily on the basis of the disturbing reports on the German Luftwaffe, the decision had evidently long since been made in Britain to take up direct negotiations with the Reich. Britain's statesmen were of course intending to achieve different aims in doing so than those Hitler pursued. Thus it became apparent from the Berlin Talks in March 1935 that Sir John Simon thought of bringing Germany back into the concert of powers in order to be able to bind it all the more easily to its international obligations. In these talks, the British Foreign Minister dropped remarks which proved to be most revealing for the shaping of Hitler's intentions and in his later political practice. And nuances so important for future developments, such as the comment that in Europe, Britain was naturally far more interested in the fate of Belgium than of Austria, certainly did not go unheard by Hitler. For his part, Hitler presented his plan for an Anglo–German agreement, even if in a diplomatically cloaked manner. What he could not do was to give even the slightest hint of the intentions behind this agreement —those expansionist aims in the East of Europe. The discussion went to and fro until at one point in the negotiations and in a flash, as it were, a new weapon in Hitler's political moves with the British suddenly emerged. It was soon to supersede the phase of mutual exchange where on the one hand the Reich would renounce its colonial and maritime claims in exchange for the expected alliance with Britain on the other, and with it the British concession of allowing Hitler a free hand in his policy towards the East. For at Simon's suggestion that the Reich might return to the League of Nations, Hitler demonstrated for the first time the tool of colonial threats. From now on, it would no longer be the renouncing of revisionist plans overseas which was to bring Britain on to Germany's side. It would be the raising of colonial demands in an increasingly threatening way which was intended to make Britain amenable. Hitler thus told Simon and Eden that as a precondition for Germany's re-entry into the League of Nations, the Reich's claim for revisions on the colonial level would have to be met. The tactical intentions behind this shrewd turn-about of Hitler's can be derived not only from the considerations in his Programme. They can also be clearly demonstrated in the fact that, both in March 1935 and in the following years, Hitler basically avoided all demands to realise German colonial desires in concrete terms, in order to hold this card in his hand. For the first time, Hitler had revealed that weapon he thought would be so useful in his future exchanges with London, the tool which he produced time and time again to blackmail the British into 'friendship'.

Talking to von Ribbentrop, Hitler expressed optimism over the chances he envisaged for the dialogue now initiated with the British Foreign Minister. In London meanwhile, Sir John Simon was being far more sceptical in the report he gave to the British Parliament. The source of the Anglo–German misunderstanding in the 1930s here becomes evident. On the one hand there was Hitler's belief that he could reach a bilateral agreement which would then enable him to conduct 'regionally' limited wars. He then believed he could achieve what was for the time being the primary goal of creating German hegemony in Europe and acquiring *Lebensraum*. On the other hand, the British wished to draw Germany into a multilateral system, in order to preserve the peace and maintain in principle the status quo in Europe and the world. But Hitler planned to win the British over to his 'common-sense solution' and achieve the alliance with her—whether by renouncing colonial demands or by using such demands as a threat against Britain. After his first experience of British statesmen, would Hitler's next big step, the naval pact, bring him towards his desired goal?

3. In Search of an Alliance with Britain (1935–37)

The Stresa Conference[1] in April 1935, attended by the heads of government of Britain, France and Italy, condemned Germany's conduct in re-introducing general conscription. It also declared itself against the unilateral renunciation of treaties. However much of a stir this declaration might have caused, it nevertheless could not prevent Hitler from continuing to follow unperturbed the path he had already adopted towards 'reconciliation' with Britain. At a time when rearmament was being stepped up intensively in Germany,[2] Hitler named his foreign political adviser, von Ribbentrop,[3] as special Minister Plenipotentiary for the German Reich. In so doing Hitler made what he saw as the important choice of appointment needed to bring the forthcoming naval negotiations with the British in London to a conclusion favourable to Germany. This would form, Hitler supposed, a promising prelude to further agreements between the two powers.

The Anglo–German Naval Pact of 18 June 1935[4] fixed the relative strengths of the German and British fleets at the ratio of 35 to 100 respectively, with submarine strength at parity. The date indeed marked a great foreign political triumph for von Ribbentrop. His first dealings with the British Foreign Minister, Sir John Simon, had led Hitler to threaten political sanctions in the colonial field. But now von Ribbentrop had apparently managed to compromise in an obviously generous way with the British in the naval area which was of such importance to Britain, and Britain seemed prepared to accept the policy of separate spheres of interest which Hitler had in view. The success of von Ribbentrop's London negotiations and above all the Führer's more wide-reaching expectations ensuing from it, may well have made 18 June—the date of the signing and the anniversary of Waterloo—'the happiest day' of Hitler's life.[5] And yet, in the very hour of triumph there was also disappointment regarding the prospect of a further agreement with London. For von Ribbentrop must certainly have reported to his Führer the reticence of Sir Samuel Hoare, who had just been named the new Foreign Minister, and the cool attitude of Sir Robert Vansittart, whom the German dictator's Special Envoy met in London during the negotiations or after the signing of the agreement. For there was hardly any talk on the British side of wishing to come to an agreement with Hitler along the lines of the mutual alliance proposed in Hitler's plans. Despite von Ribbentrop's successful mission and the completion of the Naval Agreement, Hitler's blueprint on bilateral lines and the multi-lateral policy of the British stood in irreconcilable opposition.[6] Obviously British readiness to adopt the policy of appeasement did not—as yet—go as far as Hitler's Programme had anticipated. Yet for the time being the delaying, reserved attitude of the British only spurred Hitler on all the more to increase his friendly wooing of Britain and indeed to fight for an alliance with her. After the preliminary concessions made in the field of naval armament, there now remained to Hitler chiefly the weapon of colonial sanctions, that is of pretending to make overseas demands in order to render the stubborn British more amenable.

In tune with this policy of wooing Britain with menaces, new orders were made soon after the conclusion of the London naval negotiations which had caused such a world-wide stir. The directive went out to von Ribbentrop that in view of the cool attitude of British politicians towards the more far-reaching proposals of the Germans between 18 June and 3 July 1935, he should set up a Reich Colonial Association with a central organisation and above all a National Socialist orientation.[7] From this time on it was von Ribbentrop who, under the Führer's orders, had 'responsibility for the whole of colonial policy'. It was not the economic pressure of groups in the German economy interested in colonial business who forced Hitler into this step, although it cannot be ignored that this decision did meet their wishes, particularly in a psychological respect. One important factor was von Ribbentrop's personal ambition. In the administrative anarchy of the Third Reich he hoped to win power through the *Gleichschaltung* of the conservative colonial associations which had continued to exist as in the Weimar Republic. Indeed, in von Ribbentrop's assumption of this task we can perhaps already see a sign of the 'conception' which the later Foreign Minister was to adopt in departing from Hitler's Programme. For von Ribbentrop's idea was on the one hand to act according to Hitler's blueprint, while on the other to pursue a thoroughly classical policy of revisionism, chiefly in the area of colonial affairs. Nevertheless, in the complex network of domestic and economic, party and foreign politics, one thing cannot be overlooked. With the *Gleichschaltung* of the colonial associations into the Reich Colonial Association, the Führer had placed in readiness a tool which could later be used against the British. As an expression of German 'public opinion', this instrument could be presented as a threat at any time in the future when Hitler announced colonial demands and tied the British down to his Programme. Indeed quite soon after Hitler's disappointment over the continuing negative attitude of the British to his endeavours to achieve agreement, the Reich Colonial Association stepped beyond its role of merely serving 'high-level politics'. From now on it also served as an instrument in preparing for the expansionist phase of the Programme which was to follow upon the continental plans. For the strategic aims overseas which had once lain in the distant and visionary future were now slipping closer into reach. But over and above this, it was precisely through the incorporation of this overseas element into his foreign policy that Hitler met the wishes and needs of the political and economic groups in Germany whom he, standing at the head of the state, represented, and who for political, economic and psychological motives were demanding colonial territory for the Reich. Thus Hitler could integrate this class of German society and the demands they made into his Programme by subordinating them to his own ideas on foreign policy, since the most important element in the Programme—continental priority and the purely tactical use of colonial demands—was hardly recognised. And it was precisely this finesse of the Führer which enabled him to win over the German public even more decisively to his policy and, 'waving this colonial weapon in his hand', to initiate on the foreign political front the menacing fight for—not against—Britain.

Besides the Anglo–German relations which were the main concern of German foreign policy in the autumn of 1935, the Abyssinian war offered Hitler the opportunity of supporting Mussolini[8] and enabled him to prepare the way towards the coalition between the Reich and Italy. By the end of 1935 the British seemed basically the only nation still opposing the realisation of Hitler's complex of alliances. But very soon Hitler's new tactics of applying threatening sanctions became quite apparent, when, on 13 December 1935, Sir Eric Phipps, the British Ambassador in Berlin, turned discussions to the question of arms limitation, the theme arousing such a burning interest in Britain, and specifically to the subject of the Anglo–French proposal for an air pact with the Reich. This, of course, touched on a topic over which Hitler was hardly prepared to make concessions. For, as we have already seen, rearmament played an integral part in his programme of expansion, and was in turn serving to cure the economic crisis. Again, it was probably the colonial 'mine' which Hitler cunningly laid which was used to sink this inconvenient offer from the Western powers.[9] For in principle both London and Paris were still concerned to avoid using colonies as currency in their negotiations with the Reich. This attitude was very soon to change, but without the West being able to alter the course of events. In the West though, there was too little awareness that Hitler was merely using the colonial problem tactically as a tool for blackmail and was not—yet—regarding it as a long-term aim worth striving for. Nevertheless, in his talks with the former British Aviation Minister, Lord Londonderry,[10] on 5 February 1936, Hitler announced the demand for a return of two former colonies to the Reich. This claim, made in the face of the constant refusal of the British, now seems to have been conceived for the first time in more concrete terms, and perhaps, seen in retrospect, it gives us an initial glimpse into a long-term goal in Africa.[11]

In any case, from now on, Hitler no longer made a complete renunciation of colonies in the pursuit of the 'exchange deal' originally intended, as he had in the 1920s and the beginning of his régime. He was continually making new overseas demands, which, going beyond his prevailing tactical viewpoint, perhaps offer some insight into the changing shape of his ideas, which in the meantime had been altering in relation to his 'programme' of the 1920s. For hints are now emerging of the ambivalent course he was adopting towards Britain. Some 'modest' demands already show a glimpse of the overseas aims which, without Hitler having worried personally about it very much, answered an economic and, particularly, a psychological need felt within those leading groups within Germany such as Hjalmar Schacht represented. Soon, besides the purely economic demands which the plan for peaceful expansionist moves overseas contained, these groups discovered in it a possible political alternative to Hitler's aggressive plans for the Continent.[12]

Yet the chief aims of the Führer lay a long way from Africa, and for the time being did not even lie in the East of the European continent, but rather on the very frontiers of the Reich. While both London and Paris were expecting Germany soon to raise a claim on Lome, Duala and Dar es Salaam, Hitler, the armed forces and the German Foreign Office were aiming their sights at Cologne, Mainz and Coblenz—the goals of traditional revisionist policy, which lay close to the hearts of the majority of Germans. One month before the coup of the 'Rhine Overture',[13] the chiefs of the armed forces and the Foreign Office were given instructions. On 21 February 1936, in a skilful interview with the French journalist Bertrand de Jouvenel, the German dictator spoke of the German peace policy, of the common danger of Bolshevism and the folly of the traditional enmity between the French and German peoples.[14] On 7 March 1936 German troops entered the demilitarised zone of the Rhineland.[15]

We do not want to trace here all the events in detail, or examine, for example, the position of the French, who, though in possession of information on the impending intervention, were unable to decide on any counter-measures. Nevertheless, some of the characteristics of the affair, in which the conservative revisionism of the generals and diplomats coincided with Hitler's expansionist plans, do seem to be typical. In this weekend coup we find an instance of lightning attack, the element of surprise, as well as the idea that, in the event of the mission failing—that is, the Western powers resisting resolutely—there would be an equally rapid withdrawal in order to secure the continued existence of the new Wehrmacht and the Hitler régime. Significantly enough it is supposed to have been von Neurath who advised Hitler against withdrawing when, in a decisive moment in the Rhineland venture, the latter was nervously contemplating it. Von Neurath advised that he should first wait for a time and leave the troops in the demilitarised zone. But the second, perhaps equally decisive feature in the undertaking was the test-case element of the venture. How would Great Britain react in the face of a German move, using force, to revise the frontiers imposed on Germany at Versailles? From the point of view of Hitler, von Ribbentrop and the Foreign Office, London responded as favourably as could have been wished under the existing conditions. For the British Foreign Office confined itself to a written protest. London did not contemplate a military intervention, since 'British interests' in Europe and the world were hardly impinged upon. But France's political and military freedom of action was thereby restricted, for it was one of its principles not to take the offensive without the support of its former Entente partner.

Just like the planning and execution of this lightning blow itself, the epilogue to the successful adventure is equally characteristic of Hitler's policy, carried out in harmony with the military and the diplomatic corps. In Hitler's great 'peace speech' of 7 March 1936,[16] he generously suggested making non-aggression pacts and, praising multi-lateral agreements, offered to withdraw from the Rhineland in the event that France likewise withdrew a corresponding distance from the common border. Ward Price, the correspondent for the Rothermere newspapers, came to hear about the same intentions on 11 March 1936.[17] However, the English could certainly not have failed to observe the fact that Hitler, precisely in connection with his speech about the 'Rhine Overture', had for the first time officially raised the demand for colonial revisions[18] before the whole world. The Führer thought he had found in this policy the very key which would make the British statesmen receptive and amenable to his ideas. From now on, the theme of colonial revisions menacingly supplied the background to every continental crisis. Very soon afterwards Hitler must indeed have been beginning to feel confirmed in his tactics of pretending to threaten Britain in the colonial and the naval sectors. For when in May 1936 the keels were laid for five instead of the three planned A-cruisers in the Reich, the British reaction was almost as vigorous and enraged as it had been in connection with the German occupation of the Rhineland.[19] Britain—or so it must have appeared to Hitler—was reacting sharply in the naval and colonial field and—as the Rhineland experiment had demonstrated—was clearly prepared to respond neutrally towards German ventures on the Continent. Would Hitler's plan for an 'exchange deal' and alliance with Britain, presented in a slightly altered form and under the banner of a 'strong' German policy, still be attainable after all? And in view of Britain's not coming round to a major alliance, but rather shrinking back in fear, was the Führer not bound to get other ideas soon? Perhaps after the ventures still facing him in Europe he would decide to extend his activities overseas, in the shadow of the neutrality of the British arising from her political and military weakness?

It was not only in the field of foreign affairs that Hitler's plan seemed to be succeeding. On the domestic scene too, his reputation was rising to almost unlimited heights. Certainly, the middle classes had to put up with the vulgar behaviour of some of the party bigwigs; to be sure, the racial dogma of the National Socialists displeased some of the nationalist establishment. But Hitler's policy of revisionism satisfied their desires for national recovery, just as it suited the economic interests of a bourgeois society dependent on permanent industrial growth. Everyone knew perfectly well that it had been Hitler, his Programme and National Socialism which, in 1933, had saved the business market—the symbol of a property-owning social order which was feeling itself to be in mortal danger.[20] This they knew, even though as tribute for the continued existence of that order they had to hoist the Swastika flag and realised that one day this temporary rescue might be followed by the final elimination of this social order through its transformation into a régime based on race. But for the time being and for a long time into the war, racial dogma and the National Socialist system (which would be wrongly described, however, as 'mere ideology') served to preserve the existing order. The slogans about the new world merely provided the ideological cosmetic, lending the old profile more friendly and attractive lines.

In the Germany of 1936, Hitler's rule of 'partial fascism' in partnership with the captains of industry, among others, was moving into 'full fascism' which became established as the economic partners fell under the domination of the Führer and the Nazi Party.[21] It was precisely in the weeks and months of that year that Hjalmar Schacht, as a representative of the 'liberal conservatives', increased his activities along the lines of a peaceful economic expansionism in the face of the régime's increasingly determined course towards war. But Hitler pushed ahead with rearmament[22] and continued his intensive wooing of Britain. Furthermore, he was already clearly taking Japan, the third partner in the future 'Rome–Berlin–Tokyo political triangle', into his political considerations[23]—apparently without feeling that the yellow skins of that alien race would hamper his traditionally orientated power policy.[24] In his talks with the Japanese military attaché Oshima on 22 July 1936, one can already detect hints of what the Führer was to say to the same man five years later about Russia; for in 1936 there was already talk about Russia having to be divided up into its historic parts.[25] Of course, with regard to world opinion, the anti-Bolshevik, that is, the ideological point of the Anti-Comintern Pact concluded on 25 November 1936[26] was not to be overlooked. But on the other hand Hitler's political calculations and his evident preoccupation with the idea of a coordinated operation against Russia should not be underestimated. The three revisionist 'have-nots' in world politics, imperial Japan, fascist Italy and National Socialist Germany, were setting about dividing up the world anew. Japan had taken the lead in 1931, seeking its territory on the adjacent mainland of Asia. Italy was conquering its *spazio vitale* on the African continent in Ethiopia. What would Hitler's next step be?

On 17 July 1936, a revolt broke out in Spanish Morocco with generals making a putsch against the government in the homeland in order to further the demands of reaction. One week later, Hitler, staying in Bayreuth, received a letter from General Franco brought to him by a representative of the National Socialist foreign department,[27] whereupon the Führer immediately affirmed his help for Franco in the Civil War. The German Foreign Office was at a loss over this decision of Hitler's. For the first time the revisionist aims of the traditional authorities and the Dictator's expansionist Programme were in head-on collision. There has been much speculation about the motives for the Reich's intervention on the side of Franco.[28] Influences in the economy played a determining role, with thoughts dwelling on the sources of raw materials in Spain. But they were certainly not the crucial factor.[29] Neither does the explanation that it provided the German Luftwaffe with a testing-ground suffice on its own. And one would be succumbing to a lie of Goebbels' propaganda in explaining

Hitler's decision primarily on the grounds that he wanted to forestall an attempt by Stalin to roll up the map of Europe from its southern flank. What chiefly persuaded Hitler to intervene in the Spanish theatre of war was probably the thought that through a victory with Franco, Germany's strategic and logistical base could be extended into Spain for future expansionist moves. From the Iberian peninsula he could seriously threaten both France and Britain. In addition to this there was once again the motivating thought of testing the reaction of the British in a military confrontation—in association with the idea of a rapid withdrawal in the event that the German intervention misfired. In fact, once again—indeed up to the end of the Spanish Civil War—Britain's statesmen hardly reacted in such a way as to cause the Führer to regard their words as a basic disapproval of his measures.[30] In principle, the British tolerated a victory of the fascist Axis powers fought by Mussolini and Hitler in Spain over the 'unnatural alliance' between the liberal democracies and Stalinist Russia. The opposing fronts of the coming war seemed to be established.

London's policy, which was hindering Hitler in his first expansionist venture just as little as it had during the occupation of the Rhineland, continued to raise Hitler's hopes and encourage him to woo Britain round to his idea of an agreement. In the summer of 1936,[31] Lord Rennell, Lord Monsell and Sir Robert Vansittart visited the Führer and heard his proposals. And in August of that year of the Berlin Olympics he named Joachim von Ribbentrop, the man who had brought him the Naval Agreement, as successor to von Hoesch, the German Ambassador in London who had just died. In October 1936 Hitler bade him farewell with the words, 'Ribbentrop, bring me back the British alliance!'[32] While initiating the 'last attempt' at an agreement with Great Britain, Hitler was simultaneously intensifying his preparations for aggressive expansion both militarily and with propaganda. The fact that the anti-Bolshevist propaganda was being carried on in the service of power politics in this matter clearly emerges from the strictly confidential directive from the Ministry of Propaganda on 21 August 1936. It urged that the intensified German Press campaign against the Soviet Union and the Red Army should already be creating a sufficient justification in the eyes of the world for future German steps.[33] The introduction of two-year military service on 24 August 1936 indicates the vehicle by which Hitler hoped to achieve his goal.[34] Finally, at the end of August 1936, Hitler dictated his memorandum on the Four Year Plan,[35] demanding that within four years the German army be ready for action and the German economy be prepared for war. This document, of which only a few copies were made, mentions nothing about the colonial demands which the German side were ceaselessly making and which the conservative Schacht was at that time presenting abroad as the wishes of the Reich[36] and which were leading to animated discussions in Paris and London. For Hitler had his sights firmly on the goals comprising the first stage of his plan: continental hegemony and *Lebensraum*.

Would he and von Ribbentrop manage after all to draw the reluctant British into the German camp? In a private talk with the British Prime Minister of the First World War, Lloyd George,[37] at the Berghof, Hitler was able to win him round to his side and gain the sympathy of this eminent politician in Britain and the Empire.[38] Surely Hitler must have felt encouraged in his hope that the British, too, would finally come to terms with his proposals after all? For with the signing of the German–Japanese Anti-Comintern Pact on 25 November 1936 and Mussolini's Milan speech of 1st November, when he enthusiastically proclaimed the famous words about 'the Axis', the tripartite world axis of Rome–Berlin–Tokyo had become a reality. But it was not only wooing proposals that the British received. Threatening demands for overseas colonies for the Reich also rained down upon them, as well as on the French. These demands, made for tactical reasons in order to achieve continental goals, were taken seriously in London as the earnest political wishes of the Reich government. On the other hand, the acting French Colonial Minister, Marius Moutet, made a brilliant diagnosis of Hitler's foreign policy.[39] Moutet, a Minister in Blum's 'Popular Front' government, elucidated the principle behind the course which German foreign policy was actually following—making colonial threats in order to achieve continental goals: an astutely accurate assessment! But just how confusing the whole situation must have seemed to the British politicians emerges from a talk, characteristic of von Ribbentrop's activities as Ambassador in London, at which his partner was the deputy British Foreign Minister.[40] The talk took place in February 1937—just after Hitler, in his Reichstag speech of 30 January 1937, had said that the time for surprises was now over.[41] The American Ambassador in Tokyo, Grew, was certainly right when, talking from the Asian storm-centre of world politics, he stated that everyone was living on a volcano, and no one knew at which moment it would erupt.[42]

What were the chief features of the talk von Ribbentrop had with Halifax, the man who one year later was to become successor to Eden in the Foreign Office and who would then meet von Ribbentrop as his counterpart in the German Foreign Office?

In this general discussion of February 1937, two points immediately emerge as characteristic of von Ribbentrop's position. Firstly, completely in line with the Führer's policy, Hitler's confidant in foreign affairs presented the idea of a German–British agreement. However, whether for reasons of complete or partial ignorance, or whether for reasons of tactical silence, von Ribbentrop was not able to inform his British counterpart in detail of the considerations which were linked to this idea. Secondly, a fact which cannot be overlooked is that von Ribbentrop, the man responsible for all colonial affairs in the Reich, did announce to Britain the Reich's demands for overseas revisions. Furthermore, it seems he did so not primarily for tactical reasons but rather with genuine intentions of having revisions made.[43] For subsequent to his talk with Lord Halifax, the German Ambassador made the suggestion to his Führer and von Neurath, the Foreign Minister, that the Reich, together with Italy and Japan, should initiate a worldwide offensive in colonial policy, in order to make the British amenable to surrendering colonial territories. Von Ribbentrop also requested that he be allowed to carry this out himself. But Hitler, significantly enough, did not acquiesce in this suggestion to the slightest degree! For as he saw it, clearing up the colonial problem in the normal way of revision politics was precisely the wrong thing to do; rather, it should remain at his disposal as a tactical weapon to further his continental expansionist aims.

It is quite evident that differences in the conceptions of foreign policy between Hitler and von Ribbentrop were already emerging at this stage, differences which were to appear with increasing clarity from 1938 on. Von Ribbentrop's anti-British, pro-colonial attitude which envisaged the safeguarding of Russian neutrality, seems to be intimated already in his talk with Lord Halifax. Nevertheless, at the same time—in step with the activities of the German Foreign Office as a whole—he continued to argue along the lines of Hitler's thoughts, that is supporting a policy which was pro-British, anti-Russian and which was geared to the temporary renunciation of colonies. Thus Hitler's 'rational' *Stufenplan* stands in contrast to von Ribbentrop's 'Wilhelmine policy' of indiscriminate expansion. Von Ribbentrop can be regarded as a representative of those conservatives in the diplomatic corps and the economy who wanted both to achieve agreement with Britain and also sought to fulfil their overseas demands. How far von Ribbentrop knew and understood Hitler's Programme in this matter is an issue which may perhaps never be resolved. But two factors are significant. Already at this time, when von Ribbentrop was carrying out ambassadorial activities in London, he was presenting colonial demands in all earnestness—which might have sprung perhaps from a wish to notch up a personal success, thus enabling him to strengthen his position on the domestic front. Furthermore, in supporting such demands, he emerges more as a representative of a 'Wilhelmine' policy, envisaging aims both on a European and a world level, than as a true representative of Hitler's Programme.

Even if von Ribbentrop—particularly during the war—never opposed Hitler so decisively as to win his own way, it must nevertheless be remembered that from the 1930s on he was pursuing a line of foreign policy of a quite traditional kind. His was a political view also held in the German Foreign Office, the navy and the economy: namely, to build up a strong position in Central Europe and extend it by means of overseas colonies.[44] Unlike Schacht in his efforts to divert the course of German foreign policy off the path of military aggression on the Continent onto that of peaceful expansionism overseas, it is quite evident that von Ribbentrop never consciously regarded his endeavours as representing an alternative to Hitler's Programme of aggressive expansionism. Indeed, one major reason for this is the submissive and devoted personal relationship of von Ribbentrop towards his 'Führer'.

Hitler was now pinning his hopes on Neville Chamberlain,[45] who moved into 10 Downing Street in May 1937 as successor to Stanley Baldwin.[46] The former Mayor of Birmingham, an out-and-out supporter of the Empire, must have seemed almost fated to agree to Hitler's plans, and turn with uninterest from the continent of Europe to direct his attention to the British Empire. And these were thoughts which Hitler had always been entertaining and continued to express. Thus Lord Lothian, who hardly seemed to be averse to such ideas,[47] was informed of Hitler's thoughts, as were the Aga Khan, an influential figure in the Empire, and Edward VIII after his abdication. Would Hitler's blueprint—involving an alliance with Britain—materialise after all, at literally the very last moment? The Führer was already celebrating the Germanic Reich, which the German nation had now attained;[48] another naval agreement was signed with the British;[49] also, in his traditional harvest thanksgiving speech at the Bückeberg on 3 October 1937, the Führer once more pleaded that Britain be reasonable, while again using colonial demands as a threat.[50] Meanwhile, he supported Japan in her war against China by cutting off all supplies to the latter.[51] At the same time America's President Roosevelt, in his famous Quarantine Speech of 5 October 1937, gave warning of and stated his complete opposition to the aggressive policy of the revisionist powers.[52] But what would the decision of the new Prime Minister in London be? Would he concede to Hitler's plan and thereby lay the foundation and precondition for the German policy of military expansion?

4. The Path to War (1937–39)

A. Hitler's Programme of expansion and Chamberlain's concept of appeasement

By November 1937, Neville Chamberlain's cabinet had been in office for six months.[1] In the meantime, Hitler had risen to a position of almost absolute dictatorship in Germany,[2] and it was clear that he was not prepared to wait much longer for the British to come round to his point of view. Hitler was beginning to pursue his aggressive programme of territorial expansion against the will of the British, the country which the Führer had originally envisaged as his alliance partner. This is the decisive fact to emerge from the secret speech made by Hitler on 5 November 1937 and noted down by Hitler's military adjutant, Colonel Hossbach, which has become known (not quite accurately) as the 'Hossbach Memorandum'.[3] The importance of this document lies in showing Hitler's changing attitude towards Britain, and not in the admission, which the memorandum merely repeats but which was known in principle for a long time, that he wanted *Lebensraum* for the German nation in the East.

What did Hitler have to tell the Commanders-in-Chief of the three branches of the armed forces, von Fritsch, Raeder and Göring, von Blomberg, the War Minister, and von Neurath, Hitler's Foreign Minister, in this speech at the close of 1937? Which aspects of his thinking had been changing, orientated though they were as ever to his basic programme? In laying down the political and military course for the coming years, it seems it was essentially the following problems which Hitler had to rethink in the light of the recalcitrant attitude of the British government on the one hand and her practical neutrality in the shadow of German military strength on the other. Most important of all, as already mentioned, Hitler's changed attitude towards Great Britain deserves particular attention. Britain was of course the very factor in Hitler's policy on whose attitude the whole of the Dictator's programmed policy seemed to depend. On 5 November 1937 there was no longer any more talk of wanting to cooperate with and woo Britain—or rather blackmail and pressurise her—into an alliance. The tactics of barter and threats took a back seat. Hitler now adopted an 'ambivalent' course towards the British which acquired an increasingly anti-British flavour.[3a] On the one hand he did not absolutely turn his back on London, but rather continued to remain 'open' to the original idea of an alliance—as his policy for a long time into the war demonstrates. But on the other hand, besides this 'doctrinaire' pet idea which he continued to pursue, the strategist in Hitler, under the principle of realist political calculation, and with extensive experience of British statesmen, recognised that Great Britain might quite well have to be regarded as an enemy. It was not primarily a question of conquering Britain, however, but rather of forcing Britain to remain in a position of neutrality acceptable to the Reich through demonstrating Germany's military might and political determination. With such a situation prevailing in European politics, the Reich would be able to take the offensive on the Continent according to the Programme, against the will of the British, while holding them politically and militarily in check. But as had been known since 1925, the direction of attack in German policy was to be towards the East. In this connection Hitler named the years 1943–45 as the ultimate deadline by which these aims were to be undertaken. And these were no vague dates, but on the contrary the relatively accurate timing for the carrying out of the continental stage within the *Stufenplan*.

What does seem interesting is that Hitler—in contrast to the colonial propaganda which accompanied all the foreign demands of the Reich on the Continent—did not talk of regarding overseas aims and European objectives as being political alternatives. Rather he was already casting his eye on the British Empire and making significant remarks about its strength or rather its weakness. However, with his assertion that he did not regard the British Empire as invincible and that Germany should only contemplate overseas aims at such a time when Britain was weak and the Reich strong, Hitler was by no means already directing his attention unequivocally at this stage to long-term overseas goals. Rather, one must take the situation at the address of 5 November into account. The Führer had to undermine the respect which his audience of officers as well as his Foreign Minister had for Great Britain, which was regarded as utterly invincible with her world-wide communication and supply network. And yet one feature, quite typical of the shape of Hitler's thoughts, should not be overlooked. According to Hitler's ideas based on his political calculation, 'cowardly' Britain would retreat again and again into a weak position of neutrality in the face of the armed and well-equipped Reich, and would at some stage or other have to take into account that its overseas possessions would be inherited by Germany. In order to be able to realise this long-term aim[4] which was already greatly interesting Hitler before 1937, a necessary precondition was to achieve hegemony over Europe by 1943–45 and thus extend the *Lebensraum* base of the Reich. With this step, a mighty Reich would then confront the British already weakened by other foreign burdens.

As Hitler saw it, the British statesmen had 'one single chance'. For a long time Hitler had been offering this 'chance' with apparent generosity; up to 1939 the offer came less and less often, until in 1940/41 it was made again at every opportunity. The 'chance' lay in the British yielding and cooperating in an alliance after all, in order to avert—at least for the time being—the threatening German step across the high seas and into overseas territories. By the end of 1937, in his new directive which he regarded as his political testament, Hitler was considering Britain primarily as an opponent of the policy of expansion he had planned. Yet in view of past experience, he was confident that the British, for reasons of political and military weakness, would remain neutral, and from this point of view he was even speculating already on more extensive long-term aims arising from the political calculation on his *Stufenplan* reaching beyond the confines of Europe. Hitler was reckoning on the years 1943–45 as the final date for the achievement of his European ventures. In accordance with his *Stufenplan* and its order of priorities, long-term goals had to be pursued after that date—that is, in the latter half of the 1940s. These aims, Hitler realised, might well have to be achieved in opposition to the British—in the event that they had not by then accepted Hitler's Programme—and most certainly in the face of opposition from the USA.[5] We shall see to what extent the events of the 1940s actually corresponded to the timing envisaged for European and overseas expansion in the plans of the navy, the economic leaders and the Foreign Office, and more particularly in the statements of Hitler and his diplomats. But what must be remembered is that Hitler never allowed himself to be side-tracked from his Programme either by the opposition of the Schacht 'liberal Imperialists' in domestic and economic policy, or by the far more significant refusal of the British to accept his offer of 'complicity'. So it is clear that in 1937 the Führer was consciously leaning more and more closely towards a policy of risk in pursuing his ambivalent—indeed increasingly anti-British—course. This policy of chance was the same that had decisively influenced Germany's statesmen in the almost fatalistic atmosphere of the years prior to the outbreak of the First World War,[6] summed up in the formula of 'world supremacy or downfall'. Hitler had taken the very same political path, admittedly without surrendering to so-called fate in the manner of the Wilhelmine Germans. For again and again he tried to achieve his original idea of winning Britain's friendship, or at least ensure that Great Britain, confronted by the might of the German armed forces,[7] would be intimidated by threats from the Reich into a passive neutral role, looking on at German ventures on the Continent.

But it was not only Hitler who had changed his policy *vis-à-vis* Great Britain, the key power in his political thinking. Neville Chamberlain, the British Prime Minister, also seems to have reconsidered Anglo-German relations intensively during his first six months in office.[8] It seems that at the very moment, early in November 1937, when Hitler was formulating his revised 'political testament', the Prime Minister was developing a clearly conceived political strategy in place of the previous largely improvised policy.[9] This strategy, which held good for Neville Chamberlain's much-maligned but perhaps solely realistic policy of appeasement up to and after September 1939, can perhaps be simplified in the following terms. From 1937 until after the outbreak of the war, Britain tried in a concrete and planned way to bring the Reich to a general agreement. As the first step towards a rapprochement, the British intended guaranteeing Hitler certain continental concessions on the proviso that these be acquired peacefully. This would then pave the way for the second stage, the problem of colonies, which in London's eyes would act as a bait. In so doing Chamberlain wanted to meet Hitler's wishes—at that time by no means very concrete—for overseas possessions. He hoped in return to bring about talks and a settlement of the arms problem, particularly the question of an air pact, and so finally secure European and world peace by means of a far-reaching Anglo-German understanding which would include other nations too. This seems to be the core of the policy of appeasement which has been the subject of so much controversy to this day. Seen in principle and analysed in its historical dimension, it has to be understood as the realistic attempt to continue to rule a world-wide Empire by means which had become inadequate for the task.[10] In order to postpone the fall of the Empire and avoid shaking any further Britain's weakened world position, Chamberlain had above all to exclude war as a political weapon.[11] But as events were to show, in the end there clearly remained no alternative to Chamberlain's policy except for the course consciously pursued under Churchill and culminating in the entry of Britain into the war. This development does not actually condemn Chamberlain's policy as such, but rather places him in the tradition of British politicians (to which his opponent Churchill also for a long time belonged[12]) who only recognised very late on, if at all, the true nature and global scope of Hitler's dynamic policy.

Let us now consider the conversation which took place at Berchtesgaden on 19 November 1937[13] between Hitler and Lord Halifax, the envoy of the British Prime Minister and the man who, though still deputy Foreign Secretary, was soon to become head of the Foreign Office. The talk took place only 14 days after Hitler's speech of 5 November 1937 in the Reich Chancellery in which he had announced the change in course towards Britain. At the outset Lord Halifax stressed the common front which Britain and Germany formed against Bolshevism. Whether for tactical reasons or out of genuine considerations of principle, he gave an assurance that Great Britain would raise no objections to German claims in Central and Eastern Europe provided they were presented reasonably—that is, that they were realised peaceably. If we recall, Sir John Simon had already said as much in

March 1935 when he asserted that Great Britain would be far less interested and concerned about Austria than the Belgian coast. But this time Hitler practically received full permission to move onto his next revisionist goals—and without having to pay in colonial coins, as he had once feared. It was Halifax's intention that talks between the two countries on this very question of colonies should be the curtain-raiser for an Anglo-German agreement and the establishment of peace in the world.

But the offer made by Lord Halifax in line with Chamberlain's strategy hardly seems to have occupied the Führer very much. Certainly, even after the change in German policy to the ambivalent or anti-British course, there still existed in Hitler's mind the possibility of making an alliance with the British and so securing his rear while executing his continental plans. But offers such as Lord Halifax presented only interested the dictator insofar as they might guarantee him a smooth course for the ventures he envisaged in Central Europe. With such an alliance he could dedicate himself to the task 'at the gateway' of the Reich, in full certainty of British neutrality. But anything beyond this—in short Lord Halifax's call for German cooperation to create world peace—contradicted Hitler's Programme and his policy towards Britain, which he had revised at the latest[14] by November 1937. Now the colonial question could hardly entice him into sitting at the negotiating table with the British to make a settlement. For it seemed to Germany that the overseas goals were just as assured if the Reich were to extend its activities overseas after the continental stage had been achieved. Hitler was not to be won round to the idea of establishing a peaceful, political, but above all economic supremacy over Central and Eastern Europe, a hegemony which London was evidently prepared to concede to the Germans.[15] He hoped to subjugate Europe and the East of the Continent in the shadow of British neutrality, which though it rejected Hitler's plans did not hinder them. Then—either in agreement with the British, if in the meantime they had 'come to their senses', or against their will—Hitler intended to go on the offensive overseas to round off Germany's position as a world power through colonial territories and naval bases.

The incompatibility of the foreign policies of Germany and Britain in the history of those years is thus quite evident—not to contemporaries probably, but at least to the historical observer looking back who is aware of the political conceptions developed by both sides. This mutual misunderstanding, however, was further aggravated by the fact that to the ears of British diplomats, officers and businessmen, the German Reich did not just speak with Hitler's voice. For example, in spite of all the extensive planning on a world scale, the German naval command was still governed by the principle of a German–British understanding, prevalent since 1935.[16] At the same time the Foreign Office, through von Weizsäcker,[17] the departmental head, was defining German wishes in moderate and traditional Great Power terms.[18] According to this point of view, the wishes of the Reich—the colonial demands and Eastern policy—should be extorted from the British in return for a compromise on an arms agreement, to which Neville Chamberlain was inclined. The German Foreign Office thereby established a maximum negotiating base in order to discuss solutions with a strong voice but still within the Concert of Europe. Even someone like Hjalmar Schacht, always judged as highly influential in Great Britain, who was a representative of the undoubtedly expansionist 'liberal Imperialism', had been pressing for a long time for peaceful, economic expansion in south-eastern Europe and for the acquisition of colonies.[19] Schacht no doubt conceived of his policy, determined by economic factors, as an 'alternative' to Hitler's planned course of military expansion. Indeed, even the role of one of Hitler's most loyal lieutenants, Hermann Göring, ought to be more precisely examined in this connection. Why was it that in talks with the American Ambassador Bullitt on 23 November 1937,[20] he announced economic and colonial demands? Did he make them in ignorance of the Führer's Programme, perhaps to gain prestige and strengthen his position within the hierarchy of the Party and State? Probably he was far more concerned to steer an opposition course, along the lines of Schacht, to guide Hitler off the road of aggression onto a peaceful course in order to follow economically and diplomatically a policy of indirect domination. In the years 1938 and 1939, the conservative opposition to Hitler were planning to remove Hitler and others and push Göring into his place as the Head of Government.[22] At the same time Göring was involved in the negotiating activities of his colleague Wohlthat, while from July and August 1939 to December of the same year there took place the 'Dahlerus Mission' to London. Seen in the light of such events, the attitude of Göring on foreign policy throws a very interesting and strong light on the apparently large range of different possibilities in the foreign policy of those years. If in principle Hitler acted in complete accordance with the decisive social factors and elements which formed the basis of his power, nevertheless it was he alone who decided on the details and extent of the course towards the attainment of the policy laid down in his Programme. And it was neither in an 'agreement' with Britain, as seen by the new men in Downing Street, nor by a strategy such as Secretary of State von Weizsäcker suggested, that Hitler saw his next goal. Nor was he making really concrete plans for the overseas stage of his Programme, but instead was turning his sights on Vienna, Prague and Danzig as the next staging-posts in his policy.

Seen against this background, it hardly seems plausible that von Ribbentrop's at present rather overrated memorandum 'for the Führer' of 2 January 1938[23] could decisively have influenced Hitler's British policy, the central factor in all Hitler's considerations.[24] But it certainly confirmed Hitler in the view he had developed of Britain in November 1937. In this resumé however, von Ribbentrop had to admit that his London mission had collapsed. Great Britain was just not prepared to make an alliance of the kind for which the Führer had hoped and which he thought his ambassador would bring him. For his part, von Ribbentrop now encouraged Hitler to treat Britain as an enemy in the future, thus slipping back into the traditional formula adopted by all those continental powers who had ever fallen into conflict with the British seapower: they sought to forge an alliance of European nations against the island. These considerations of von Ribbentrop finally reveal his political 'conception' of regarding Britain as the chief enemy of German policy and thus of acting in cooperation with the great power in the East, Russia. This anti-British policy which sought to preserve Russian neutrality and envisaged making overseas acquisitions led to the conception of a continental bloc, an idea which von Ribbentrop developed in 1940.[25] It found support and was echoed in similar reflections on the part of the Foreign Office and the navy, as well as among groups within the economy. The difference between this and Hitler's strategy is evident. It is true that Hitler came to judge Great Britain more and more as an opponent and that he too was already contemplating overseas aims. But he never allowed such considerations to supplant his central idea of achieving European hegemony and destroying Bolshevik Russia, while at the same time conquering *Lebensraum* in the East. In contrast to the 'traditionalists' and von Ribbentrop he remained bound to his *Stufenplan* just as he remained open even to the possibility of eventually coming round to an alliance with Britain, his 'hated opponent'—which was what he had originally envisaged. Whenever there seemed a favourable opportunity, Hitler still tried to implement his blueprint after all, in the face of all strategic insights and rational calculations which were forcing him to judge Britain as an opponent and reckon with or even intensify open conflict with Britain.

By this time, in any case, Hitler was making preparations to continue his policy of expansion by military means. In January and February 1938, in the process of eliminating all the remaining centres of conservative opposition, he reorganised the leadership of both the armed forces[26] and the Foreign Office, and thereby created the decisive preconditions enabling him to carry out his expansionist policy unhindered. As a result of a personal scandal von Blomberg, the Reich War Minister, was removed from his post; but the office of Supreme Command of the Armed Forces was not occupied by anyone else. Hitler kept this position for himself, and named the loyal General Keitel[27] as Chief of High Command, but with purely administrative functions. The headquarters of the armed forces under General Jodl never had the same significance as the old Prussian General Staff. Von Fritsch's place as Chief of Army Command was taken over by von Brauchitsch, who was even less of an opponent than von Fritsch,[28] who had at least resisted Hitler's war course—though not National Socialism as such. To a great extent the army leadership had capitulated to Hitler.[29] In line with these moves on 4 February 1938 Hitler replaced von Neurath at the Foreign Ministry by von Ribbentrop, a man personally quite loyal to him.

Only 20 days after this shake-up in the German Foreign Office there also occurred a change in the Foreign Office in London, which likewise did not run against the wishes of the German Head of State. If in Germany the 'doves' were leaving the Wilhelmstrasse to make room for the 'hawks', the opposite was the case in Great Britain. The 'hardliner' Eden—in method though hardly in political aims—disappeared and in his place stepped the herald of Berchtesgaden, Lord Halifax, as the new Foreign Minister in Neville Chamberlain's cabinet.

B. The Austrian *Anschluss* and British neutrality

The diplomatic and military changes in Berlin of January and February 1938 took place against a background of increasing tension in German–Austrian relations.[30] In spite of the agreement of 11 July 1936, concluded with Mussolini's approval, which sought to encourage friendly ties, the relations between the two countries had deteriorated. What played a decisive role in the course of events was the fact that Italy, who in 1934 had still seemed to be determined to intervene for the sake of Austrian independence when the Austrian National Socialists made their putsch,[31] now stood firmly on the German side. As the Swiss historian von Salis once put it so vividly, this was the Berlin–Rome axis upon which Austria could be put on the spit and roasted brown.[32]

We do not wish to repeat in detail all the events surrounding the Austrian crisis, as they have been described often enough. But one question decisive for the success or failure of the German policy should once more be raised: how would Britain respond to a German move against Austria, a member of the League of Nations? Up until that time, all the European test-cases had turned out positively so far as Hitler was concerned. Admittedly, it is true that he had not succeeded in achieving an alliance with Britain as the cornerstone of his policy. Nevertheless, British neutrality—even though accompanied by a gnashing of teeth—seemed certain to him, and that would be enough for him to risk his headlong rush towards hegemony. So it was not surprising that during the whole of the Austrian crisis in the winter and spring of 1938 not a single serious warning was issued by Britain to Berlin. For Britain's position as a world power was no longer anything like that before the First World War. The economic power of the nation was weakened; the military preparedness of the country was less than perfect; the navy was no longer indisputably the best in the world; and the Empire was shaken by the revolutionary activities of colonial liberation fronts. Britain neither regarded it as expedient, nor did she seem in a position to get militarily involved in the problems of Central Europe. Anyway, in Chamberlain's view, this issue fell within the German sphere of interest. What was to become decisive after the outbreak of the Second World War was already beginning to become apparent. Only the United States of America, following in the footsteps of the once powerful Britain, would be in the position to take up Hitler's challenge adequately and, together with the Soviet Union, the other flanking power, re-establish world peace—admittedly of a very temporary and improvised kind. But in 1938 Britain's abdication of its role as judge and arbiter in the European system had not quite come to pass. Indeed, Neville Chamberlain resisted any attempt or appearance on the part of America to get involved in affairs which the British Prime Minister regarded as European and British concerns.[33]

Probably influenced in no small way by what Sir John Simon and Lord Halifax had said on the Austrian question, von Ribbentrop and Hitler were agreed that Great Britain would never take on the risk of a large-scale war on account of a crisis in Central Europe. If we look back over the history of German foreign policy since 1871, there is a certain justification for maintaining that neither Bismarck nor Bülow, neither Bethmann Hollweg nor Stresemann ever had so much room for manoeuvre within the system of European and world nations as Hitler now had available to him in the Austrian crisis of 1938. Before the First World War, even the smallest claims on territory or frontier revisions had led to wars such as those which shook Europe in 1912 and 1913.[34] But now a *nation civilisée*, a member of the League of Nations, could disappear off the map without London having seriously reacted! This brings us to the course of events immediately prior to the so-called *Anschluss* of Austria.

As so often happened, on this occasion too Hitler's aims of bringing Austria 'back into the fold' of the Reich coincided with the hopes the German and Austrian population and government had held for a long time. Ever since the decision of the National Assembly in 1919, Vienna had never given up the idea that 'German–Austria'—the independent state which had emerged from the former Hapsburg monarchy— should join the Reich.[35] But besides these long-term preconditions, Hitler had other reasons for risking the decisive step in February and March 1938. Mention has already been made of the regrouping in the leadership of the armed forces accomplished just previously, which was a pre-requisite for Hitler adopting an adventurous course in foreign policy; the assertive role of Field Marshal Göring during the whole of the crisis also cannot be overlooked. However, seen in retrospect, the factor which turned the balance was the neutrality of the British which was expected with almost complete certainty; for it was the British who were regarded as the decisive factor in the shaping of European affairs. Chancellor Schuschnigg, the successor to Engelbert Dollfuss, who had been murdered in 1934, was at the head of an Austrian government which could only be described as a fascist–clerical dictatorship.[36] It was eventually his policy which gave Hitler the excuse for aggressive measures. As is well known, Hitler received the Austrian leader on 12 February 1938 for talks in Berchtesgaden,[37] basically in order to present him with an ultimatum. According to Hitler's wishes, among other things the foreign policy of the two countries was to be coordinated and the National Socialist Seyss-Inquart was to take over as Minister for the Interior in the Republic— and thus take control of the police force. In addition, the Austrian government was to allow the presence of the Nazi Party again and conduct itself favourably *vis-à-vis* the German economy. Hitler's demands were lent visible emphasis through a demonstration of military force. While Hitler was talking to his Austrian guests, Generals of the Luftwaffe— incidentally without their knowing the reason for their own presence —were staying at the Berghof, demonstrating to the Austrian leader and his Foreign Minister the military determination of the Reich.

On his return to Vienna, intimidated and desperate, Schuschnigg chose the course of head-on fight. He called his country to a national referendum 'for a free and German, socialist and independent, Christian and united Austria'. Significantly enough, the Chancellor only wanted to allow those over 24 years old to vote. For the youth of the upper classes in Vienna particularly were so enthusiastic about Hitler, his Reich and National Socialism, that they would certainly never have supported a decision made against Berlin. To the young people of the leading circles in the old capital of Vienna at that time, there seemed to be no problem at all about German–Austria 'returning home' to the Reich sooner or later. Economic misery had hit Austria badly too, and middle class people had found their chances at economic betterment seriously impaired. It was in view of this that they particularly saw the hope of improving their social position in absorption of the Republic into a greater Reich. In the light of the almost ceaseless propaganda on the theme of colonies being drummed up in Germany, some were already dreaming of stepping into the role of Hitler's colonial governor in African possessions of the Reich, which by that time would also be powerful overseas.[38] But only two days after announcing the plebiscite, the Chancellor had to admit defeat, submit to German pressure and call off the vote. Göring's pressure for a quick military solution had been successful; Berlin could rest assured of Mussolini's benevolent attitude. At 8.45 pm on the evening of 11 March 1938, Hitler gave the order to march the following day. The invasion by German troops did not proceed without some technical hitches; clearly, the armed forces were only in a state of strictly limited war preparedness after all.

A decisive factor in the course and sequel to the Austrian crisis was the fact that only two weeks after the event, Great Britain acknowledge the unilateral act on the part of the German Reich. Indeed, soon afterwards it also recognised the Italian Impero, that is it sanctioned the fate of the Abyssinian Empire defeated by fascist Italy, and with it abandoned a further member of the League of Nations.[39] Of course, protests were heard against the aggressive military methods adopted by the Germans, but in principle, the Austrian 'return home' did not seem to arouse London all that much. Britain's was a thoroughly consistent attitude, when we bear in mind the continuity in British policy revealed here and in the statements of Simons and Lord Halifax. For Hitler's move against Vienna could hardly have troubled Chamberlain in his major conception. On the contrary, except for the crude and rather 'unreasonable', that is non-peaceful, means he adopted, Hitler's move was basically in line with British expectations. As a first stage British intentions were to make concessions to the Reich in Europe. London regarded this as essential to enable Britain to hold talks with Berlin about the colonial issue as the prelude to the second stage— discussions on the thorny problem of arms limitation and the establishment of world peace. But in Great Britain, discussions with the Reich on their colonial demands had to be dropped for the time being, so as not to expose the government to attack from the Opposition for their being too soft towards Germany. In principle, however, it was this very issue of colonial demands which, together with the lever of 'economic appeasement' applied chiefly in south-eastern Europe,[40] the British government planned to use as a bait to bring Hitler to the conference table. They intended allowing him a power base of partial hegemony with a secured economic supremacy in central and south-eastern Europe, while at the same time hoping to prevent him by this means from threatening the very existence of the British Empire on the continent or overseas.

In strife-ridden France there was no great surprise at the fact that relatively soon after the Austrian affair Hitler once again took up the colonial question through his diplomats. On the contrary, a little illogically, and failing to recognise Hitler's phased planning, some political circles in Paris seemed to believe that if Nazi Germany was showing an interest in Africa, then it would not cast an interested eye across the Rhine towards the French motherland, Basically, neither Paris nor London had understood the essential dual function of the colonial demands. Although it is true that they emerged increasingly as long-term aims of German foreign policy, nevertheless up to and even after the outbreak of war on 3 September 1939 their primary purpose was a tactical one—diverting attention from the continental demands. Hardly a single career diplomat or politician in London or Paris managed to see this. This was all the more remarkable in view of the fact that the *Australian Statesman*,[41] appearing in its home country, managed to recognise the largely functional nature of the colonial demands in Hitler's policy, even during the Austrian events—much like the perceptive analysis of Marius Moutet, the French Colonial Minister of the previous year.

In Great Britain those in responsible government positions continued to believe firmly in the view that this very problem of colonies would be of decisive help in making it possible to have discussions with the Germans on a calm footing. For at the beginning of March 1938—before the final phase of the Austrian issue—the British Ambassador in Berlin, Sir Nevile Henderson,[42] announced an important diplomatic initiative by his government.[43] There was to be no more talk about preliminary concessions, but instead the intention was to achieve the aim of world peace by adopting the colonial path and coming to economic agreements. However, in deference to British public opinion talks on the colonial issue, which was regarded as the bridge towards better understanding, had for the moment to be postponed. They were to be taken up again when the volatile and capricious public opinion of the British democracy had turned its attention to some other question.

Hitler's power was now greater than ever before, both at home and in the foreign field. His popularity had reached a new peak and his policies were flowing smoothly and successfully. But in the course of 1938, members of the Officer Corps as well as representatives of the economy were recognising with increasing clarity that for personal as well as for social and armament reasons, Hitler's Germany was resolutely adopting a course geared to war. Hjalmar Schacht was one of the first to recognise that the financial and economic policies being adopted by the Reich would inevitably lead to war. He saw that debts of the kind being accumulated could only be covered through plunder and looting if bankruptcy was to be avoided. Unflaggingly, but in vain, Schacht worked at creating a political alternative to Hitler's war course of primarily continental expansion. As an alternative he advocated a plan of 'liberal imperialist' expansionism directed overseas.[44] His attempt failed because the Führer regarded his own Programme as unalterable and proven through his successes in the field of foreign policy. In no small way Schacht's collaboration with Hitler on financial policy at the beginning of his régime had made Hitler's Programme possible. For a long time after that Hitler's policies may have matched the interests of the important partners of the National Socialist Government in the heavy industries. As political factors, these forces had stood on an equal footing with the Nazi Party up to 1936; but for a long time that had no longer been the case. Instead, they had become dominated by the Party and Führer through Göring's organisation of an arms economy preparing for the coming war. And yet the policy of the Third Reich with its ultimate consequence, war, enabled these very forces to look after their own pressing economic interests. Under state protection, these groups were able to make considerable profits in the armaments business and its off-shoot industries.[45] These economic and social elements were dictatorially used by Hitler to serve his ideas and aims and in so doing they supported the materialisation of these aims while at the same time temporarily ensuring the continuation of the existing social structure. It was Hitler, his Programme and these compliant elements who were pushing towards the war which by the autumn of 1938 could only have been avoided with great difficulty.

C. The Munich Agreement and the 'encirclement' of the Soviet Union

After the Austrian *Anschluss*, Hitler was tempted to a further step on the path to hegemony. On this occasion, as so often in the history of Europe since the French Revolution, it was a minority group[46]—in this case the Sudeten Germans in Czechoslovakia—which served as the political 'explosive' providing the confusion necessary to set off an international crisis.

Our purpose here is not to present a history of the Sudeten Germans.[47] Only a little need be said by way of background to the events. The Republic of Czechoslovakia was industrialised and therefore economically viable, but as an artificially created political structure it was exposed to continuous danger from the political undertow created by the renewed strength of the German Reich. The Sudeten Germans living in Czechoslovakia were not treated all that well and their sense of dissatisfaction was certainly justified. Hitler took advantage of the situation of the Sudeten German minority for his own ends. By the beginning of the 1930s the leaders of the Sudeten German Party were already in contact with Nazi Party figures in Berlin centred around Hess.[48] But significantly enough, these contacts only acquired an importance when Hitler's traditionally orientated foreign policy had reached its limits. At that stage, with the help of the dissatisfaction of the 'national' minority in Czechoslovakia and in the shadow of British neutrality, it now seemed worthwhile to Hitler to extend beyond these limits in pursuance of his policy of phased conquest. So on 28 March 1938, a few days after the successful Austrian coup, the Führer advises the leaders of the Sudeten German Party to present more exacting demands than the government could possibly satisfy.[49] Those leaders round Konrad Henlein followed these instructions and a month later, in the 'Karlsbad Programme', they demanded autonomy and the freedom to propagate the German *Weltanschauung* in Czechoslovakia. However, this meant demanding that the Czech government should humbly tolerate Nazi agitation. The Czech state—which in Berlin had been harangued as the 'aircraft carrier' of the Soviet Union—was sliding into the utmost danger. Europe stood on the brink of its next crisis—willed by the German Reich.

Once again Hitler's Programme and Chamberlain's appeasement concept came into conflict. On the one hand Hitler planned the phased establishment of a position of world domination based on European hegemony and overseas territories. On the other, Chamberlain's concept was to preserve the British Empire by pursuing a policy of negotiation. So once more the two contestants in the duel appear in the arena. Their conceptions and policies during the Czech crisis are worth analysing. In contrast to the conventional portrayals in diplomatic history, we shall not describe in full the diplomatic situation in Europe with respect to the Czech events. The road to Munich has been surveyed often enough. We know that France felt duty-bound to help Czechoslovakia while Britain was in a sense bound by French conduct and thus always at pains to have a calming effect on Paris, and that Downing Street stubbornly pursued the idea of securing peace by being prepared to make concessions, promising themselves security in return. However, too little attention has been paid to the conceptions and ideas of the statesmen and their nations which lay behind these diplomatic moves, though these conceptions were decisively influential and binding on Chamberlain's Britain, Hitler's Germany and Stalin's Russia at this phase in history. Particularly in connection with the Sudetenland crisis and the network of alliances at that time, it is of great interest to recall that since 1935 Soviet Russia had had a binding pact with the Czechs, and that military assistance from Russia would have presupposed the right to march through Poland. One could fill books with endless reflections on how the Reich could have been forced into withdrawal by employing the Soviet factor as a means of threatening Hitler's policy without actually having to think about the Red Army marching through Poland. Would Hitler's Secret Service not have known all about these possibilities under consideration and so have undermined the effect of the intended threats even at the discussion stage? Since the files of the Secret Service—in the nature of things —are hardly available, and historians cling as always to the maxim *quod non est in actis, non est in mundo*, such prior considerations are all too often forgotten. The fascination of the diplomatic game tends to impair recognition of and obscure the actual driving forces behind the policies—seen in terms of social history and the history of ideas—and the conceptions of the statesmen evolving them.

But the course which Neville Chamberlain intended taking in the new crisis troubling Europe became evident on 10 May 1938. It was then that Kirkpatrick, the First Secretary in the British Embassy in Berlin, told the envoy von Bismarck[50] that Britain would be completely willing to come to an agreement on the Sudetenland question on Germany's terms if it could be accomplished peacefully and reasonably. Indeed, in such an event Britain would even be prepared to exert a certain pressure on the Prague government. As the British politicians round Chamberlain—so contemptuously called 'the appeasers'—saw it, this additional European concession would be followed by talks between the two nations. For Hitler, on the other hand, this was simply the next stage in his basic plan. By 1943–45 at the latest, he intended striking the 'great blow' against the Soviet Union in the East with the aim of attaining European supremacy. Then, after 1945, the next move would be to strike out abroad, across the oceans, into overseas territories.

The parallel between the Czechoslovakian and the Austrian crisis is unmistakeable. Both the British and German leaders, Chamberlain and Hitler, held unswervingly to their political conceptions. Russia too, the third decisive party in the issue, but one which was not reckoned among the 'inner circle' of powers in European politics, stubbornly pursued a course entirely consistent with Stalin's blueprint for foreign policy. Stalinist Russia, socially so different from the other nations of Europe, and a country which particularly since the purges in the Red Army in 1937[51] was always underestimated in its military strength, had followed this course since 1927 and continued to do so, as will be shown in connection with the events surrounding 23 August 1939. During the 'Litvinov era' Russia pursued a policy of cooperation with the anti-revisionist capitalist powers of Britain and France and a strategy of safeguarding the status quo in Central Europe. But under Litvinov's successor, Stalin's hidden aim of maintaining and possibly expanding Russia as a Great Power was to be achieved by other means.[52]

Meanwhile in the Reich the propaganda machine was working flat out against neighbouring Czechoslovakia. In order not to throw a questioning light on the priority placed on the Reich's continental aims in Central Europe, colonial propaganda was now damped down. All possible alternatives to the objectives envisaged by Hitler had to disappear temporarily from view of world opinion and the politicians in London, Paris and Rome. On 28 May 1938[53] in a talk with his top officers and officials, the Führer declared his unalterable will to smash Czechoslovakia militarily. Two days later, this intention was formulated into a directive from the Führer. On the one hand, it seemed to the army officers that this bound them to obedience to Hitler, yet on the other it also gave rise to the military opposition which was now forming against the Dictator.[54] Hitler elaborated upon the plan of his future policy, remaining in so doing completely within the framework of the Programme he had conceived in the 1920s and revised in 1937. He explained that he would first tackle 'the task' in the East and then, in three or four years, take the offensive in the West. In 1934, in line with *Mein Kampf*, he had considered the conquest of France to be the precondition for eastward expansion. In spite of these changing reflections which were not then elaborated upon, it nevertheless seems to us that the shape of Hitler's ideas had not basically altered. Clearly now, in 1938, he planned to settle the question 'on the German frontier' to his own satisfaction. Whether he then intended to move against France or whether, in the shadow of British neutrality, he considered instead marching against the Soviet Union—either with Poland or after conquering it—are two possibilities which must remain unresolved.[54a]

The direction of Hitler's strategy was clear. British neutrality, the precondition for any expansionist plans on the Continent, seemed secured. The actual order of the separate lightning campaigns in the East and the West of Europe would be determined largely by the prevailing political and military situation. A major reason for Hitler's counting on Britain's neutrality, however, was that, having built up the army and air force again, the Reich had now begun to re-arm its navy. Germany's admirals, in calculating their strategies, were already having to draw Britain in as a potential, indeed probable, enemy.[55] And according to Hitler, it could quite easily be the case that in the latter half of the 1940s—after attaining supremacy over the Continent and Eastern Europe—the Reich would be confronted by Great Britain as its next natural enemy. This would come about if Britain were to oppose Germany's overseas colonial policy and resist striking against the USA as Germany's junior partner. In 1937 America was already raising her voice in warning against the threatening aggression of both Japan and the Reich.[56] In effect, this gave encouragement to a weakened Britain, though this hardly suited Neville Chamberlain's idea of a policy of settlement; for it gave a boost to those forces of resistance in Britain which, with Churchill at their head, were to hold out in the critical situation of 1940.

In actual fact, in the spring of 1938 the German navy for the first time carried out manoeuvres which presupposed conflict with Britain. It seemed that the building of an Atlantic fleet was impending[57] and

with it the attainment of Hitler's long-term aims for the second half
of the 1940s moved into the realm of the possible. For the time being
the fleet appeared as a means of exerting pressure on Great Britain
should she try to oppose future lightning attacks by the Reich on its
path to supremacy.

The foreign policy of the Führer diverged more and more from the
ideas of his mostly conservative or 'governmental-liberal' colleagues in
the German Foreign Office and the armed forces. It was not that in
principle they would have resisted the re-establishment of the Reich
as the supreme power on the Continent or would have been against a
strong position for the Reich as a colonial power. It was merely that
their fears in the face of the war course Hitler was strictly pursuing
led them to regard the risk involved in achieving these aims as too
high. Beck, the Chief of the General Staff, resigned in opposition to
Hitler's policy.[58] His successor, Halder, made contact with the con-
spiratorial group round Canaris and von Witzleben who, although
they never made any concrete plans,[59] played with the idea of replacing
Hitler in the event of a serious international set-back or the outbreak
of war, in order to protect Germany from a military catastrophe.[60] But
the mediator they sent to London to seek support from Britain, the
vital power in the matter, had hardly any success.[61] For at least Neville
Chamberlain, the key man, had no intention of jeopardising his concept
of agreement reached in stages with Hitler by getting involved with
conspirators who were working against the established government in
Germany. To the British Premier, the envoys of the conservatives in
Germany seemed like the Jacobites at the French Court. He preferred
to deal with those in office in Berlin and perhaps even hoped that he
would be able to achieve his plan of a comprehensive settlement more
smoothly with the 'Austrian' Hitler than with the conservative 'Prussian' conspirators.[62] Chamberlain could hardly imagine why Hitler
should want to reject his idea of a settlement, which even in the
concrete case of the Czech crisis permitted the annexation of the
Sudetenland to the Reich. But Hitler had no intention of tying himself
down to the rules of reasonable and peaceful procedure. Rather, under
a certain time-pressure, not least of all for personal reasons,[63] Hitler
was obviously planning to settle all the 'preliminaries'—including even
the French campaign—by 1943–45. This would then enable him to
dedicate himself to the 'important matter' in the East, smashing Soviet

Russia and finally, in the second half of the 1940s, moving beyond the continent of Europe to pursue his policy on a world-wide scale. While in the Reich the navy and the officials responsible for colonial and maritime planning were casting a shadow over Hitler's future aims, in London Sir Horace Wilson, the confidential aide to the British Prime Minister, was negotiating with Wohlthat, the Secretary of State from Göring's staff responsible for the Four Year Plan.[64] The British negotiator, completely in line with the policy of Chamberlain, made the Germans the offer of allowing Germany the exercise of influence in colonial policy and the shaping of economic relations in south-east Europe. Of course, in these discussions, Wohlthat did not follow Hitler's programme of military conquests. With his policy of economic expansionism Wohlthat was much more a follower of Schacht, who had been deprived of his powers. In this, he was arguing completely in line with Göring who had already condemned Hitler's war course and was now trying to divert the Führer from the road of military expansion by bringing about an economic and political 'alternative' solution. Göring sought to direct the Führer along the path of a peaceful 'liberal-imperialistic' policy by creating a strong position for the Reich in Europe and overseas.[65]

In connection with this, perhaps note should be taken of the plans of the opposition which was establishing itself against Hitler in 1938–39. The plans were to depose Hitler and place the no doubt more peacefully-inclined Göring at the head of the state. Even if Göring never actually stood in opposition to his Führer, one may still regard this peaceful 'liberal-imperialist' conception of economic expansion and political influence, consciously or unconsciously developed by Göring, as an 'alternative' to Hitler's Programme.[66] In his speech at the Nuremberg party rally on 9 September 1938, however,[67] Hitler forced the Sudetenland crisis to a head, causing the British Prime Minister to hurry over to Germany in order to save the peace. That is, in line with the familiar policy of appeasement, Chamberlain permitted Hitler this concession too, in a reasonable, non-military way. The British Premier recognised the right to self-determination of the Sudeten Germans and promised Hitler that together with France they would urge Prague to agree to cession without a plebiscite. On the other hand, the Czech President, Benes, wanted war against the Reich in September 1938 as he believed that Germany could be conquered in three to four weeks.[69]

Chamberlain's attitude can only be understood properly if it is seen in the context of his basic plan for peace. His aim was to allow the status quo to alter just enough for it to be protected and maintained in its broad outlines. In this way, with insufficient political, military and economic means, he hoped to be able to maintain and stabilise Britain's position as a world power. As the first stage in Britain's concessions to the Reich, the settlement of the Czech question was complicated only by the fact that, quite beyond Chamberlain's understanding, Hitler seemed to want to proceed on an aggressive, military footing. A week later the British Prime Minister returned once more to Germany with his Cabinet's approval of the agreement arrived at with the Führer on 15 September 1938. But Hitler, governed by his principle of conquering Europe by quick military attacks, not by long and wearisome negotiations, felt himself to be under pressure of time. He informed an embittered Chamberlain that he demanded the immediate intervention of German troops in the Sudetenland; an ultimatum to that effect was to expire on 28 September 1938. And yet even this blow did not alter the basic situation for Chamberlain. He had no intention of jeopardising his major peace plan for the sake of a couple of thousand square miles of land belonging to a second-rate nation in Central Europe. So the British government conceded and called the Italian Duce in on the discussions, who in turn called a conference of the 'inner circle' of powers at Munich.[69] Posing as the European mediator, Mussolini presented a proposal which, among other things, provided for the intervention of German troops in stages between 1 October and 10 October 1938 and which was based on settling the question of the remaining minorities in Czechoslovakia. Significantly enough, this compromise, so favourable to Germany yet only reluctantly accepted by Hitler, was a plan which had been drafted by the German Foreign Office and on which both von Weizsäcker and Hermann Göring had been working. Even though this agreement brought the Reich considerable success, it was nevertheless in evident contrast to Hitler's policy, since in principle it proposed settling the crisis in a peaceful manner.

Three conclusions may thus be drawn which are of decisive importance for the course of events over the months up to the outbreak of war, in fact up to the beginning of the war on a world scale on 22 June 1941:

1. The events surrounding the Czech crisis had clearly revealed Hitler's desire for war. The Führer intended getting the first, the European, stage of his plans behind him by means of lightning military attacks in the shadow of British neutrality. At the same time he was preparing the tools by which, through threats, he thought Britain could be held in check, and which afterwards, in the latter half of the 1940s, were to serve as a means for Germany to expand overseas.

2. The non-participation of the Soviet Union at the Munich Conference clearly demonstrated that the Western powers were not inclined to accept the USSR as a partner in international politics. This induced Stalin to alter his tactics in foreign policy.[70] Afraid that the capitalist democracies and fascist dictatorships could unite against Russia and defeat it, Stalin's Foreign Commissar Litvinov, using the slogan of 'collective security' and Russia's entry into the League of Nations, had sought to make an alliance with the anti-revisionist capitalist nations. 'At the latest by the Munich Agreement, this policy must be seen as having failed.'[71] While Stalin's aim remained unchanged—to exacerbate the tensions between the 'imperialist' powers as far as possible in order to ensure the continued existence of Soviet Russia—the pro-Western 'Litvinov era' now drew to its close with the 'encirclement' of the USSR at the Munich Conference. When Molotov moved into the Foreign Office on 3 May 1939, a new chapter in Soviet foreign policy was initiated. Now the old aim of maintaining the security and protecting the interests of Soviet Russia was to be achieved with new partners. Thus the foundations of the Nazi-Soviet Pact of 23 August 1939 were laid in Munich.

3. The Munich Conference and the policy of Neville Chamberlain which led to it—often misunderstood and vilified as a humiliating series of ignominious retreats—had shown how stubbornly the British Prime Minister was pursuing his aim of securing peace. As he saw it, no war should break out over European concessions which he was in fact prepared to make to Hitler. In the course of his crisis diplomacy, Chamberlain was far more concerned that after settling

European matters, he would succeed in achieving proper talks on an arms agreement by means of the economic and colonial bait. He wanted to press for a settlement in order to ensure peace and so save Britain's position as a world power in Europe and overseas.

Seen from this point of view, for all its sentimental overtones, Chamberlain's exclamation of 'peace in our time' gains a very realistic dimension. The day after the Munich Conference Chamberlain was able to persuade Hitler into making the declaration according to which all future problems would be settled by consultation.[72] To Chamberlain, this declaration seemed to offer a guarantee that from now on international developments would proceed along his lines. But for Hitler, the signature beneath the Anglo-German declaration of 30 September was nothing more than a cumbersome concession. In his future policy, he would pay not the least regard to this 'scrap of paper'. For of course, the agreement was not as Hitler had originally pictured it in the 1920s; it was not based on a British alliance. Rather, it sought to bind Hitler and commit him to the present status quo. In view of the increasing emphasis on his long-term aims and the preparations being made towards their fulfilment, it seems questionable whether Hitler was still prepared to renounce unconditionally a policy of colonial demands for the sake of Britain, as he had once (at least for a time) intended. For the wider aims and intentions which had always been latent in his policy were now emerging more and more evidently in the anti-British course he was adopting.

D. The 'Advance on Prague': towards an analysis of German foreign policy

Despite all the foreboding signs threatening Great Britain, Chamberlain continued to believe quite firmly that he would succeed in bringing Hitler to the conference table. Through his Press spokesman, Steward, he therefore requested that the Germans refrain from colonial propaganda immediately upon concluding the Munich Agreement.[73] For the Prime Minister was hardly able to defend himself against the pressure of attacks made on him by the opposition in the Labour Party,[74] from supporters of the Churchill faction in his own party,[75] and from the Dominions.[76] In actual fact the Reich did impose a noticeable slackening-off in colonial propaganda. By means of the lever of colonial policy, both Chamberlain's democracy and the Führer's dictatorship quite clearly did their best to influence one another. Hitler afforded Chamberlain protection on his domestic front, and in so doing repaid the British Prime Minister for the success at Munich. The Führer was by no means enthusiastic about the latter, but it enabled him to avoid a coup against him by the conservative conspirators.

In the meantime, the dictator had been giving fresh insight into his plans when he held a final audience with the departing French Ambassador, François-Poncet, at which the Frenchman, on personal initiative, sought to bring about a Franco-German rapprochement with Hitler in order to free French policy from being tied down by the British.[77] For the present-day observer looking back on the matter, the meeting gives an insight into the very heart of Hitler's Programme, even if contemporaries gleaned only very little information from it. In answer to the question posed by the French diplomat as to the Reich's colonial intentions, Hitler used the formula adopted again and again by him and von Ribbentrop—that that would only be thought about in five or six years' time.[78] It will be remembered that the Führer was planning to have subjugated the Continent—including the chief target, Russia— by 1943–45 and that he arranged to have the German navy in a state of readiness at the latest by the second half of the 1940s. Taking these factors into account, we may conclude from his statement to François-Poncet that Hitler really was contemplating bringing up the colonial issue in the 1940s after he had attained supremacy in Europe.

In both parts of Hitler's 'dual state'[79]—in the conservative German circles as well as in the SS, where the ideology of the Nazi Utopia of the new man was being propagated—the Führer's plans were being earnestly discussed and prepared for, even though they were hardly recognised as part of a set programme. The seriousness of this discussion can perhaps be seen in the attitude expressed by Admiral Carls towards the *Draft study of naval war strategy against Britain* of September 1938.[80] His opinion may properly be taken as representative of the view held by the Naval High Command who were making plans on the scale of their Wilhelmine predecessors. More and more, their thoughts and intentions fitted in with the anti-British course, falling in line with the second phase of the *Stufenplan* which was now moving into sight. As Admiral Carls stated: 'If Germany is to gain a secure position as a world power, as the Führer wishes, then, in addition to sufficient colonial possessions, it will require *secure naval routes and communications and guaranteed access to the high seas.*'[81]

It is not known whether Admiral Carls knew in detail about Hitler's idea of creating a position as world power through the conquest of Europe (including the Soviet Union) and then ranging out overseas. He may well not have known this. But what is important is that his ideas corresponded completely with Hitler's long-term aims embracing the whole globe, and that he recommended that the navy include them in their planning.[82] Similarly, the SS leader in the Reich also spoke of intentions of world power when he addressed his 'men' on 8 November 1938[83]—that is, at the same time as Hitler, in his traditional speech at the Munich Bürgerbräukeller, was praising the Wehrmacht as the vehicle for his policy of world power.[84] Himmler announced to his SS leaders that for Germany the future would bring either the Greater German Empire, or ruin. How remarkably this echoes Hitler's declaration in *Mein Kampf*, that Germany would either become a world power or disappear completely. Himmler promised his men that the Führer would create the greatest empire which had ever been established by man. No doubt in asserting this promise, which was in line with his own racist dogma, Himmler was alluding to the idea of world domination[85] by the racially pure Aryan Reich of the future. In saying this, the head of the SS was talking as the champion of the ideology of the 'new', biologically superior human being, an ideology which was ultimately to become a hindrance to the policy of rational political calculation.[86] It remains uncertain as to whether or not Himmler knew Hitler's *Stufenplan*, which was largely orientated along traditional lines of power politics. In practice, the plan hardly bore any of the traits of a 'new', revolutionary racialism, even if in theory with the very last stage—the racially determined domination of the world—the plan was supposed to enter a new and extra-historical dimension. Yet this stage too quite clearly bore the character of conservative power politics in the vision it projected of the conflict between the German world power and the United States.

Nevertheless, besides the schemes and designs of the more conservative navy, of the business community and the German Foreign Office, another characteristic Nazi driving force behind foreign policy between

1933 and 1945 is evident in the ideas of Himmler and the SS on foreign policy.[87] Until 1941 these views of Himmler's hardly upset or interfered with Hitler's policy and war strategy; indeed they seemed, rather, to integrate well into his plans. Hitler's Programme, in short, appeared as the culmination of all the political aims, economic demands and ideological views existing in Germany since 1866–71.[88] For the politics of Bülow, Tirpitz and Miquel, nationalism alone had still sufficed as the means of mobilising the (petit-) bourgeois class—in their dependent relation as employees—behind the Crown and the landowners and heavy industrialists who stood in alliance behind it.[89] But now, one generation later, far stronger binding forces were needed to integrate the community. For Germany had undergone extensive historical changes, particularly after the experiences of the First World War and the inflation and world economic crisis. In view of this and the worldwide challenge presented by Communist Russia, new tools of integration were necessary to tie down and commit 'the people' to the expansionist policy of its political rulers and the preservation of the social status quo connected to this policy. This latter role, the socio-political function of the Hitler dictatorship, is all too easily overlooked in the light of the development towards 'full fascism' initiated after 1937.[90] The 'new' slogans for integration, however, contained above all others a catchword of long-standing familiarity in Prussian-German history[91] —that of anti-semitism. Nevertheless, in asserting this fact it should not be forgotten that the anti-semitic element in Hitler's ideas had a central and thoroughly significant importance in its own 'right', and did not merely serve to 'ideologise' the existing social relations and class structure. On the contrary, it was precisely the realisation of this racist element which was finally to undermine the stabilisation of the existing social order which was being brought about for a time against the Dictator's will. Hitler moved closer to this (final) racial goal of his Programme in the plan he envisaged of conquering Russia as a move of shrewd political calculation. But it was from the racist point of view that Hitler, in connection with this conquest of Russia, was then to order the extermination of 'worthless' lives.[92]

From the point of view of the whole social complex, however, it should not be overlooked that Hitler's dogma also served a function of a temporary nature. Rather than announcing social reforms, the biological revolution was proclaimed and so the misery of the day was not recognised for what it was—a fault in society—but instead the 'discovery' was made of a racially identifiable 'enemy', the Jew, who could thus be attacked. The defects in the existing social order were attacked in that they were abolished according to the ideology. Instead the system propagated the idea of a 'new' type of human being.[93] The 'new Aryan' did not actually reflect upon society and its proper organisation as such, but rather, in apparent independence of it, set about solving all problems on the basis of racial superiority, by making the world subject to his victorious and conquering sword. Here lay the connection between the *Weltanschauung* of the Germanic conqueror—serving the socially-motivated function in domestic politics of preserving the status quo—and Hitler's aggressive expansionist programme. The three components—the policy of the Führer, the social structure of the Third Reich and the ideology maintained particularly by the SS—still stood as a trio, each playing a harmonious variation on the theme of expansion. For however Carls and Himmler might have understood their notions of world power—regarding it from the conservative viewpoint of traditional power politics or the racist aspect of Nazi plans for world conquest—both advocated that the political goals of the Reich ought to be sought beyond its own frontiers—just as Hitler's Programme did. As a result, the alternative course of non-aggressive imperialism through economic expansion increasingly lost ground as a further option of foreign policy.

But if we consider the whole range of attitudes on foreign policy from the point of view of the leading statesmen of the day—the foreign aims of Hitler, his Foreign Office, the armed forces and the economic community, the official propaganda as well as the information circulating unofficially—and if we put ourselves in the position of Neville Chamberlain, then we can see that it was precisely this apparent wide range of opinion which must time and again have provided grounds for his believing that it would still be possible to get the Germans to the conference table to discuss the maintenance of world peace after all. And yet at the same time, particularly in Himmler's speech for example, the racist ideas, ideological dressing and camouflaging of social conditions which were cropping up, reveal dimensions which pushed the possibility of a rational solution along the lines of Chamberlain's policy into the far distance. In Germany at this time, political statements and preparations were already centring not only on the first, but also on the second stage of Hitler's Programme. Meanwhile, the British Prime Minister was unerringly pursuing his own political conception. This situation therefore seems a good point at which to attempt a diagnosis of German foreign policy during the 'Hitler era'. For now, in its 'attack on Prague', Germany was for the first time exceeding the boundaries of its so-called policy of revision. The liberal-imperialist alternative of peaceful economic expansion had been pushed out to the margins of 'high-level politics', where now and again it flared up briefly. Hitler's policy now entered upon a war course hostile to Britain, even if it gambled on British neutrality. But to the foreign observer, it seemed like business as usual; diplomatic and economic activities went on as normal, concealing the actual aim of expansion.

Analogous to the 'dual state' model, explaining the domestic politics of the Third Reich, it is this very contradiction between the 'madness' on the exterior and the inner 'method' and pattern which seems to offer a standpoint from which to analyse the role of the Third Reich within the 'dying European diplomatic system'. The conservative moderate-right associates of Hitler manning the government offices in the 'Third Reich' helped, *nolens volens*, to conceal the true policy of the Führer. The diplomatic activities of a well-trained, trustworthy and distinguished body of career diplomats went on apparently undisturbed against the background of a planned Utopia of world conquest. Likewise, on the economic level, the IG–Farben Works,[94] paying due regard to the topic of colonies which moved increasingly to the forefront in the latter half of the 1930s, were planning the establishment of a large sales organisation in Africa. In so doing, they sought, in the course of peaceful economic expansionism, to profit from the envisaged colonial policy, for which the relevant government departments made loud propaganda—even though it was not yet an immediate objective for Hitler. And this they did without troubling themselves about the ideological motives of Himmler's SS which was a further factor in the power system of the Third Reich. On the whole, in the field of domestic, economic and foreign policy, the business and transactions of the institutions and representatives traditionally concerned with them continued without hindrance. They seemed to be existing in apparent independence against a background provided by the totalitarian Programme.[95] Yet objectively they were in fact dependent on it, basing their activities on its existence, thereby making possible its realisation and continued existence.

To the totalitarian principle of Hitler's foreign policy there was a corresponding normal side of the coin—the dealings, plans and activities of the economy, the diplomatic corps and the armed forces. In return for this camouflaging service done often unconsciously and increasingly unwillingly by the captains of industry, the diplomatic corps and the armed forces, there was perhaps just one favour which they may have thought the régime had done for them. At least according to the view of a wide circle of the bourgeoisie, it was only thanks to the extreme exertions of the totalitarian Nazis in 1933 that the social order guaranteeing their existence could be maintained through the establishment of a political system and the foreign policy inherent in it, to which the same classes were now themselves subjugated. The *Weltanschauung* of National Socialism was aligned to a policy of conquest out of economic but above all social necessities. According to Hitler's thinking inherent parts of this ideology were the integrating forces of anti-semitism, anti-Bolshevism and the conquest of *Lebensraum*. Together they formed part of that trio of power politics, economics and ideology which was the absolutely decisive model accounting for the nature of foreign policy. These ideological elements were appealed to far more emphatically than had been the case in the Wilhelmine epoch, with its slogans of nationalism and anti-semitism. Indeed, this was so much so that in the Third Reich it appeared as if the remedies originally prescribed to safeguard its existence would transform German society of the future into a new form—in fact into a different essence, if we remember the final racist aim of breeding a 'pure race' of a Germanic élite.[96] The answer the world gave to the German provocation, the coming of war, was the outcome of this policy and the successful countering of the totalitarian menace it represented. In Germany therefore, the traditional form of a policy of world power dominated until 1945, which, born of German society, and raised by Hitler to a programme of foreign policy, had for its part helped to stabilise German bourgeois society in principle and maintain it for a long time.

And in reality Hitler's policy and plans did appear more and more traditional—more Wilhelmine, so to speak. It was not that the Führer adhered to a wide-ranging and indiscriminate Pan-German world policy, nor that he translated into foreign aims all the demands and interests voiced by German society, putting them into a political compromise after the fashion of Bethmann Hollweg in the 'September Programme' of 1914.[97] Hitler acted far more according to a fixed concept of foreign policy such as Bülow, Tirpitz and Wilhelm II had resolutely followed[98] from 1897 to the collapse of their ambitious plans for the Fleet—though they had admittedly put greater emphasis on the overseas colonial aspect of their policy—and such as the Third Supreme Command under Ludendorff had again sought to carry out in the First World War. For the Supreme Command in the First World War had already drawn up and put into practice a *Stufenplan* anticipating Hitler's conceptions with its initial continental priorities and subsequent territorial annexations overseas.[99] Looking back, Hitler's Programme was only apparently independent of motivations within German society; in fact it emerges as an expression of the sum of demands and wishes of that society, ordered into a political and military strategy by the Dictator. Thus the continental and overseas demands of Hitler's Programme place it completely within a particular tradition of power politics such as is observable in Prussian–German history since the days of Bismarck.[100]

The German government offices and military sections—the army, navy, SS, Economics Ministry and Colonial Office—were already hurrying on ahead with preparations on the colonial front. A few days before the 'advance on Prague'—a snubbing shock to the Western Powers, even if they were still not shaken into action by it—Hitler officially gave the order of unimpeded preparation for the annexation of colonial territory.[101] The full implications of this instruction can only be recognised if we are acquainted with Hitler's simultaneous directive concerning the accelerated build-up of the navy. According to his wishes, this was to be completed by 1944, while the naval leaders only envisaged achieving this aim by 1945 or later.[102] While still in the first, continental, stage of his Programme, Hitler was already ordering preparations for the colonial annexations of the second stage and the build-up of naval strength necessary for it. His instructions clearly reveal the long-term aims emerging in his ideas which were to be achieved according to his Programme after attaining continental hegemony and *Lebensraum* in Eastern Europe. In the second half of the 1940s, the task would be to 'show the United States a bold front'—

either together with Britain in the role of a junior partner, or against Britain's will. Then, in harmony with the objectives and wishes of the navy and some branches of industry,[103] a position for Germany as an Atlantic and colonial world power would be established. These long-term colonial aims, which had always been latently present, had been deliberately set aside during the period when a settlement was being sought with Britain. But they had never been completely abandoned and now they re-emerged—somewhat earlier than Hitler had expected —in the wake of the anti-British course. In this, the aims were thoroughly in accord with the existing needs in German society— though admittedly these could well have been satisfied through peaceful expansion.

While the fuse on the Czech powder-keg was still burning Hitler was already thinking about his next continental move. When the Polish Foreign Minister Beck visited him in January 1939, Hitler presented him with his plan of overrunning Russia in alliance with the Poles.[104] Thus by 1939 it seems as if Hitler had decided first to march against the East, including Russia, and then to turn to the West and France, in bringing the first stage of his plan to its completion. Afterwards he intended to confront the USA, and—if necessary—Great Britain. But Beck reacted with hesitation, as a result of which the 'minor' Eastern solution moved into view.[105] The road to 3 September 1939, and—in Hitler's view—the senseless war with the reversed fronts was emerging. While von Ribbentrop, working in the context of his anti-British 'alternative' conception, succeeded in bringing Hungary into the Anticomintern Pact, negotiations were taking place in France which kept alive the hope that Hitler's war course could still be halted after all by diverting the Germans economically towards colonial business. For when the German economic experts, led by Weigelt, director of the Deutsche Bank, met the French, things went very promisingly[106] These semi-official attempts by the French side to divert the Reich onto a peaceful course were complemented by the official British policy which was stated once more by the British Ambassador Sir Nevile Henderson in a note to Halifax, the British Foreign Minister, on 9 March 1939.[107] Yet again Great Britain showed itself willing to let the Reich have supremacy in Central Europe, both directly—politically —and indirectly, by economic means. But Britain was not prepared to allow the Reich to pursue an expansionist policy without bounds. A limit was drawn which was completely compatible with Neville Chamberlain's concept of appeasement.

Meanwhile Hitler was setting about 'liquidating' the map of Czechoslovakia—the *'Rest-Tschecher'*, as it was contemptuously called in Nazi terminology; there was talk of the 'Greater German World Empire'. It is true that the propaganda under Goebbels' direction prohibited the usage of this concept. Yet it was by no means absolutely banned, but rather—as was said, significantly enough—reserved for use at a later time.[108]

How would the British react now to Germany, when for the first time Hitler openly stepped beyond the limits of the policy of revisionism and erased yet another European state, Czechoslovakia, from the face of the map? Chamberlain's speech delivered in Birmingham on the 17 March 1939[109] has usually been understood as the resolute reply to Hitler's move of 15 March, and as the great turning-point in British foreign policy.[110] Certainly, the warning undertones of this speech, departing from the original written draft, could hardly be ignored. But seen in the longer term what remained unmistakable was that soon afterwards Chamberlain once again took up his concept of a realistic policy of appeasement towards the Germans as the only way of safeguarding peace and with it the status of Britain as a world power. This attitude in British policy was also to make itself evident in the Polish crisis, just breaking out under Hitler's instigation. It was the Polish crisis, again initiated under the banner of a propaganda barrage about the Reich's colonial demands, which was finally to lead to the Second World War.

E. The Polish crisis and the unplanned war

The British Government's attitude had not changed fundamentally, and if they now handled the German dictator more firmly, they did not lose sight of the actual concept of 'peace and settlement' in doing so. This was revealed very soon in the declaration the British made on 31 March 1939[111] guaranteeing the protection of Poland. The British government emphasised that it was prepared to protect the existence of Poland and to intervene for the sake of Polish national sovereignty in the event of its being 'clearly threatened'. Nevertheless, this did not mean, as has at times been asserted, that Britain would guarantee the frontiers of Poland at any price. Thus there remained quite enough room for manoeuvre in negotiations between Germany and Britain for the two most decisive nations in European politics to find a compromise at the expense of Poland which, though it appeared as a major power, was clearly of second-rate importance compared to Britain and the Reich. The much-discussed Polish guarantee declared by Britain cannot, therefore, be basically understood as demonstrating a British readiness to go to war, such as clearly emerged after the Prague provocation. Of far more concern here is the extreme effort the British government made to save the basic European status quo by agreeing to modifications they could still just tolerate. They were striving at the same time to meet by way of the negotiating table the threatening claims the Germans were making on colonial possessions. British policy, firm and conciliatory at one and the same time, thus sought to discover Hitler's real intentions and then to negotiate over them. London advocated a peaceful solution which left enough leeway to enable them to come to a compromise with the Dictator. That is, they sought a solution which permitted Germany a position of partial hegemony in Europe, yet which was at the same time still just tolerable to the vital interests of Britain and which allowed them then to discuss colonial problems. However, it was the Führer's intention to achieve all these aims and other far more extensive ones by means of war.

The more decisively Hitler adopted the course of war, the more intensively did Chamberlain struggle to begin a political dialogue. But Hitler's expansionist intentions were quite evident in a discussion he had with Burckhardt, the High Commissioner of the League of Nations in Danzig.[112] The Führer talked of pursuing his Eastern policy either in alliance with Poland, or of bringing his more wide-reaching plans in the East to their fulfilment after having completely subjugated the small neighbouring state. This talk between the Swiss diplomat and the German dictator was taking place in an international situation already almost hectically beyond control. On 23 March 1939, German troops marched into the Memel district, and on the same day a German–Rumanian economic agreement was concluded. Unlike Göring and Wohlthat, Hitler did not regard this step as implying a peaceful 'alternative' to his policy of expansion by war. Neither could it bring him to seek economic compensations in south-east Europe in pursuit of an 'economic appeasement' along the lines of British reasoning. On the contrary, the Rumanian oil supplies fell more and more into the hands of the Reich—a prerequisite of the economic war machine necessary for the Dictator's forthcoming lightning campaigns. Four days later, on 27 March 1939, Spain became a member of the Anticomintern Pact. In view of this at least visually impressive front[113] stretching from 'Madrid to Yokohama', which was very soon able to include even Stalinist Russia as a well-disposed neutral country, and in the light of his experience of the English gained in his previous surprise blows on the Continent, Hitler must surely have thought that Great Britain would persist in her neutral attitude in the event of further European ventures. Only one month later, Hitler, agreeing with the wishes of the navy and in line with his own strategic concept, let himself be persuaded to denounce and cancel the numerous stipulations of the Anglo–German Naval Agreement.[114] Hardly any more obstacles now stood in the way of the implementation of 'Plan Z'. The growing fleet could already be used as a means of threatening Great Britain, locking her away in the cupboard of neutrality while also providing Germany with the means later to pursue a successful policy of world power after her victories over Russia and France.

In view of the obvious war course adopted by the German dictator, the American President, Roosevelt, now made an appeal to Hitler to maintain peace.[115] As well-versed diplomatic experts knew, the USA would always intervene on the side of London in the event of a change in the European or world situation endangering Britain.[116] A chief reason for this, no doubt, was to protect their own various economic interests in Europe, but it was also in order not to endanger their strategic security in the Atlantic largely guaranteed by the British fleet, which enabled them to concentrate their own navy in the Pacific against Japan. The USA was observing the game being played by the European powers in an alert and—for Hitler—threatening way. And even if the Führer firmly rejected Roosevelt's attempt at intervention in a masterly display of demagogy,[117] the future shape of the Anglo-Saxon alliance was nevertheless already emerging. Hitler had never lost sight of the contest between the German and American world powers for the long-term political future of the Reich. Precisely for that reason Hitler was painfully intent, up to December 1941, upon keeping the economic and political potential of the United States out of a conflict with Germany[118] until he had achieved the first stage of his Programme, the hegemony which would guarantee self-sufficiency. In the USA people were meanwhile beginning to grasp the strategy and tactics of the Dictator—namely of making political demands on the colonial front in order to notch up gains on the Continent.[119] At the same time in Germany, the 2nd Air Fleet of Göring's Luftwaffe—like the navy in February and March 1939—was preparing a study which foresaw Britain as the chief enemy.[120] Very soon this was to become reality—but before the German armaments had grown sufficiently for Hitler to be prepared to extend his activities overseas.

On 23 May 1939, the Führer delivered an address to the Commanders-in-Chief of the armed forces,[121] which his military adjutant, Schmundt, noted down in brief and rather unclear shorthand. Here Hitler was completely preoccupied with the Polish question. He touched on long-term strategic aims[121a] only in remarking that it was precisely from a secure base won on the Continent, safe from blockade, that the blow could best be struck against the West. In principle Hitler was planning to repeat the attempt which Ludendorff had undertaken after the German victory in the East and the Brest-Litovsk Peace,[122] when it seemed unlikely that Germany could be starved into submission and all forces could be concentrated on the Western front. Hitler wanted to conquer Poland in a lightning war, incidentally the only strategic possibility left open by the Reich's armament preparations 'in breadth' but not 'in depth'.[123] When the Führer spoke of being prepared for a long war which could take the shape of a war of attrition against Britain, he probably intended the remark rather as a reassurance for the officers present. Or perhaps it was envisaged as a possibility for the distant future when Germany, master of a vast continental empire, could defy Britain at sea and endanger the supply routes of the British Empire.

While the Chamberlain government in Great Britain was, as ever, still trying to meet Berlin halfway in order to achieve a reasonable settlement, it also, in a dilatory way and under pressure from Conservative dissenters round Churchill,[124] began negotiations for an alliance with Soviet Russia. It was Churchill's plan, regardless of all the social and political differences between the systems, to re-establish the pre-war alliance and, in reply to Hitler's policy of provocation, to 'encircle him from all sides.[125] Neville Chamberlain, however, on the one hand possessed of a deep antipathy towards Bolshevik Russia, and on the other, mindful of the disastrous mechanism of the alliance system at the outbreak of the First World War, submitted only unwillingly to this wish of Churchill's. He left negotiations in Moscow to subordinate representatives and continued to hold fast to the bilateral line with Berlin.

In the meantime, Stalin had recognised very well the preference the British Prime Minister showed for an agreement with National Socialist Germany. He feared a coalition of the capitalist and fascist states against Communist Russia, in which Hitler's armies would strike out against the USSR as the spearhead for British interests. The Russian Dictator drew the conclusions from his analysis of the international situation. His speech before the XVIIIth Party Congress of the CPSU (B) on 10 March 1939, in which he declared that the Ukraine felt in no way threatened, was correctly understood as a bait by Berlin.[126] The path to 23 August 1939 was being paved; Stalin's concept of foreign policy which he had been following since 1925 of not letting the capitalist states unite against him was becoming clear.[127] The fact that he correctly assessed Chamberlain's policy, at least in respect of his efforts to reach an agreement with Germany, is revealed in the latter's attempts to hold talks with Hitler, made again and again right up to a few weeks before the outbreak of war.

On 13 June Sir Nevile Henderson proposed negotiations.[128] So far as territorial questions were concerned, admittedly, there was only meant to be discussions on the overseas areas; the decisive subjects of the talks otherwise would be the problems of the arms race and trade exchanges. In London they evidently thought they would still be able to make economic concessions to the Reich as well as to suggest a revision of the German–Polish frontier which would guarantee the basic existence of Poland as a state. London was thus prepared under certain circumstances to allot to the Reich spheres of indirect interest on the Continent in the firm belief that Germany, deeply shaken economically, was particularly dependent on the offer of economic appeasement. Then, after granting these just about tolerable concessions, they believed negotiations would move into their second phase on the problem of colonies. But on the German side it was only the diplomats and specialists in the economic field who were interested in these British proposals. For Hitler was determined to bring his *Stufenplan* to

realisation, either in the shelter of British neutrality, or—if necessary
—against Britain's will. For this reason the controversial talks between
Sir Horace Wilson, Chamberlain's confidant, and Wohlthat, the
Minister from Göring's Four Year Plan staff, hardly seem to have
bothered Hitler. It still remains unclear to this day who arranged these
negotiations so shortly before the outbreak of war.[129] While Wilson,
acting completely in line with Chamberlain's strategy, appealed for
talks on the Polish question and sought to win the Germans round to
establishing a peaceful world with the familiar concessions, what does
seem interesting is that it was an economics expert from the group
round Hermann Göring who was discussing these plans for the
German side. That is, Wohlthat was basically seeking in these discussions a peaceful, economic 'alternative' in opposition to Hitler's policy.
Do these negotiations perhaps conceal a final attempt on the part of
Göring to direct Hitler from the path of war? Was Göring trying
to eliminate the economic bankruptcy of the Reich brought about by
the rapacious build-up of armaments by means of economic advantages
won in the course of a strong but peaceful foreign policy—while the
Dictator was intending to cover the financial deficit of his régime by
fighting a war of conquest?

Further private and semi-official, at times quite improbable-sound-
ing, offers and negotiations between the representatives of the two
nations were at the time occupying the minds of well-informed contemporaries.[130] Yet none of them could gain any influence over the
foreign policy decided upon by Hitler. In his 'most extraordinary
declaration' made to the Swiss Commissioner for the League of
Nations, Carl J. Burckhardt, Hitler once again revealed the motives
behind his actions. 'Everything that I undertake is directed against
Russia. If those in the West are too stupid and too blind to understand
this, then I shall be forced to come to an understanding with the Russians to beat the West, and then, after its defeat, turn with all my concerted force against the Soviet Union. I need the Ukraine, so that no
one will starve us out as they did in the last war.'[131] Was Hitler laying
a bait here, via Burckhardt? Was he trying forcibly to demonstrate to
Britain just one more time the advantage of adopting a neutral course,
or perhaps the advantage of an alliance against Russia, so different
socially—an alliance which would only be possible for a short period
of time of course, in view of the strengthening of the navy?[131a]

Perhaps these words of Hitler's should be seen in connection with the 'generous offer' he made on 25 August 1939. While the British government was indefatigably trying to move Hitler to talks, von Weizsäcker, the German State Secretary, was on the one hand, as official representative of his government, rejecting this offer, while on the other, as a member of the opposition to Hitler's war course, informing London about the impending signing of the Moscow pact. In the meantime the Dictator was already announcing to the Commanders-in-Chief of the armed forces on 22 August 1939 the actual fact of the German–Soviet Agreement, which put the army in a position to smash Poland in an isolated action according to plan.[132] In this speech Hitler declared that the Reich was being forced by economic factors among others into making war. No doubt this assertion also served the Führer in proving the rightness of his Programme. Regarded objectively, however, that is in the context of the social situation and functional fabric of power politics and economics in Germany in 1939, it does allow us a glimpse into connections and interdependencies which up till now could only be intimated. 'Our economic position, as a result of our restrictions, has become such that we can only hold out a few more years. Göring can confirm that. No other alternative remains open to us, we will have to act. . .'[133]

The economy which had been totally geared to a war of plunder according to Hitler's Programme, was now demanding its tribute. Hitler intended solving these economic problems which were in accord with the demands of his *Stufenplan*, not by means of peaceful expansion, but in a warlike atavistic fashion. On 23 August 1939, the world heard about the signing of the German–Russian Pact, without being informed about the additional clauses which in practice provided for a partition of Poland.[134] Two days later, with a mixture of tactics and truth, Hitler made his last 'generous offer' to Great Britain to achieve his old goal of an alliance with Britain.[135] What cannot be overlooked, however, is that even in this connection the Polish question could evidently not be a subject for negotiation for Hitler! But with reference to colonial affairs he let the British Ambassador, Nevile Henderson, know[136] that these would only become of acute concern in three, four or five years time. Perhaps from the point of view of the long-term overseas aims, it becomes evident why Great Britain, in the light of the rapid rearmament of the German navy, did not agree to the seemingly generous offer of the Dictator.[137]

The Dahlerus Mission,[138] initiated, interestingly enough, by Göring in the last days of August 1939 in an attempt to save the peace, was bound to break down since Great Britain was not willing to submit to Hitler's ultimatum. The Führer, however, had not signed the pact with the 'devil' in order to have to negotiate further or make what to him appeared trifling alterations to frontiers, but in order to be able at last to let loose an attack and overrun nations in lightning campaigns. According to past experience and the quite one-sided information conveyed to him,[139] Hitler believed he could count on British neutrality in such an event. When the British declaration of war was delivered on 3 September 1939, only a few hours before the French, the war on two fronts, in the East and West, appeared to Hitler as a conflict forced on him at a most inopportune time. His concept of conducting separate *Blitzkriege* and conquering Europe in stages under the shelter of British neutrality, had failed. Would he succeed just once more in altering the course of fate, or would the coming events persuade him to give up his *Stufenplan*, his programme of expansion?

5. The Idea of a 'Partition of the World' (1939–40)

Carl von Clausewitz, one of the theoreticians of modern war,[1] once said that if one is sensible one never begins a war without being clear about what one wishes to gain in and by it. Now which aims was Hitler pursuing in that war on two fronts which he had unwillingly unleashed, in that war the origins of which have been judged by a French historian thus: 'Urged on by the crisis, impelled by the logic of his policy, prompted by the principles of his ideology, he launched into war, followed by the entire élite of the nation'.[2]

The Führer's aim, as laid down in his Programme, was to acquire *Lebensraum* in the East of Europe in separate lightning military campaigns. The Polish campaign was meant to represent a stage on the road towards hegemony in Europe, itself a phase in his Programme. But the war in the West—which was not desired by Hitler even if it was provoked by his policy—had broken out at an inopportune time. How would the German leadership respond in the light of the war on two fronts which, though they had been at pains to avoid it, had now become a reality? What position would Hitler adopt towards Great Britain, which was to remain the decisive power in the future as it had been up till now? Indeed which attitude would the British take towards a Germany which was marching victoriously through

Europe towards supremacy? For up to 22 June 1941, or perhaps even
7–8 December 1941, the conflict between the powers was still totally
confined to the continent of Europe and was only to gain world-wide
dimensions with the entry into the war of the Soviet Union, the United
States and Japan.

During the campaign against Poland, which went off brilliantly for
the German side,[3] it was the position in the West which continually
occupied Hitler's mind.[4] He was certainly aware of the fact that a
concerted intervention by the Western powers would have brought the
Reich into an almost hopeless situation. However, for various reasons
neither the British nor the French were prepared to defy Hitler by
determined military action.[5] Beneath the façade of the 'phoney war',
the policy of appeasement was basically continued. The governments
in London and Paris overestimated the strength of the German army,
and underestimated their own potentialities. Moreover, the Anglo–
French defensive strategy, geared to a 'long war', had been laid down
in April 1939.[6] But France on its own as the decisive power on the
continental mainland, could evidently not make up its mind to march
without being assured of British aid, as it did not wish to allow itself
to be used by the British Government as its 'continental dagger'. The
British Cabinet, however, still seemed to be believing in the possibility
of a peaceful solution to the continental conflict, hanging on to the
idea of a commonsense solution[7] such as Chamberlain had been presenting to Hitler for three years now.

The Führer also tried to shape this unwelcome war on two fronts
according to his own conceptions, through the rigid execution of a
policy and war strategy along the lines of his Programme.[8] For it was
only by means of the pact with Stalin that Hitler succeeded in overcoming the extremely critical situation facing the Reich in the autumn
of 1939. Dependent on the very power which he was intending to
destroy, the Dictator was primarily reliant on the economic aid provided by the Soviet Union not to mention the strategic freedom offered
to his rearguard guaranteed by the German–Russian pact. It was above
all the Russian war aid to the Third Reich which enabled it to overcome its dependence on foreign supplies of raw materials and food.
For a 'British economic blockade of Germany, if the Soviet Union had
participated, would have brought Germany's "war economy" to a
standstill in a short time'.[9]

If Hitler in accordance with his Programme even now regarded the USSR, which was supporting him, as his future enemy, he was trying as before to draw Great Britain, who had declared war on him, onto his side. Significantly enough, on 27 September 1939, he spoke of one of his war aims as being to smash France and force Britain to her knees.[10] By the end of September, it was already becoming evident that the Polish question would be settled according to Hitler's wishes. Pursuing his ideas from *Mein Kampf* and influenced by the actual political situation, Hitler now decided to overrun France in order to 'secure his rear' for the 'big task' in the East. However, it was not his intention to destroy Britain. Rather, he wanted to make Britain compliant to the aims of his Programme by striking military blows against her. In principle, he regarded the war strategy directed against the island empire as a further intensification of that policy of courtship and threat which he had been pursuing since the 1930s. This time Great Britain was to be tied down to his policy through the use of force. Hitler conducted a war against Britain in order to force the stubborn British into an alliance. It is precisely this intention which is also expressed in the 'great peace address' of the Dictator of 6 October 1939.[11] Perhaps it was this mixture of simultaneous courtship and threat against Britain which led one of the most attentive observers of the situation on the German side, the conservative Ulrich von Hassell, to come to the conclusion that Hitler in his heart of hearts was only concerned with the Russian problem.[12] The experienced professional diplomat and son-in-law of Grand Admiral von Tirpitz also recognised that the central question preoccupying the doctrinaire Hitler was how it would be possible to achieve either Great Britain's neutrality or its consent to an alliance, in order for Germany to be able to attack Russia.

Admittedly, Admiral Raeder's quite different ideas were continually being brought to bear on Hitler's strategy and he was forced to give way to them through small concessions. Raeder was pressing for an intensification of the war against Britain, and to this end suggested guaranteeing Russian neutrality.[13] Here we find a plan which is the exact reverse of Hitler's Programme. In its basic features, adopted after 1938 when the navy was forced to give up the principle of British 'friendship', it corresponds to the plans of the German Foreign Office and von Ribbentrop, the 'creator' of the German–Soviet Pact. On the other hand Hitler's line sought agreement with Britain in order to march against Russia, while Raeder's, on the other, was for peaceful coexistence with the USSR in order to be able to defy Great Britain. Both lines, Hitler's and Raeder's, had already emerged in Bismarckian and Wilhelmine Germany,[14] and were now again confronting one another as apparent alternatives. Thus while the navy was demanding an intensified war against Great Britain even to the extent of risking an American entry into the war, and was already planning for war on a global scale—just as during the First World War and the years prior to it[15]—Hitler, right up to December 1941, was consistently at pains to keep the USA out of the struggle.[16] For Hitler wanted to arrange the conflict according to his Programme and wished to conduct lightning campaigns on the continent alone. The Führer thus concentrated on the events in Europe, as is shown by the fact that on 17 October 1939, he described Poland as an advanced glacis for a further concentration and deployment of forces.[17]

While keeping his Russian aim in view, Hitler continued trying to draw Britain over to his side before his intended Russian operation, largely by means of 'peace feelers' to London—whether or not he knew of them all and however seriously these are to be judged. In November 1939, for example, messages arrived in Berlin at the office of State Secretary von Weizsäcker,[18] to the effect that in London by no means all members of the Cabinet were prepared for unconditional war against the Reich: indeed, that there were forces which still regarded it as expedient to make extensive concessions to Germany.[19] However such messages were to be assessed, must they not have confirmed Hitler in his belief[20] that he would still manage to carry out his Programme after all, and win Britain round to his policy? Significantly enough, in the strategic decision to attack Britain and France, made on 23 November 1939,[21] it was said that the intention was to defeat the island empire, Germany's chief enemy—but not to destroy it. After the Polish stage of the 'phoney war'[22] Hitler was intending to turn to the West and the conquest of France, and so create for himself the necessary military rear-cover for his Russian campaign. But he regarded the war against Great Britain as yet another attempt, this time using military means, to draw into the German camp a Britain who had hitherto stubbornly refused to give in. For that reason he also avoided letting too much leak out about the colonial preparations which he had ordered his staff to undertake, already casting sights on the next, over-seas, stage of his plan. He similarly intended keeping the 'American factor' out of the issue, just as he also struggled, up to the end of 1940, against bringing Japan into the conflict.[23] He did this not because, out of short-sightedness or preconceived decisions, he was a 'European-ist', but rather because having learnt certain lessons from the experi-ence of Wilhelmine politics and the First World War, he was guided by a programme of conquest in stages through separate lightning campaigns.

Hitler was therefore intent on bringing the existing war back into line with the course envisaged in his Programme by making offers and striking blows against Great Britain, the decisive power in the issue. What he did not want to do was extend the war through intensi-fied naval activity in the Atlantic and the involvement of Japan[24] or America. The ideas Hitler elaborated upon in talks with Mussolini on the Brenner on 18 March 1940 offer us a partial insight into the shape of Hitler's thoughts.[25] As is of course known, Mussolini referred to and regarded Russia as the chief enemy of the Reich, in order to prevent a German intervention into the Duce's sphere of interest in south-eastern Europe, the Mediterranean and in Africa.[26] Taking this tactical position of Hitler *vis-à-vis* Mussolini completely into account, it seems revealing that Hitler described the German pact with Stalin as a disagreeable interim solution. His plan remained the same as ever, even if he was no longer prepared to renounce colonies completely, as he had been in the 1920s and the beginning of the 1930s. He still planned to gain a 'free hand' in the East after concluding the British alliance, and then partitioning the world off into spheres of interest. The demand for two overseas territories for the Reich—familiar to us since the talks held with Lord Londonderry in February 1936—offers us a clear insight into the long-term aims envisaged for the 1940s. But until that time, the British alliance was a prerequisite for Hitler, and lay at the heart of his considerations.

Both the preconditions laid down in his Programme, as well as the circumstances actually prevailing in the present struggle, led Hitler to two further steps in the course of his dynamic power politics. In order to be able to attack Russia at some time in the future untroubled by other continental problems, and for him to be able to force Great Britain into an alliance before this time, Hitler set about creating two other situations. These were the successful campaigns in north and western Europe in the spring and summer of 1940. With the 'Weser Manoeuvres'[27] against Denmark and Norway in April 1940,[27a] the plans and demands for an Atlantic strategy which had been advocated for a long time by the German navy, came to fruition. At the same time it anticipated an otherwise almost certain occupation of the Atlantic coast of Norway by Britain. Without doubt, Raeder had won influence over Hitler with his anti-British strategy. With this step, the way to the Atlantic was open for the navy.[28] Would the navy now also be able to put through their demands for support bases and colonies in pursuit of their Atlantic strategy and world projects?

The opportunity of looking towards Africa and even the far East and the American continent was to arise after the Reich had overrun France, judged to be the strongest military power on the Continent, in the summer of 1940.[29] These were the intentions of the 'traditionalists' in the navy and the German Foreign Office—amongst whom we can also count the relatively small group of staff under the Colonial Minister designate, von Epp, who were particularly involved in colonial plans. But Hitler did not allow himself to be diverted from his own Programme by these men with their anti-British concept directed towards securing Russian neutrality while seeking acquisition of overseas territories. In his diary entry for 21 May 1940, Halder, the Chief of the Army General Staff, noted down the aims which Hitler envisaged for the present war and which he thus regarded as preconditions for his future campaign against Russia:[30] 'We are seeking contact with Britain on the basis of partitioning the world.' As Hitler saw it in the summer of 1940, the aim was to have Britain as the strongest seapower and Germany as the supreme power on the Continent. At the same time, however, the 'modest' demand continually being raised for two overseas colonies already hinted at the more distant objectives of his policy and war strategy.[31] While the doctrinaire in Hitler continued seeking a settlement with Great Britain, the strategist in him, recognising the absence of any British willingness to yield, saw himself forced to act and discussed the problem of a landing in Britain with Admiral Raeder on the same day, 21 May.[32] Yet he still waited for a sign from the British, for before him lay the tempting goal of the Soviet Union.

That the diplomats in the German Foreign Office were thinking in different terms clearly emerges from the memorandum of Clodius and Ritter, written on the orders of von Ribbentrop, the German Foreign Minister.[33] After the successful conclusion of the French campaign, and with Russia still neutral, a further war aim was here envisaged for the Reich besides that of creating a large economic empire in Europe—namely, acquiring an overseas area of expansion in Central Africa. Such plans were in line with the First World War tradition represented by Solf, whose aims had stood in opposition to those of Ludendorff.[34] The memorandum formulated ideas such as had been discussed in traditional circles of the German leadership in the Foreign Office, in the armed forces and the economy. Hitler, however, held firm to his alternative, which was ultimately the deciding one. At this point, in 1940, we can recognise quite clearly what had already begun to suggest itself in the latter half of the 1930s and what was to become even more evident in the shape of the 'racist war of extermination': despite all the advantages which the conservative leadership groups—for example in the economy—had drawn from their collaboration with the National Socialist régime, and which they would continue to draw in the future, the differences between their interests and those of the Nazis were becoming ever more apparent.[35]

Hitler's Programme has elsewhere been described as a programme which represented the sum of all the political demands emerging in the Reich since 1866–71—the demands for an economic empire in Europe; Central Africa as an area for expansion; a policy of rearmament as a means of stimulating the economy; the use of those arms in successful lightning campaigns. Now this Programme was coming into ever sharper conflict with the demands of the groups who had always supported the goals appearing in the Programme. If it had now been possible to achieve peace under the conditions outlined by the Foreign Office, the demands of the heavy and manufacturing industries (like those of the chemical industry) would certainly have been satisfied. The wishes of the army and navy, too, had been fulfilled for the time being. Not least of all in its lightning campaigns, the Programme had fulfilled its domestic function of integrating internal elements. It had saved the existing social structure from possible or feared social change —the ghost of the social revolution was exorcised. But in place of that, the conservative leading classes in the Reich were now confronted by the National Socialist demand for the 'biological revolution' which likewise threatened their hereditary ruling positions. From the point of view of the conservatives, the 'Hitler system' had basically fulfilled its 'function' on the domestic and foreign political fronts, as well as in the military sector. A more extensive war fought under the banner of a racist ideology would simply contribute to the strengthening of the power of the new Nazi élite and their claim to replace the traditional ruling classes.[36]

But the Programme which had originally served both Hitler and his conservative helpers now moved towards its fulfilment with an almost automatic momentum. For, with the implementation of the Programme, the continued existence of the Nazi system of domination which in the meantime had become the absolute and controlling power in Germany, was now, for better or for worse, irrevocably bound to the personal fate of Hitler. Indeed, even if Hitler had contemplated the idea—which seemed absurd to him—of making peace by renouncing further claims, the rest of the world which had been provoked by the Reich, particularly Churchill's Britain and Roosevelt's America which was supporting her,[37] would hardly have allowed, for example, Germany's retention of the conquests made hitherto. For the 'unconditional surrender' formula was long-standing and by no means a spontaneous demand devised at the Casablanca Conference.[38] Under the Nazi régime of terror, the Programme was to reach its fulfilment within its own terms—'all or nothing'. And even those who had once called upon the magician Hitler and now found him undesirable were now forced to take part in the gamble which Hitler had initiated. For these one-time powerful elements had long since been forced into political submission by the Führer and his régime.

Thus 'conservative Germany' was envisaging African goals—the second stage in Hitler's programme of conquest. They were obviously wanting to return to a policy of liberal expansionism which, though based on political supremacy, was nevertheless strongly influenced by economic factors (and which was to be pursued under conditions imposed in a victorious peace extremely favourable to the Reich). But in the meantime, Hitler was concentrating all his attention solely on the European continent and particularly on the response of the British to the peace feelers he was putting out. In contrast to this, it was only half-heartedly that he followed all the preparations undertaken by the armed forces in connection with 'Operation Sea Lion' which arose from strategic and rational calculation.[39] For again and again, Berlin received reports according to which the British Cabinet was split over the policy to be adopted towards Germany. Hitler was trusting to his good fortune. He not only continued to believe that he could avoid having to extend the European war into a world war. He even tried to guide the continuing conflict back along the lines envisaged in his Programme, shaped by a strategy of separate and isolated lightning campaigns, thus making the conflict alternating war and peace. In accordance with the stage of what Ernst Nolte has called the normal, conventional European war,[40] Hitler was evidently also considering at this time (the latter half of 1940) exiling European Jews to the island of Madagascar lying off the African mainland.[41] As a response to the question of anti-semitism, this was a view which was to change significantly when the war of extermination against Bolshevism and Jewry was to reach its zenith in Russia.[42]

At the height of his power in that decisive year, 1940, after the victorious French campaign, Hitler was waiting for the British to give in. It was for that reason that in the cease-fire treaty made with the defeated French the delicate question of the overseas territories of the 'Grande Nation' were excluded.[43] For one thing, Hitler certainly had no wish to draw Britain's attention already to his extensive ambitions overseas. For another, he was considering the possibility of taking the French fleet into the service of the Reich for the continuing war.[44] It was for these reasons of a tactical and temporary renunciation of global undertakings or intentions that he also refrained from establishing a German Colonial Ministry in the spectacular form such as Reichsleiter Bouhler, the rival of General von Epp, had requested of the Führer on their flight back from Paris to headquarters in Bruly de Pêche on 23 June 1940.[45] As Hitler saw it, a further demonstration of Germany's military might would be necessary to make Britain 'see the light', while in the Reich meanwhile, 1 July was being named as the probable date for an armistice.[46] In Germany the plans for a colonial Reich went ahead, just as Hitler had ordered them, though he had never regarded them as an alternative to expansion in the East, or even as the next aim. These plans not only seemed to complement the war aims of the navy, the admittedly more modestly formulated plans of the Foreign Office and the wishes—aimed more strongly at economic expansion of an indirect kind—represented by the various economic groups.[47] As emerges from the notes made by Rademacher, the expert in the 'German' department of the Foreign Office, reporting Hitler's remarks on the 'Jewish problem', the plans preparing for a colonial Reich in the course of the 'conventional European war' also seemed to be in agreement with the kind of 'solution to the Jewish problem' which Hitler had been suggesting in the course of his conversations.[48] Rademacher stated in detail the conditions under which the 'export of the Jews' from Europe was supposed to 'take its course'. Yet in just the same way as Hitler's Programme contrasted with the 'alternatives' of the conservatives, so too, as the war against Bolshevik Russia took a more radical course, this 'problem' was to move towards the extreme solution long since laid down for it.[49] Neither could the African alternative be brought to bear in this question, for the extermination of Bolsheviks coincided with that of the Jews in the course of the conquest of *Lebensraum* in the East and occurred during the first —continental—phase of the Programme, not the second—overseas— phase. Madagascar and Africa were aims for a future time—not only from the point of view of the Programme, but also from considerations of power politics. The Führer evidently did not wish to wait for the realisation of those future aims before 'solving the Jewish problem'.[50]

It is nevertheless apparent that at this time Hitler was already examining plans concerning a later stage of his Programme. Although according to his Programme such plans would only have become relevant after the Russian campaign, seen strategically under the prevailing conditions of the war situation and the reactions of Germany's old and new enemies, these plans could have become important before that time. That Hitler was considering such plans is shown by the fact that he affirmed the intentions of the naval leadership presented by them on the 6 July 1940 and on which Hitler put his seal some five days later.[51] The significance of this document lies in the fact that it shows that the build-up of the German fleet was now undertaken with the idea that America would be the enemy. Ever since 1928 Hitler had been preoccupied with this very idea, in complete agreement with the political reflections of the representatives of the liberal and conservative bourgeoisie.[52] Even if originally Hitler had regarded the German contest with America for world domination as being among the tasks facing a future generation of Germans, this idea was soon to acquire a new and very real significance. And yet this intention did not prevent Hitler from keeping a careful watch in 1940 to ensure that the United States stayed out of the war. He wanted America neither in a battle in Europe and the Atlantic, nor in the Pacific and Far East in the event of a possible attack by Japan southwards. In Hitler's view, on the other hand, any steps taken by Japan against British possessions in South East Asia might encourage Britain to come to peace terms with Germany.[53] This possibility seemed all the greater since rumours were continually coming through from London which could have been regarded as peace feelers.[54] Although these rumours were not to be taken all that seriously, they certainly influenced Hitler's thinking. The 'contacts' between Germany and Britain which were revived at limited intervals were only broken off in August 1942, after the Americans had won the decisive air and sea battle of Midway in June and thus succeeded in turning the war in favour of the two Anglo-Saxon powers.[55] But by the middle of July 1940 Churchill already seemed to have achieved success with his call for perseverance, however strong the opposition in the Cabinet might have been.[56]

As so often before, the Führer was disappointed by the British. In the German public media organised by Goebbels' propaganda, this disappointment revealed itself in the wish that 'God punish Britain', as in the First World War. On 13 July 1940, Hitler seemed almost at a loss over the hostile attitude of the British.[57] In his statements, he was already moving towards the solution which, brought to fulfilment in 'Operation Barbarossa', was in fact finally to destroy his Programme. It occurred to him that Britain regarded Russia as a possible spearhead on the European mainland. So if he were to open a second front— still fighting the British in the West—and overrun the Soviet Union, then the British would lose any hope of help from Russia.[58] Thus, if originally the British alliance with Germany was intended to enable Hitler to conquer Europe and the Soviet Union without hindrance, Hitler was now contemplating using Russia both as an end and as a means in his Programme. The campaign in the East which had once been envisaged as the culmination of the first stage of the Programme, to be achieved under the wing of British approval, now became a means to an end, to be used to bring about a more favourable British attitude.

The question remains as to what plans Hitler had for his 'junior partner' Britain after the conquest of Russia. It was here already that

America appeared on the scene as the next opponent of Germany.[59] This was quite in line with the dynamic of Hitler's political calculations, though it did involve compromising his original Programme which envisaged such steps over a longer period of time. The Russian campaign—the step which Hitler now judged simultaneously as an end and as a means to an end—appears as a last desperate effort by Hitler to keep to his Programme. After the successful conclusion of this Russian stratagem, the Programme would then take on its global dimension and come to its full fruition in a shorter time than Hitler had originally envisaged. What Hitler failed to recognise was that with this step he had in fact finally given up that Programme.

While from now on Hitler became increasingly preoccupied with the 'Eastern solution',[60] von Ribbentrop, the Foreign Minister, did succeed in winning the Führer round for a short time to a project stemming from his, Ribbentrop's, 'conception'. His aim was to try to bring the present war to a victorious conclusion. Although he was certainly not enthusiastic about it, Hitler did agree to von Ribbentrop's idea of trying to force Great Britain into giving in by creating a continental power bloc stretching from Madrid to Tokyo, and the idea dominated the political activities of Hitler and his Foreign Minister once again in the months of September and October.[61] The signing of the Three Power Pact between Germany, Italy and Japan on 27 September 1940 marked a climax in this policy advocated by von Ribbentrop. Under the pact it was agreed among other things that the parties would 'give mutual support with all the political, economic and military means available, in the event that any one of the three nations party to the pact is attacked by a power which is not at present involved in the European war or the China–Japan conflict'.[62] So far as Hitler's strategy was concerned, what stood in the foreground here was the intention of preventing an American intervention in the continuing struggle by threatening a war across two oceans, in the Atlantic and the Pacific.

The plan for a continental bloc, characteristic of von Ribbentrop's way of thinking, was intended to serve the function of—temporarily— isolating the United States while maintaining the neutrality of Russia. This would force Britain to her knees and might well then enable Germany to make territorial gains overseas. Hitler, on the other hand, seems to have undertaken this final attempt in order by this means to win London round to 'his' solution. However, the agreement with Japan, the Far Eastern partner in the Three Power Pact, came as little to fruition as did the attempt to make Mussolini, Franco and Pétain compliant to Hitler's wishes. Von Ribbentrop's conception of a continental bloc misfired. The Führer finally dropped the idea probably by the end of October, and once again announced the 'priority of the Eastern policy'.[63] Hence the failure of the Berlin talks in November 1940[64] with Molotov, the Soviet head of Government, merely meant that Hitler was confirmed in his decision which was becoming more and more evidently in favour of the 'military solution in the East'[65]— all the more so as Great Britain, the Reich's crucial enemy, could not be forced into submission.

Faithful to his favourite idea of creating an alliance with Britain, the Führer never really seriously considered conquering the British. But leaving this fact aside for a moment, it nevertheless seems that Hitler was relying on a demonstration of military force to draw Great Britain on to his side. However, even in 1940, such a victorious year of the war for Germany, the strength of the German armed forces was just not sufficient to guarantee the success of 'Operation Sea Lion'. It was not just the protection afforded Britain by its island situation, nor the weather—quite unfavourable for a landing operation over large distances—which led the German officers to be extremely sceptical in their judgment of the chances of a landing. The strength of the British navy and the striking power of the Royal Air Force also restrained Hitler from giving 'Operation Sea Lion' the go-ahead. Alongside this came the restraining factor of Hitler's doctrinaire inclination towards his British enemy, whom he continually tried to win round through offers of peace, having no desire to run the risk of an invasion and an extension of the war with the British. Besides, by the middle of September 1940, the Reich with its 'National Socialist' Luftwaffe had already lost the 'Battle of Britain'. The German fighters did not manage to achieve superiority in the air as they had done in the Polish and French campaigns. Apart from the fact that the Führer was never absolutely and genuinely prepared to agree wholeheartedly to an invasion, this failure of the Luftwaffe meant that the decisive precondition necessary for an invasion remained unfulfilled— even though in the plans of the German Army High Command Great Britain was already being regarded as an occupied country.[66] Britain

103

stood its ground. Its air force proved itself the equal of Göring's—indeed its better—while, guarding the world-wide communication lines of the Empire, the Royal Navy guaranteed the sovereignty of the admittedly hard-pressed British.[67]

Once again, in talks with Molotov, von Ribbentrop tried to define the world-wide spheres of interest of the Germans, Italians, Russians and Japanese. Within the framework of the southern expansion permitted to all the Great Powers—Italy into North Africa, Germany into Central Africa and Japan into the Pacific—Russia was supposed to expand southwards towards India—although von Ribbentrop never actually made this offer directly to Molotov in the Berlin talks. It was a move which would indirectly support von Ribbentrop's anti-British interests. These global intentions of von Ribbentrop, in contrast to Hitler's ideas, always envisaged and wished for the continued existence of Russia. And yet they failed not least of all because of the concrete territorial demands, made by his Russian negotiating partner, which certainly seemed petty and narrow to von Ribbentrop. In the course of the very broadly conceived defensive policy of the Soviet Union which had been pursued since 1925, Molotov made these demands as the price Hitler had to pay for German–Soviet agreement: primary demands with respect to Finland, Rumania, Bulgaria and the Mediterranean–Black Sea straits; more far-reaching demands on Hungary, Yugoslavia, the western part of Poland and the outlets to the high seas on the Baltic.[68] It may well be that in making these extensive demands, Stalin was already speculating on a possible defeat of Nazi Germany.[69] But to Hitler's way of thinking, all these signs seemed to indicate one thing. As so often, he would have to risk the 'head-on fight' and begin the war against the USSR, which he now judged both as a military means and an end. The defeat of Russia, he thought, would then enable him to win over Great Britain and 'throw down the gauntlet' to America.[70]

6. 'Operation Barbarossa': The Conflict between Power Politics and Ideology (1941–43)

Hitler's improvised plan for total war made in the autumn of 1940[1] was intended to assist him in fulfilling his Programme in one massive effort. In a world *Blitzkreig*, the Soviet Union was to be overrun, thus achieving the central war aim pursued in his policy since 1925. At the same time the defeat of Russia would serve Hitler against Britain— her supposed weapon on the mainland would be thrust from her hands, though he was powerless at present to include the 'American factor'[2] into the practical execution of his strategy. His Programme—which he was to widen onto a global scale[3] very soon afterwards—had to depend for its realisation on the success or failure of the Russian operation. With the visionary aims of Hitler's Programme seemingly within his grasp, and in accordance with his political calculations, Roosevelt's America appeared as Hitler's next enemy in the plans, projects and statements of 1941. For the thoughts of the Führer and his officers, diplomats and economic experts ranged towards Africa,[4] the Far East[5] and across the oceans of the world. After the collapse of the USSR within a few weeks[6]—for that is how Hitler thought of it—Great Britain would either be forced into a rapid surrender or else come to support the Reich as its 'junior partner'. After the armed forces had been adequately re-equipped (with the Luftwaffe and navy having priority over the army), Germany would be armed for the fight for world supremacy by virtue of its power bases in Europe, Africa and the Atlantic.

These thoughts reflect one of the two motives in Hitler's policy and war strategy. It is echoed again and again, particularly in the first weeks of the Russian campaign which were so victorious for Hitler. As a basic pattern it also determined Hitler's strategy in 1942, when the Three Pact Powers, Germany, Japan and Italy, stood at the height of their power.[7] But the other factor which impinged intensively on the decisions of Hitler and the Reich with the beginning of the Russian campaign, was the motive of racism. The conventional European war waged by Hitler in fact as the continuation of his 1930s policy which had been based on the conventional methods of 'courtship' and threats just short of war, was now intensified by this factor into a racist war of annihilation. This racism was no longer conducted sporadically or for propaganda, as in the 'Night of Broken Glass' pogrom; it was racism carried on by genocide. Without considering insignificant 'difficulties', which anyway seemed immediately to offer new political advantage,[8] both the motives in Hitler's policy—traditional power politics and 'National Socialist' racism—appeared to complement each other successfully within his Programme. The Programme itself had been built upon the driving forces of anti-semitism, anti-Bolshevism and the conquest of *Lebensraum*, all of which acted as factors integrating German society.[9] But from now on, the racist component came increasingly to the forefront of events, and as such was in practice a 'new' feature[10] in the history of Prussia–Germany. It was at this moment that the two faces of the Programme were revealed: the 'dual state' broke apart. On the one hand, in clear priority, there was the rational power political component—though it served goals which were themselves irrational and tainted by racism. The other face of this Janus-state was the irrational racist policy which reached full fruition under the banner of 'Operation Barbarossa', which Hitler regarded as his personal task.

Originally, the 'old' conservative ruling class had helped the National Socialist party to get power in order to be able to safeguard their hereditary positions of power. But now the 'new' National Socialist élite, feeling itself victorious, no longer wished to see the ideological factors of anti-semitism, anti-Bolshevism and *Lebensraum* used primarily to serve the existing social order and treated merely as slogans to achieve integration. What they desired was the strict realisation of these motivating elements in their *Weltanschauung*, and—connected to this—they wanted to replace the conservative leading groups with the 'biologically' superior SS master race.[11] The ideological factor in the Programme had helped to guarantee and consolidate the working of the existing social order. Now the ideology worked more and more as a brake, blocking the development of the rational power politics which Hitler also continued to conduct. Power politics in Prussia–Germany had always been upset by ideology.[12] In the Wilhelmine Reich, it was the reflex of a society with a mixed feudal and capitalist organisation unable to reconcile its contradictions. But now, this 'ideologised' power politics had reached a climax hitherto unknown in the history of Prussia–Germany. This was not motivated by the Dictator's 'demonic power', but was the result of objective, if somewhat complex historical relations and conditions. For reasons of political, military and technical development in general, and acute problems of social tension in particular, German society at the beginning of the 1930s was prescribed the most drastic 'treatment' since its beginnings[13] in the form of the fascist 'remedy'. The medicine—the plan which Hitler had personally designed and had understood merely as a foreign political programme—had clearly been necessary temporarily to safeguard the existence of German society. But now the stimulant proved itself to be a poison which was finally to destroy the very existence of the society and state.

Just as once the 'Brown Shirt battalions' won power over their 'black, white and red' rivals, so now the system's ideology, pressing for its full realisation, obstructed a power politics based on rational and pragmatic calculation. For now the ideology stepped out of its former subordinate role and moved toward material fruition. Already in the 1930s, after their initial enthusiasm for the new régime had disappeared, Germany's conservatives had tried to halt Hitler's ruinous policy aimed at war by means of the policy of liberal imperialistic expansion. But just as their 'alternative' had failed to stop Hitler at that time, so now the representatives of the Foreign Office, including Ribbentrop, the naval leaders and those in the economy also proved unsuccessful. For it was the Führer himself, of course, who had been using his racist policy to undermine the policy of pragmatic political calculation—which was still dominant up to the beginning of 'Operation Barbarossa'. His Programme and the driving forces behind it had developed a momentum of their own. The 'extermination measures' which had been introduced according to programme both in and after the Polish campaign in practice obstructed the return of Germany into the concert of nation states. And the dynamic which the Programme and its forces had acquired now pressed for its fulfilment. This really left only the one alternative open—'all or nothing'. The only exception would have been if a revolutionary reversal in domestic politics had occurred, taking the power away not only from Hitler, fanatically pursuing his Programme, or the 'new' élite in the Nazi Party and the SS who were responsible for the implementation of the racialist policy, but also from the 'old' ruling groups. But even in the course of the 'Russian roulette' to decide whether the Reich was 'to be or not to be', these latter groups were still toying with notions of a victorious peace beneficial to the Reich and their own interests—dreams from an era long since past, which had had no chance of fulfilment even in the First World War. But who could provide the opponents of the Reich with a real alternative? From the point of view of the important personalities on the opposing side, as well as from the vantage point of the historical observer, both the 'old' and the 'new' leading groups in Hitler's 'dual state' sat in the same boat. First of all they did so willingly, then later against their wishes, until in the end they were forcibly bound to one another by the iron chains of terror.[14] But perhaps we should turn our attention again to the policies and war strategy of the Third Reich in the years 1941 and 1942. This will enable us to diagnose more clearly the contradiction between power politics and ideology within that Reich, though its origins can be traced back into the earlier history of Prussia–Germany.[15]

After Hitler had made the decision, in the latter half of 1940, to adopt the 'military solution in the East', his thoughts turned ahead to the time when 'Operation Barbarossa' would be victoriously concluded. Not only Hitler, but also the General Headquarters of the armed forces and the Army General Staff all thought that Germany would be able to overrun Russia in a few weeks. The General Staff, who, according to tradition, had been primarily thinking merely within the now broken framework of the France–Poland–Czechoslovakia triangle, now found themselves—not least logistically—in unknown terrain. After the expected defeat of Russia, the Dictator intended establishing a colonial and Atlantic power base[16]—which he hoped to achieve side by side with the British, as rumours were again reaching Germany at the very beginning of 1941 that in Britain, the Under-

Secretary of State Butler, for example, was quite prepared to make peace with the Reich.[17] On the ruins of the Soviet Union—to be conquered as far as the operational line from Archangel to the Caspian Sea—the continental empire would be set up as the kernel and first stage of his Programme. From strategic military motives stemming from the continuing war on the one hand, and for reasons arising from his Programme on the other, Hitler then intended enlarging this continental base both by reaching out towards the Near East, North-west Africa and Central Africa, and by acquiring overseas bases. After all, as early as *Mein Kampf* Hitler had intimated that colonial territory would be all the easier to gain after the creation of a strong central base in Europe.[18]

Hitler's directive of 17 February 1941,[19] ordering preparation of an assembly plan in Afghanistan against India, provides an indication of the strategy envisaged for the 'Post-Barbarossa' period. This move represented a further step in the sustained struggle against Great Britain, aimed at striking at the very heart of her Empire, to make her willing to accept an alliance. Moreover, another, as yet perhaps still distant, possibility was offered in this operation and by the decision made a few weeks previously to support Mussolini in North Africa.[20] In a pincer movement from Russia across Iran, and from North Africa towards the Suez Canal, the Near East could be placed under control. It was in this way that the leading naval officers who advocated the 'periphery' strategy planned to conquer Great Britain, while Hitler as always thought of using the operation to force Britain on to the side of the Reich.[21]

But the aims of the officers at the Armed Forces General Headquarters, as revealed on 11 June 1941,[22] went even further in the Near East and north-west Africa. They too were discussing strategy for the time after the Russian campaign, envisaging in this case both Britain and the United States as enemies of the Reich. These ideas certainly corresponded to Hitler's notion of establishing an Atlantic world power base, seeing North-west Africa and the Near East as strategic outposts, and no doubt also considering Central Africa as territory for colonial expansion. From such a power base and with this political momentum, the fight against America could then be waged. Admittedly, in line with his Programme, Hitler would have liked to see Britain on his side—unlike General Jodl who was led entirely by considerations of calculated strategy. Why it was that Hitler never signed this directive No. 32 is not known. Karl Klee's theory that this was a simple oversight seems very plausible,[23] particularly if we remember the large measure of agreement which still obviously existed at this time between Hitler and Jodl on strategy.

But the Führer's mind at this time was naturally preoccupied with the imminent war against the Soviet Union. The last attempt to draw Britain onto the German side before 'Operation Barbarossa' was made by Hitler's deputy, Hess, when he flew to Great Britain in May 1941 in order to forge a peace. But Hess's puzzling mission, this final rather amateurish effort—yet one so characteristic of the Nazi system of government as a whole—fully in line with Hitler's ideas and no doubt tolerated by him, proved a complete failure.[24]

Meanwhile, the preparations for the campaign against Russia went ahead. On 6 June 1941, the armed forces High Command issued the infamous 'Commissar Order', for the impending war in the East.[25] According to this order, commissars of the Russian Red Army who were made prisoners of war would be 'eliminated' after a 'process of selection'. This ideologically-motivated directive, in line with Hitler's Programme and issued by the armed forces, was to be executed by them together with the Sonderkommandos (Special Corps) of the SS.[26] This order to conquer Lebensraum and simultaneously exterminate Bolsheviks and Jewry in order to create a 'pure-bred' world— these and other orders and 'measures' escalated the war which was initiated soon afterwards against the USSR. They lent the war a new character which European and German history had previously known only in colonial wars. But along with the monstrously large loss of life these measures brought to the Red Army, they also mobilised enormous reserves of strength and resistance among the Russian people. To avoid colonial subjugation and escape physical extermination, the Russian people took on the totalitarian challenge in the fight for their very existence. Hitler had never planned the same type of rule in the Soviet Union[27] as was for the time being still largely imposed in Western Europe—though in West Europe, too, there were exceptions[28] which offer us an insight into the world-wide racist colonialism of the Führer.[29] It was largely these ideological 'measures' taken to accomplish the Programme that finally prevented Hitler the strategist and the armed forces from achieving their military shrouded aims, which anyway could hardly have been achieved in the form of a 'conventional' war.

The differences of political interest between the Dictator and the leading industrialists, who up till then profited from Hitler's conquests, now became more apparent.[30] The wishes and intentions of industry would certainly have been better met[30a] by utilising Russian commissars and Jews as cheap sources of labour than by exterminating this sorely needed potential labour force. The first alternative would have guaranteed the continued functioning of the Third Reich's war economy, which at the beginning of the 'Barbarossa' operation was not even running at full stretch. In addition, using cheap labour could have assured greater profits—just as happened with the utilisation of foreign workers and concentration camp inmates, which, significantly enough, was made only from 1942 onwards. Although, morally speaking, such thinking did not imply a genuine alternative, it nevertheless drew the line at the physical extermination of human beings, if only for reasons of expediency. The intention of the economic ruling groups here—however horrible this may sound—was to shape the war of conquest, now that it had been started, along rational lines rather than to undermine it through irrational steps. Hitler's system with its internal contradictions resembled Homer's Penelope who, in order to evade her pressing suitors, at night unraveled the carpet which she wove during the day. Similarly, Hitler impeded his pragmatically calculated rise to world power by his ideologically-flavoured policy—without, however, recognising the contradiction. For in his Programme both poles were completely integrated. For a long time, both elements working together had safeguarded the existence of the 'dual state' and served to maintain the social order. Now, in the course of their actual implementation, both components split apart and worked against each other. Hitler's system was orientated towards irrational goals. It cannot ultimately be understood within objective historical categories, for it was based on racist dogma. By 1941 at the latest, the irrational measures which at first served these goals came to dominate over the rational, calculated methods of power politics within the system. In the final analysis, the irrational elements helped the 'cunning of reason' in history to victory, in that they brought about their own and the system's downfall.

It was still power politics based on rational strategic calculation which seemed to be prevailing in the brilliantly successful first weeks of the Russian campaign. Perhaps it reached its climax in the discussions Hitler held with Oshima, the Japanese Ambassador to Germany on 14 July 1941.[31] In a momentary temporal foreshortening of his visionary plans for fighting the USA for world supremacy, Hitler, clearly carried away by the political dynamic of the situation, was here already envisaging America as Germany's next enemy—a plan which he was to give up again soon afterwards.

The Russian campaign seemed to be running according to programme when the Führer received the Japanese Ambassador on 14 July. In expectation of the impending collapse of Russia, Hitler wanted to suggest that a war be waged jointly by Japan and Germany against America. In contrast to the conception of Foreign Minister von Ribbentrop, and the suggestions of his naval strategists, Hitler had hitherto always been at pains to insist on Japan's keeping clear of the Russian theatre of war. He wanted to limit Japan to the task of holding Britain in check and keeping America neutral[32] in order to render impossible the establishment of an Anglo–American front in Europe. (This was the policy he later returned to after he had given up this short-lived plan of including the visionary American aims of the Programme in the concrete planning of policy and strategy.) But now, in the discussions with Oshima, he held out the prospect of Japan's participation in the 'liquidation' of the 'assets' of the massive Russian state. While Hitler thought it was the task of the German troops to achieve the decisive victory over the USSR, he thought of employing Japan's aid in occupying and dividing the defeated colossus. Hitler talked of Japan's occupying the far eastern territories of the Soviet Union. One major reason for this suggestion was probably to get the Japanese to agree to a coordinated plan of action. As Hitler envisaged it, he would win 'his' war against Russia and German tanks would reach their operational goals on the Archangel–Urals–Caspian Sea line. The colonisation of Russia would then be put into effect under the 'new' SS élite, and with the help of Japan in the Far East, the Russian mammoth would be divided up. Then, as soon as all this had been accomplished, Hitler intended moving against Britain and the United States to 'destroy' them. This *volte-face* over Britain must certainly be understood, from the tactical point of view, in the light of Japan's hostility towards the British as the white colonial rulers in Hong Kong,

Burma, Singapore and India. Perhaps it might also have been that the idea of a fight against the British, which indeed seemed a strategically rational move, was now prevailing in Hitler's mind over his preference for an alliance with Britain. It remains unclear just how Hitler would have treated a defeated Britain which, having lost her 'Russian sword' on the mainland of Europe, was now also to be robbed of the USA, her second support. For Hitler took up the idea of Anglo–German 'friendship' again and again, and—if he had succeeded (together with Japan) in his daring blow against the USA—he would certainly have preferred an alliance with Great Britain to a further close association with Japan.[33]

But what was important in the discussions on 14 July 1941, was that Hitler suggested to General Oshima that Germany and Japan should attack and 'destroy' the USA in a coordinated war effort. The fight against the United States for the supremacy of the world was an idea which had been occupying Hitler since 1928.[34] Originally this was supposed to have been a task reserved for a generation of racially superior Germans after the Führer's death. But now, in the summer of 1941, things looked different. The implementation of the first stage of the Programme, hegemony over the continent of Europe, was nearly at hand; plans were being made for the establishment of an Atlantic power base embracing the Near East, North-west Africa, territories for colonial expansion and overseas support bases. In view of this, Hitler, following the momentum of political calculation, was clearly considering attacking the USA with the help of Japan. At this moment it was pure political calculation, essentially rational pragmatism, which held sway over Hitler's thoughts.

And yet no more than one week after this, the other aspect of his Programme, the ideological obstacle to purely political considerations, became apparent in talks with the Croatian Defence Minister, Kvaternic. On 21 July 1941[35] Hitler told Ante Pavelić's[36] collaborator that he intended 'solving' the 'Jewish question' in Europe and sending the 'racial aliens' either to Madagascar or to Siberia. During the conventional European war, the suggestion of the Madagascar plan had already been mooted. Besides this, the thought was now emerging of seeking a 'solution to the Jewish problem' in connection with the conquest of *Lebensraum* and the fight against Bolshevism in Russia. At the beginning of 1942, these ideas were elaborated and intensified in the Berlin Wannsee Conference.[38] Even at the moment when political pragmatism and the most daring military planning were seemingly reaching their most triumphant heights, the Dictator did not discard his racist dogma. The orders to exterminate the Russian 'sub-humans' and to colonise the Soviet Union caused the resistance in Russia—particularly in the later partisan war[39]—to become far more tenacious than had been the case earlier in Western Europe. Moreover, the 'measures' taken to 'exterminate the Jews' were destined to tie down German military forces and block transport routes, as well as eliminate a potential working force for the armaments industry. But above all, in pursuit of this racist dogma, Germany was to provoke the rest of the horrified world into total and unlimited war against the Reich.

This intensification into total war, which was brought about by the intrusion of the ideological factor into power politics, ultimately made any attempt at peace negotiations almost impossible.[40] The ruling groups in Germany which had originally supported Hitler and now found themselves more and more in opposition to him, could therefore hardly find anyone among the enemy powers who would listen to their 'alternative' plans. For the latter had decided that there seemed only one meaningful answer to the challenge the Reich had made, and that was to wage war to the point of unconditional surrender.

Indeed, as early as December 1941, the German attack was brought to a standstill short of Moscow by the determined and remarkable resistance of the Soviet army.[41] With it, the Programme was wrecked; the ideological element was no longer supporting that of power politics, but was rather hindering it; the ideology misled Germany into overestimating its own strength and into showing scant regard for the Russians.[42]

On 6 December 1941, in the context of a strategic review of the situation, Hitler expressed the rationalised and hence accurate supposition that it was hardly likely that the war would still be won.[43] But the Führer did not recognise and eliminate the basic fault—the ideological 'interference'. For on the one hand, anti-semitism was an integral part of his thought, and on the other, it projected an enemy and scapegoat which served to commit the population in firm solidarity to the goals of its leaders. However, at the very moment when the Russian campaign—and hence in principle Hitler's Programme—collapsed, the war escalated into a world war. For on 7 and 8 December 1941, Japan attacked the United States at Pearl Harbour.[44] On 11 December 1941, Hitler declared war on America in accordance with the Three Power Pact.

Why did Hitler decide to take the step which, hitherto, he had been at such great pains to avoid? The Japanese attack hardly came as a fundamental surprise to the German leadership.[45] It is true that Hitler was not previously informed about the precise date of the attack. But he was certainly informed about Tokyo's intention of taking 'head-on flight' and attacking the USA as the only way out of the almost inescapable situation confronting the Japanese Empire, particularly economically. Even so, the Führer decided to wage war against America on the side of Japan only reluctantly. His agreeing to support the Far Eastern partner in the Three Power Pact was based on the idea of undermining the attempts at agreement being made between Tokyo and Washington. For in the event of a Japanese–American reconciliation in the autumn 1941 negotiations, the USA, without the threat of a war front in the Pacific, could have hurried to the aid of both Britain and Russia in Europe. Just as earlier he had always wanted to assign to Japan the task of holding Britain in check and keeping America in neutrality to avoid the second front in Europe, so the Führer now decided to come in on Japan's side. In order to escape the danger in Europe—at least temporarily, until he had conquered the Continent including Russia—Hitler intended that, in the event of a Japanese attack on the USA, he would wage war too, in order to undermine any attempts made in Tokyo to reach agreement with America. Japan would then tie down the USA in the Pacific and keep it well clear of the European theatre of war.[46] This was thus a dangerous undertaking which presupposed victory over Russia within the foreseeable future. However, (until the great 'turn-about' at the beginning of 1943), Hitler rejected the idea of Japan taking part in 'his' Russian war by setting up another front in the East—which was what the Japanese army had always been demanding, without being able to prevail over the stronger Imperial Japanese navy and its allies in industry.

While the army, the strongest arm of the German military forces, was in complete agreement with Hitler's view—winning the Russian war without the aid of Japan—von Ribbentrop, the Foreign Minister, altering his original 'alternative conception', was unflagging in his advocacy of a Japanese front in the Far East. Now as before, he clearly regarded Great Britain as Germany's chief enemy. If ever since 1938 he had been trying to challenge London with his concept of the continental bloc, von Ribbentrop now realistically adopted his ideas. He intended ending the war in Russia as quickly as possible with Japanese support. Land forces of sheer invincibility would then become available which could offer security in the coming conflicts or provide favourable conditions for future peace settlements. But von Ribbentrop's 'realistic conception' had just as little success in Germany with Hitler and the army, and in Japan with the Imperial navy and industry, as did the German naval leaders with their strategic alternatives. The latter were in favour of intensifying the 'peripheral strategy' in the Mediterranean and pushing towards Suez in a combined operation of army, navy and Luftwaffe. Japan should be persuaded to penetrate into the Indian Ocean, conquer the Indian subcontinent under British rule and join up with the Germans in the Near East. They could then eliminate Great Britain and create a position of world power for Germany from the periphery.[47]

Hitler, however, held unflinchingly to his *Stufenplan* and the Russian goal immediately central to him, even though his improvised plan of a world *Blitzkrieg* had now collapsed. Whether or not the navy's calculation would have stood a better chance of success seems an almost academic question to the historian. For the domestic premises which determined the foreign policy and strategy at the time were founded—from the very nature and origin of the Third Reich—precisely on the fact that Hitler and the army were the decisive factors. But once again in the summer of 1942, Hitler's *Stufenplan* seemed to be having success. For in Russia and North Africa, the German armies were storming almost irresistibly ahead, while by March 1942 the Japanese Empire was reaching the height of its power. With the problem of the war strategy against America occupying him more and more,[48] Hitler nevertheless rejected Japanese participation in the Russian war as consistently as ever. Indeed, he was generally suspicious of closer collaboration between the 'Swastika' and the 'Rising Sun'.[49] For although on 18 January 1942, the Reich and Japan agreed to divide up the Eastern Hemisphere, establishing longitude 70° East as the line demarking their spheres of influence, Hitler never seriously thought of allowing India—which according to this partition would fall to Japan—to break off from the British Empire.[50] Of course, as a strategist, he was jubilant over the fall of Singapore on 15 February 1942, but the doctrinaire in Hitler regretted the loss of the white South-east Asian bastion to the 'yellow race'.[51] For even in 1942, with Britain in such a critical position, the idea of the British alliance never left Hitler.

Von Ribbentrop continually tried to persuade Hitler and Japan to open up a second front in Soviet Russia. But, for differing motives, Hitler and the navy were both in agreement that the most pressing task for Japan was to fight the United States. While the German naval leadership, side by side with the Imperial Japanese navy, wanted to defeat Britain and America, Hitler was thinking in far more defensive categories—tying down the Americans with their enormous potential in the Pacific. On 6 January 1942, President Roosevelt, who had for a long time been the Dictator's most bitter enemy,[52] unequivocally announced the intention of replying to the provocation of the aggressors.[53] In fact on 14 January 1942, on the final day of the Arcadia Conference, Churchill and Roosevelt had agreed upon the 'Germany-first strategy'.[54]

In March and April 1942, with Japan reaching the height of its advance and Hitler forecasting the destruction of the Red Army, Britain and America under pressure from Stalin began considering the establishment of a second front in France and North Africa, to enable them to attack the Axis powers from the rear. Clearly, time was working against Hitler's strategy. Nevertheless, he firmly rejected the attempts which the Japanese began as early as the end of 1941 and which continued up to 1944, to secure a peace in Russia.[55] Hitler had to attain his central aim—victory over Stalin—for it was on that that his Programme stood or fell. And once more it seemed as if his calculations would prove correct. With the Battle of Midway in early summer (4–8 June 1942), and the American landings on Guadalcanal in August 1942, Japan was clearly being forced onto the defensive, whereas the German troops were achieving victory after victory, until they had advanced to the Caucasus in Russia and were pushing forward on Alexandria in North Africa. But as in previous years, the racist dogma once again burdened and thwarted the strategy of politics just as it was triumphing again. For in the summer of 1942, with the German advance on all fronts and with the armed forces strained to the limits in Russia and North Africa, Himmler, the Chief of the SS and representative of the 'new' élite, approved the so-called 'General Plan for the East'.[56] This plan, already being aired in the summer of 1941,[56a] envisaged resettling the populations of Eastern Europe in Siberia. This move was destined to arouse forces of resistance which Germany would no longer be able to overcome.

The Allies were beginning to secure footholds on the peripheries of the Axis power bloc. The Americans landed in Guadalcanal and the British occupied Madagascar, while the French colonial territories in Africa, under the rule of the Vichy régime, completely transferred their allegiance to de Gaulle's Free French after the Allied landings in North-west Africa in November 1942. Meanwhile in June 1942, Churchill and Roosevelt were discussing the possibility of opening up a second front in Europe within the foreseeable future to take the pressure off the Soviet Union. Hitler had to conclude his war in Russia in order to escape this threat which had been made even more serious by the race policy of the SS in the conquered territories of the East. On the one hand this racist policy tied down forces of the German war machine, while on the other it spurred on the hate and the will to resist among the subjugated and the still free peoples of the world, provoking them to enormous efforts. In the summer of 1942, when Hitler himself had transferred his headquarters to Vinnitsia in the Ukraine, and the German army was penetrating deep into Russian territory, the deportation of 350,000 Jews to the Treblinka extermination camp from conquered Warsaw began. From Hitler's point of view, power politics and racist policy in Eastern Europe—in his eyes attractive colonial territory[57]—were clearly progressing successfully, even if, in fact, they were impeding one another. He therefore naturally rejected any suggestions of peace in Russia, however seriously they were intended.[58] Indeed, even when the strategic situation was changing to the disadvantage of the Reich, Hitler remained unaffected for a time by the peace feelers which Stalin was manifestly putting out after November 1942.[59] Hitler was still counting on the Japanese war in the Pacific to protect him from the second front in Europe, even if the building of the Atlantic Wall had already begun in August 1942. The war in Russia still did not seem to take the turn towards victory which Hitler longed for. He intensified his efforts until, in the 'leadership crisis' of August and September 1942, he finally recognised that he could hardly still win victory in the continuing battle.[60] The Programme split into its component elements in exactly the same way as the 'old' ruling groups and the 'new' élite which had once complemented one another in the consolidation of the domestic status quo now fought against one another, contending for supremacy in the 'dual state'.

Until the 'crisis' of August and September, the success of the year had once again been feeding the illusions of victory entertained by Hitler and the three Pact Powers. But towards the end of 1942, the Japanese were already on the defensive, and for the Reich too there was also a hint of the turn in the war. In North Africa, Montgomery's troops went onto the offensive on 23 October 1942 and on 7 November, 'Operation Torch' began with the landing of Allied forces in North-west Africa, to which Hitler could only respond with the occupation of Vichy France and Tunisia.[61] While the 'North-west African back-door' was thus being kicked open for the Anglo–American attack on Europe, on 19–20 November 1942 the great Russian counter-offensive began which led to the encirclement of Stalingrad on 23 November. On 1 December 1942, Mussolini advised the Führer to end the Russian war,[62] though this request seemed impossible to Hitler. Although, calculating strategically, he had already admitted that the war could hardly be won by either side,[63] he had nevertheless tried and hoped again and again throughout 1942 to carry out his Programme, to subjugate Russia and win Great Britain over to his side. But the racial policy, that integral element in his Programme, had helped to fan the already enormous powers of resistance of the enemy and had systematically undermined the political calculation in the Programme. Hitler personally obviously felt himself bound to his Programme for good or ill; the Reich and its ruling groups were fettered to the Dictator and his war, as the abortive peace talks between the German conservative opposition and the Bishop of Chichester in Stockholm showed.[64] Then, with the surrender of the German 6th Army at Stalingrad,[65] what the decisions to attack Russia and to declare war on America had implied was now demonstrated for the whole world to see. The Dictator's Programme, that Janus head which had so successfully helped to guarantee the social structure of German society, now fell apart into its contradictory components.

At the latest by 1943, Hitler had virtually lost the political and military elbow-room which he had always had during the first years of war and in the 'peace' years when he pursued his 'short-of-war' policy. He clung ever more grimly and determinedly to his Programme which was now collapsing about him, and emphasised more and more strongly the ideological element of his policy and war strategy as opposed to the factor of political calculation. For dug in within the improvised 'fortress of Europe' until the end of the struggle, he hoped to be able to defeat Russia through a 'fanatical' effort, draw Britain onto his side and thereby arrive at what was really the starting-point of his Programme. Meanwhile, his colleagues, officers and diplomats were drawing up 'alternatives' which stood no chance of success in view of the way Germany's enemies judged the Third Reich to be a united monolith. Indeed, neither did these men, with their territorial demands, really constitute clearly convincing alternatives to Hitler's policy of conquest,[66] even if in principle the differing intentions of the Dictator and the 'traditionalists' can hardly be overlooked.

7. Germany between the USA and the USSR: The Beginnings of the Cold War (1943–45)

After the turn in the war in December 1941, Hitler's freedom of movement[1] in foreign policy had shrivelled away to the alternative of continuing the war or going for unconditional surrender and thus his personal defeat and capitulation. There were four chief factors which made the Dictator into a prisoner of his own policy and a captive within his 'European fortress':

1. The National Socialist doctrine, although it had been in the background of his policy and war strategy for a long time, was nevertheless an integral factor in his Programme which he pursued largely along lines of rational political calculation.[2]

2. It was this doctrine, however, which so exceeded the power political aims of the Programme that it was ultimately bound to provoke the whole world to war and remain unattainable. But there was a confident belief that, with the political successes in foreign policy, there would also come the racial perfection of the German people, making them into the first nation in the world. This trust was able to sustain the belief that these plans could be realised, though they were clearly far too ambitious politically.

3. It was this dogma of the superiority of the Germans and the

Germanic race that led Hitler and the leadership in Germany to overestimate their own strength and underestimate that of the other nations[3]—with the exception of Britain who was envisaged as Germany's partner.

4. This overestimation of their own strength and the scant regard they had for the enemy combined with the fixation on the racist dogma caused Hitler and the German army to fail in the competition for military allies.[4] Indeed, it was the very intrusion of ideology into politics and war strategy that created confusion among the allies of the Third Reich. It was precisely this dogma which provoked the resistance of the free world and incited the subjugated nations to ever greater resistance.

As can be conclusively shown, none of these motives was a 'new and revolutionary' intrusion brought about by Hitler in the history of Prussia–Germany. Rather, they can be traced back as integral or sporadic elements in its history as far as the Bismarckian period. But now, initially for domestic and then for foreign political reasons, they all acquired a momentum and took on a historical force and effect of their own. They were in no small way responsible for the fact that in 1943 Hitler was forced into making the following fundamental decisions:

1. All intentions concerning the second, overseas phase of the Programme were given up after the turn in the war in 1942–43.[5] These ideas which had always had a place in Hitler's thoughts, and which had become increasingly prominent since the latter half of the 1930s, had seemed close to fulfilment in the years from 1939 to 1941–42. But the possibility of their materialisation now lay in the far distant future for the Reich which was being pushed onto the defensive.

2. Hitler limited his strategy solely to the defence of the 'fortress of Europe'—as becomes clearly evident after the attacks on British convoys in the North Atlantic by German U-boats were broken off on 24 May 1943.[6] The Führer intended to defend his fortress 'fanatically', until events took a turn in his favour. He hardly seems to have taken the enormous disadvantage of this plan properly into account.

As President Roosevelt said, this so-called fortress had no roof, while the Allies on the other hand had overwhelming superiority in the air.[7]

3. Hitler expected the turn in the war which he hoped for to come with the break-up of the 'unnatural alliance' between the USSR and the Western powers. Indeed, in retrospect, such a split which Hitler regarded as inevitable was by no means all that improbable. For in the long run, it was from the tensions already emerging at that time that the 'Cold War' era after 1945 resulted. The contrasts in the differing social systems of the West and the East which were doubt-lessly inherent since 1917–18 now became increasingly prominent in the political sector. Hitler intended turning these very discrepancies to his own advantage. He wanted to exploit the tensions in terms of his familiar Programme and the power alliances envisaged in it—even though in the case of the USA his view of the power nexus had significantly altered. He was now planning to conquer the Soviet Union after all, with the help of Britain and—from March and April 1945—with the United States too, the country he had always hitherto regarded as an enemy of the Reich.

4. With this move—in line with the Programme so far as Britain was concerned, improvised in the case of the USA—Hitler was still hoping to achieve his central aim of *Lebensraum* in Russia and the smashing of Bolshevism. This would then have given Hitler a starting basis which would have enabled him to pursue politically and militarily the original intentions of his Programme.

Now as ever, Hitler was hoping that the British would come round and that a coalition could be formed with the Americans. In his view a fight against Bolshevik Russia must be in the general interests of Britain and America too—whether for reasons of the differing social systems or because Russian expansion westward in Europe, now an obvious possibility, would seriously shift the balance of power in the world. But the crucial mistake in his calculations remained hidden from him. For the 'unnatural alliance' of the Reich's enemies had been firmly forged precisely as a result of and in response to the *Weltan-schauung* of National Socialism—that synthesis of the economic and political demands of Germany's ruling classes and Hitler's ideas—and its motivating forces initially functional in domestic affairs and then in foreign policy.[8] Perhaps all the thoughts of the economic experts, officers, diplomats and even the Führer himself might have seemed politically plausible and soundly calculated—even if after the start of 'Operation Barbarossa' the original power politics was increasingly disrupted by the ideology. Nevertheless, seen in terms of the Programme, their function was in effect to bring about German world hegemony founded on a biological dogma. The world was being provoked by a series of acts which, though they were in part pursued along completely calculated lines, were aimed at an irrational goal which envisaged the culmination and end of history as a continuous process. Regarded as a whole, this goal represented something quite new in the history of Prussia–Germany; what cannot be overlooked however, is that even this phenomenon was a product of those significant domestic and socio-political conditions inherent in the German Reich which had helped to determine German foreign policy ever since Bismarck. They were a result of the fact that social conflicts in Germany were never genuinely resolved but instead were covered over with the help of secondary integrating factors and mechanisms[9] in order to block social reforms or even revolutionary activities 'from below'.

Of all the types of integrating mechanism applied in the history of Prussia–Germany, anti-semitism, propagated and practised on a world scale and claimed at the actual physical extermination of Jews, was the most powerful. This factor seems to confirm the saying of Grillparzer that in the course of historical development, liberality leads to nationality which in its turn leads to bestiality. Hitler—in this respect quite unlike Bismarck—can hardly have consciously used foreign policy to serve domestic ends.[10] Rather those integral elements in his Programme —anti-semitism, anti-Bolshevism and *Lebensraum*—which served as integrating forces in domestic politics, were regarded by Hitler as the driving forces behind his foreign programme. From the power political viewpoint this programme was thoroughly Wilhelmine in its aims, though it did systematise these in the form of the *Stufenplan*. Because Hitler did not consciously use these factors merely as means of integration on the domestic front, the original function of the slogans on race and foreign policy to safeguard the existing social order now underwent a reversal into its very opposite—as became particularly clear from 1943 on. For it was precisely these driving forces in Hitler's Programme which held Germany's enemies together, despite all the tensions between them, and which blotted out the differences between the various groups within the Reich. For that reason the chances of signing a separate peace treaty with one side or the other[11] became increasingly slender—whether it was a peace achieved by the elimination of Hitler by the conservative opposition or even by the SS who sought a peaceful solution, or whether it was a peace according to Hitler's notion, so that Germany and the Western Allies would march against the Soviet Union.

The possibility of such a peace was slight since, as early as the beginning of 1943 at the Casablanca Conference, the USA and Great Britain had agreed that in pursuit of their 'Germany-first' strategy, they would force Germany into unconditional surrender.[12] While within the 'fortress of Europe' order after order was made escalating the war,[13] and those around Hitler and the allies of the Reich began testing the possibility of a separate peace. In January 1943 Antonescu, the Deputy Prime Minister of Rumania, suggested to Mussolini[14] that contact should be taken up with the West, hence presenting the very plan which Hitler, Himmler and Göring afterwards tried to achieve. But to complement this, new attempts at a German–Russian settlement were initiated.[15] Hitler, however, remained quite unmoved by all these peace probes. Stalin, on the other hand, seems to have been forcing the pace in the search for peace in the spring and summer of 1943.[16] As Stalin saw it, if they met with no success because of the demands of the Germans, they would nevertheless give him a lever by which he could pressurise the Western powers into quickly opening up a second front in Europe. If the peace probes were to have success, then Stalin could still conclude the war which was so damaging to Russia before she was completely exhausted and confronted by an America hardly affected by the war. Further, remembering the German–Soviet understanding from 1939–41, Stalin seemed to be hoping to gain more easily from Hitler than from the Allies the territories which for a long time had been the envisaged aims of Russian policy. For Winston Churchill particularly was suspicious and hostile[17] towards the aims Stalin had been pursuing ever since 1925. As he presented them in 1940 in talks with Hitler and von Ribbentrop and again in December 1941 to Eden, Stalin's wishes were for territorial gains in East Europe, a weakening of the centre of the Continent, while conceding to the British a sphere of influence in North and West Europe.

On the German side it was primarily Goebbels who contemplated a separate peace with Soviet Russia,[18] in contrast, for example, to Himmler who advocated the idea of concluding peace with the West and then marching as the 'regulating factor in Central Europe' against Russia, in alliance with the British and Americans. Admittedly, what can hardly be ignored in regard to all these 'conceptions' and attempts at a separate peace in the East or West, is that at the latest by 1943 they were hardly more than of episodic importance, since by that time the Allies were clearly dictating the course of the war. Probably not least of all because the Russian front was consolidating in the spring of 1943,[19] Hitler temporarily forbade all peace feelers towards the West and East. The Allies were bombing the industrial plants and towns of the Reich to rubble in combined bomber offensives.[19a] President Roosevelt gave his consent to the plans, which were later carried out by the Russians, to evacuate the German population from East Prussia and the Sudetenland.[20] In April 1943 the National Socialist doctrine once more celebrated its nihilistic triumphs in the quashing of the desperate Jewish uprising in the Warsaw ghetto against the police units under SS-Gruppenführer Stroop; the rising was finally put down on 19 May 1943.[21] Amidst all this, Hitler still seemed to be thinking about a military solution to the Russian campaign—as ever, preferably with British aid.

Thus on 5 July 1943, 'Operation Citadel', to which Hitler pinned such great hopes, began. The operation, the storming of the salient of the front round Kursk, was meant to win back the initiative for the Germans in the USSR.[22] But the luck of war (as it might have seemed to Hitler) had left him. Within a few days the advance came to a standstill. But preferring as he did an agreement with Britain, Hitler obviously still did not want to accept the idea of a settlement with the Russians. Had he done so, would he not simply have been repeating the same move as on 23 August 1939, and given himself temporarily more room for political calculation? The fact was that in view of the struggle for 'all or nothing' initiated with the beginning of the Russian campaign, Hitler was hardly capable any longer of such tactical, rational considerations. The racist dogma had finally triumphed over the political cunning in his Programme. The Dictator was determined to achieve his central goal—the conquest of the Eastern empire, and the realisation of the 'final solution'—in one attempt. As it became more and more evident that a military victory in Russia was impossible, Hitler clung all the more to the single aim of the 'final solution'.

From the political point of view, Hitler was pushed irrevocably onto the defensive. His former idol, il Duce, had been overthrown and the Italian front was in the most extreme danger.[23] Now it seems that the Dictator was wanting to do in the East what he had begun in the West with the building of the Atlantic Wall. He ordered the building of an Eastern Wall. He might well have been contemplating a war of attrition lasting a decade,[24] with Germany holding out within the 'fortress of Europe' with its thousand-mile fronts, demonstrating to the enemy 'the futility of their attacks' and forcing the West to give in.[25] The very power which had waged an aggressive war and, from the viewpoint of its war economy was increasingly dropping behind,[26] was playing with the idea of forcing its opponents into surrender by a war of attrition! Hitler's hopes of breaking up the enemy alliance and then being able to regain the offensive in Russia, either under the umbrella of the Western powers or with their positive help, may well have been fed by the tensions which, despite declarations to the contrary, clearly existed between the Western powers and the Soviet Union. For in the course of the summer of 1943 Stalin made increasingly emphatic demands for a second front in Europe to take the pressure off Russia. Sustained by the foreign political concept which had dominated him since 1925, Stalin feared that Russia would bleed to death, being used by the Western powers as their sword against fascism on the mainland of Europe. Moreover, he was annoyed that the Western powers were still not prepared to accept in full his territorial claims in Europe.

Just as Stalin's policy and strategy were determined by ideas which had dominated his mind since 1925, so Hitler too held firmly to his Programme—modified so far as America was concerned—and particularly firmly to the aspect of the racist 'war of extermination' which was being pursued as 'successfully' as ever. In September 1943 he rejected all attempts to reach a separate peace agreement with the Soviet Union which would have been a repetition of the Brest-Litovsk Peace. Both von Ribbentrop and Goebbels had to hold back. The former could otherwise have resorted to the concept to which he had been committed up to 1941 of fighting the West in alliance with Japan, with the Russians in neutrality. The latter, Goebbels, also wanted to make peace with Stalin. But the neutrality of the Soviet Union as an alliance between the two conflicting dictatorships remained an illusion despite what Stalin said in 1945 when, largely in the light of an actual or imagined threat from the USA which had risen to become the leading power in the world, he argued that Russia and Germany together would have been invincible.[27] For Hitler and the German army followed a different strategy. With Germany in continuous retreat in Russia, with the Italian capitulation[28] imminent and Germany's other allies secretly seeking negotiations for a separate peace, Hitler and the German army were still hoping for the break-up of the overwhelming enemy coalition. Both Hitler and General Jodl, Chief of the Armed Forces High Command, desired the conciliation of the Western powers in order that Germany might attack in the East once more.

In principle this idea linked up with Hitler's policy of the 1930s in trying to force Britain into an alliance by putting pressure on the West. Thus on 3 November 1943 he issued directive no. 51[29] which gave priority to defence measures against the enemy in the West. Hitler, the army and Himmler's SS[30] still maintained the hope that the 'unnatural' coalition would collapse and thought that by demonstrating Germany's striking power they would be able to carry out their plan of an alliance with the Western powers. Foreign Minister von Ribbentrop on the other hand continued to advocate his idea of bringing about an end to the war in Russia with the military or diplomatic aid of Japan.[31] It was not simply Hitler's rejection of this idea, however, which caused the failure of the renewed negotiations in Stockholm aimed at ending the Russian war. Nor was it only the preference of the SS, the 'new' élite in the Third Reich, and powerful groups within the old ruling classes (the army and the economy) for peace in the West.[32] Also contributing to the failure of the peace attempt were the demands of the Germans which, following the example of the First World War, again demanded the Brest–Litovsk frontiers of 1918.

Hitler continued to believe that he would be able to turn the tables both by ideological and military responses. In line with similar demands in the autumn of 1943,[33] Hitler demanded on 27 January 1944 that the army be trained in future along National Socialist lines.[34] The army's field marshals yet again assured absolute loyalty to Hitler in view of the assassination attempts being planned by conservatives.[35] In the meantime the south-east European allies of the Reich were preparing to break with Germany and could only be held within the 'fortress of Europe' by the refusal of the Western powers to accept partial surrenders.[36] Meanwhile 'measures' taken towards the 'final solution of the Jewish problem' were being set in motion in Hungary.[37] These measures, which not only whipped up resistance and enormous hatred but also tied down Germany's own fighting forces, were directed against the last large group of European Jews who had not been caught in the previous extermination operations. As the political defeat of the Reich clearly emerged the opposite element, the 'victories gained' in the field of Hitler's dogma and racist policy, became dominant.

If in March 1944 it seemed as if political thoughts once more held sway in Hitler's mind, it was in fact far too late for such a solution, particularly as the Führer pursued it only half-heartedly even now. Just as in the autumn of 1940 he had for a short time reluctantly concurred with von Ribbentrop's concept of a continental bloc, so now he seemed—at least for a short while—to be prepared to conclude peace with Russia. This, he thought, would enable him to wage the war against the West side by side with the Japanese (and possibly with Russia, but at least with its neutrality ensured).[38] However, no agreement between Stalin and Hitler was possible because since April 1944, the Russian dictator was no longer pursuing with any seriousness the idea of a separate peace.[39] As a result, Hitler turned his attentions back to his 'first love', the idea of an Anglo–German alliance. With this, the speculations of von Ribbentrop and Goebbels on ending the war in Russia finally fell through. Meanwhile in the East, despite continuing military setbacks, the ideologically-motivated extermination measures went ahead, while in London the political and military leaders of the Western nations were being informed by General Eisenhower of the details of the planned invasion of France.[40] But Hitler had decided to offer the Allies determined resistance in order to convince them of the indispensability of the German forces in the ensuing war which they would all be fighting against Bolshevism. As seen particularly from the viewpoint of the illusory but nonetheless stubbornly pursued aim of rapprochement with Britain—and from March and April 1945 with America too—the decree issued on 30 May 1944 by Bormann, the Führer's personal secretary, seems particularly revealing. Reichsleiter Bormann, who in the last year of the war was probably the most influential man in the Führer's headquarters after

Hitler himself, ordered that crews of Allied bombers which had been shot down should not be lynched.[41]

On D-Day, 6 June 1944, Allied troops finally landed in Normandy. Now, directly confronting Hitler and his armed forces was the second front—the very thing which Hitler had hitherto been at such pains to avoid.[42] Would his stratagem work out and would a convincing defence by the German military bring the Western powers round to his solution of attacking Russia in a combined effort? By no means, for, convinced as they were that Hitler's state was an outcome of the past history of Prussia and of German militarism, the Allies had long since decided to smash the Third Reich. So in fact the idea of concluding a separate peace with the West was an illusion, though it was one which was kept alive to the very end of the war and to which not only Hitler but also many of the generals and members of the conservative resistance like Goerdler and Beck were committed. The hope was all the more illusory since the idea, the product of pure political calculation and even as such rather shortsighted, was being continually and systematically undermined by new war crimes committed by the Third Reich, as for example in Oradour some four days after the successful Allied landings. But now, with the beginnings of the invasion, all thought of political alternatives in fact became irrelevant. This was the case regardless of whether the preference was for attacking Russia in alliance with the West or for ending the war in Russia and confronting the West. For in the South-east Asian theatre of war American troops had landed on Saipan as early as June 1944 and in Russia the massive summer offensive of the Red Army began on 22 June 1944 in the central sector of the Eastern front, the way having been prepared by partisan operations of an unparalleled kind.[43] The only stroke of luck which Hitler could now hope for was that the Allied coalition might break up. However, Hitler and those around him reacted more and more sharply with ideological measures in response to the military reversals they suffered. After the attempted assassination of 20 July 1944, Marshal Göring introduced the 'German salute' into the armed forces. On 25 July 1944, Goebbels proclaimed total war mobilisation although he had been demanding and announcing this since the catastrophe at Stalingrad. Hitler decreed that if a soldier committed the 'sin' of cowardice, his whole family would be punished with imprisonment. After the crushing of the Warsaw rising on the other hand, political calculation and cunning once more prevailed—though admittedly without success. The Polish 'Home Defence army' under General Count Bór-Komorovski had been vainly hoping for the support of the Red Army in their attempt to cast off the German yoke. Now, after the initial atrocities, the relatively 'normal' treatment of the Polish army by the Germans was supposed to serve the purpose of winning the Polish enemy into supporting Germany in the struggle against the Soviet Union.[44]

Basically, however, National Socialist dogma triumphed over all rational considerations and it was only the iron clamp of terror, embodied in Freisler's People's Courts, linked with the uncertainty about the consequences of a German defeat, which could hold the nation together.

In August 1944 von Ribbentrop tried once again to turn the course of fate, taking advantage this time of the obvious tensions that existed between Churchill and Stalin over the partition of the Balkans into theatres of operation, and over the Polish problem. Von Ribbentrop prepared a memorandum which was aimed at achieving peace with Russia,[45] but his initiative was vetoed by Hitler. But at the same time as Hitler was rejecting this attempt at finally ending the Russian war, Japan was disengaging itself more and more from the Reich. Hitler moved more and more consistently into isolation, for in his view collective suicide was the only proper step for the losing side to take. Yet despite the negative course in all theatres of war, Hitler was still toying with the idea of striking a demonstrative blow against the West to 'wake them up' and bring them onto the side of the Germans. The deployment of the 'miracle weapons', the V1's and the V2's, was probably also intended to serve this purpose. Meanwhile the Armed Forces Operations Staff under General Jodl was planning the Western offensive.

On the Eastern front, the Russians were penetrating into East Prussia while Warsaw was being systematically destroyed. In South-east Asia, Japan was finally losing the initiative of the war to the USA in the last of the three massive air-and-sea battles at the battle of Leyte between 22 and 25 October 1944. (The first battle had been at Midway between 3 and 7 June 1942 and the second at Saipan.) Meanwhile Hitler and his officers were discussing the imminent blow against the

West. From the military point of view, the blow was meant to create a breathing space, while politically it was supposed to help in securing Hitler's plan of a Western alliance. The discussions centred on the question of whether it would be more advisable to advance only as far as the Meuse or to retake Antwerp. While Field Marshals von Rundstedt and Model were in favour of the 'limited' solution (advance up to the Meuse) in the light of their estimates of the relative strength of the forces, Hitler was advocating the 'major' solution. As Hitler saw it, the retaking of Antwerp would represent the very demonstration of power and success which he thought was needed to bring Britain 'to reason'. Hitler's plan prevailed. On 16 December 1944, the much-discussed Ardennes offensive was begun, but by 20 December it had already collapsed.[46] Obviously, the Western powers could not be forced into allying with the Reich. Colonel-General Guderian therefore met von Ribbentrop, the Foreign Minister, in January 1945 in order to persuade him to press the Führer into peace talks with the West. But von Ribbentrop hesitated—perhaps for fear of approaching Hitler about a 'Western solution' after the failure of the Ardennes offensive.[47]

Characteristic of the prevailing situation and decisive for the state of affairs in postwar Germany was the fact that—from March and April 1945—not only Hitler, but the armed forces and even the SS with Himmler at its head and representatives of the German economy were all in favour of forming a front against the East in alliance with the Western powers. The latter group, the businessmen, can certainly be counted as members of this phalanx, if only on the basis of the property principle questioned by the Russians as the constituent element in the capitalist economy. The front lining up against the East was in fact the same which became reality after 1945, admittedly under greatly differing conditions, and which was emerging at the beginning of the Cold War at the Yalta and Potsdam Conferences.[48] Churchill was particularly suspicious of Stalin's expansionist desires[49] which went as far as demanding support bases in the Mediterranean, where Russia was only to gain a foothold in the latter half of the 1960s. But despite all the differences, these suspicions were not strong enough to persuade the West—for example the American Under Secretary of State Hewitt[50]—to grant Himmler, the Chief of the SS, the peace which he was intending to buy even at the (probably temporary) cost of ideological sacrifice. Perhaps it was largely for this reason that Himmler forbade the blowing up of concentration camps as the enemy was approaching,[51] after he had already given the order in October 1944 to stop the extermination of the Jews. Meanwhile Hitler, with visions comparing his position to that of the fate of Frederick the Great in the Seven Years War, was on the one hand talking of the turn in the war which was still to come in that year, while on the other he was preparing more and more for the suicide of the German nation—as in the 'Nero order' of 19 March 1945.[52] In the meantime, in Italy, the 'Supreme SS and Police Chief', Wolff, was already starting to negotiate for a partial surrender.[53] Nothing could conceal for very much longer that the war was lost for the Reich—not the 'miracle weapon' V2, nor the 'Werewolf' operations, the show trials in the People's Courts, Hitler's 'fanatical' will to persevere, the People's Battalions, nor finally the 'turn in the war', which simply did not come about, even after the death of President Roosevelt on 12 April 1945.

In April 1945, Hitler spoke of the senselessness of the war against the United States[54] together with whom he now wished to fight for *Lebensraum* for the German nation in Russia. Almost as an epilogue to the tragedy and at the same time a demonstration of the politics of illusions, Himmler, figurehead of the 'new' élite in the National Socialist state, tried once more to arrange talks with the representative of the Jewish world congress, Masur, in order to prepare for peace in the West.[55] The attempt was bound to fail. At the end of the war, not only Hitler but almost all the leading figures and groups in German society without exception were advocating the idea of allying with the Western powers against the Soviet Union. The idea still dominated in the government of Dönitz and Schwerin-Krosigk[56] which succeeded Hitler. They continued to speak untiringly of its being Germany's European mission to keep the USSR out of central Europe. Not least of all because of the determined way that the German government lined up against the Soviet Union, Stalin adopted a very hostile attitude to the Dönitz administration, which had also refused to move the seat of government to Berlin, but rather remained in the British zone. Another important reason for Stalin's attitude was the growing hostility which was developing at the time with the Western powers, among whom the United States, about to enter the age of nuclear diplomacy,[57] was well on the way to becoming the greatest power in the world.

In the shadow of the split between the United States and Russia which became manifest relatively quickly after the end of the war, the ideological and political opposition of the German Reich to Soviet Russia was the legacy inherited by the newly founded Federal Republic of Germany which was absorbed into the Western bloc.[58]

Conclusion
Hitler's Place in German History: The Relationship between Domestic and Foreign Policy

To conclude this outline history of German foreign policy in the years 1933–45, we should raise once more the questions which were posed at the outset and which have been the guide for the whole of our inquiry. They concern the issue of 'continuity or discontinuity' and the interplay of domestic and foreign policy in the history of Prussia–Germany. To summarise and elaborate upon our conclusions, four theses may be suggested in answer to the problems raised in the introduction.

The first thesis: The break represented by the year 1933 results from the continuity in Prussian–German history.

In the course of our interpretation we have repeatedly come up against the fact that in the area of German foreign policy from 1933 to 1945 we can find both elements of continuity as well as indications of a break with tradition. What appeared as something 'new and revolutionary' was the 'ultimate aim' of Hitler's Programme. This aim envisaged world domination based on race and the plan for a new 'master race' forming a biologically bred élite which was intended to supplant the conservative leading groups in the ruling positions of the Reich. But in contrast to this, what became thoroughly familiar to us was the fact that for a period of time there existed in the Third Reich an identity of aims in foreign policy between Hitler's ideas and the wishes of the 'old' leading groups who had determined policy in the Reich ever since the days of Bismarck. Indeed it is clear that the short- and long-term goals of the Dictator in the political sector were thoroughly Wilhelmine in their dimensions, even if these goals were systematised by him in the form of the *Stufenplan*. Besides the National Socialist methods of foreign policy, which in practice did not play a constitutive role,[1] Hitler's strategy was always dominated by the traditional and classic tools of diplomacy and force of arms.

However, we reach quite differing judgments of the nature of the 'dual state' depending on which aspect of it we are considering. On the one hand we may emphasise the teleological nature of the system which removes it both from the tradition of and continuity in Prussian–German history and indeed from the general course of historical development as determined by men. We find confirmation of the theory that the Third Reich represents a revolutionary discontinuity in German history if we examine the methods of the Nazi régime and of Nazi foreign policy already being practised during the 12-year régime as a means towards attaining the goal of drawing the historical process to its end and producing a biological culmination through the breeding of a new race of men. However, other aspects of the 'dual state' lead us to place stronger emphasis on the continuity over the whole period. For the power-political ideas which Hitler took up were thoroughly familiar in Germany since the nineteenth century, reflecting the desire for a strong central Europe under German leadership, an expansionist policy in the East, an overseas colonial empire and, connected with this, the idea of political and military confrontations between the major powers envisaged on a world scale. In addition, further elements of continuity are to be found in the conventional diplomatic weapons of courtship, threat and blackmail which were primarily applied. Tracing these two concepts, those of discontinuity and continuity, as resulting from the development of Prussian–German history is most easily achieved by considering the interplay of domestic and foreign policies.

In the course of our reflections we were continually being reminded of the fact that the aims conceived in foreign policy and propagated as slogans consciously or unconsciously fulfilled functions in domestic politics. Today we can clearly recognise[2] the overwhelming part played by domestic interests[3] in Bismarck's foreign policy. For the policy of the founder of the Reich was in the first place geared to safeguarding the existing social order in Prussia–Germany.[4] Confronted by the 'sickness' of the 'civilised world',[5] the proletarian class created by industrialisation, Bismarck's primary task was to stabilise the makeshift compromise existing since 1848 between the landowning nobility[6] and the industrialist bourgeoisie, between the Crown and Parliament, and to give permanence and stability to the status quo. But with the intensification and expansion of industrial development, the contradictions existing between the different social groups were rapidly exacerbated.[7] The tools of integration were applied more forcibly. At first it was the *Kulturkampf* which served the purpose of domestic stabilisation. Afterwards this role was filled by the fight against social democracy and by the solidarity-protectionism (Rosenberg) of agriculture and industry. Then, however, the primary question became not merely the appeasement of the bourgeoisie who in the meantime had rapidly moved over on to the side of the Crown.[8] Rather the task became that of winning over the large mass of the working class and the white-collar workers to the interests of the Crown and the propertied bourgeoisie.[9] Hence besides their role as basically power political aims,[10] the slogans of nationalism and imperialism and demands for a strong naval policy in the Wilhelmine era also served to unite the nation under the banner of internal mobilisation and social imperialism. Thus Miquel, Tirpitz and Bülow were able to take up the policy developed and practised under Bismarck.[11] This caesarism reached its culmination in the days of the German naval build-up and *Weltpolitik*, with its militant mass associations and popular imperialism, though as early as 1862 Prussia–Germany had found its Caesar in Bismarck.[12] Tirpitz's 'Risk Theory', which was based upon a widespread belief in a vulgar Darwinism and which in foreign policy aimed in effect at eliminating Britain with her supremacy at sea,[13] was to take over the function in domestic politics of avoiding large-scale social reforms which, it was feared, would herald the socialist revolution. To supplement this, there was also the state welfare legislation[14] initiated under the banner of Bismarck's 'conservative revolution'[15] and put through in the face of opposition from the patriarchal landowners and the National Liberal industrialists, a welfare policy which was aimed at tying the working classes to the state. This marked the beginning of a development which was continued during the First World War with Bethmann Hollweg's policy of 're-orientation',[16] which attributed to the state a certain power of social redistribution and enabled it either to integrate the 'masses' in a social and democratic manner or to make them obedient by means of the stick-and-carrot method in the absolutist fashion.

But the most powerful force for integration holding the German nation together in the final days of the Second Reich was doubtless the First World War itself. For in the eyes of the overwhelming majority of its people and subjects, the Reich was being 'attacked' by a world of enemies. In 1918 this unity was shattered; the 'civil truce' of 1914 had long since been broken. After 1918 there remained only the force of revisionist foreign policy as a tool of integration, but considered in retrospect and measured against the instruments of National Socialism it was all too feeble a tool and was soon to be supplemented by more radical methods. For those and the Right in the Weimar Republic began forging new tools of integration, again conceived of as aims of foreign policy, for the maintenance of the social status quo and as a domestic reaction against the development of parliamentary democracy in a society whose social structure had not been altered by the 'revolution' of 1918. Two factors confronted them. On the one hand, as an event of world significance, there was the Russian Revolution. On the other, there was anti-semitism,[17] which for centuries had raged in Europe, including Germany, though it had never hitherto been applied there as an integral tool of government policy. Under its Führer, Adolf Hitler, the most extreme group on the Right in opposition to the Weimar Democracy[18] formulated the foreign political goals of the struggle against Bolshevism and the Jews. For these enemies—the Jews and the Bolsheviks—were held to have been responsible for the ruin of the German Reich and the vanished power and glory of pre-war Germany. The *Volk ohne Raum*, 'the people without space', would find the *Lebensraum* which was regarded as necessary for its existence in the fight against Jews and Communists in Russia.

In virtue of the fact that aims in foreign policy presuppose preconditions and fulfil functions on the domestic front, the political planks in Hitler's Programme—anti-semitism, anti-Bolshevism and the conquest of *Lebensraum*—also carried political weight domestically, though Hitler had hardly conceived of them consciously in domestic terms. A powerful enemy, existing all the world over, had been discovered as the alleged evil causing misery to the German Reich in social, domestic and foreign politics.[19] The task now was to strike this evil at its very heart, first within the Reich and then over the whole world. This would serve to ensure Germany's future, so the 'National Right' believed, and at the same time protect society from changes. But the precondition for this was that law and order, discipline and unity should prevail within the Reich. For various reasons, the mechanisms which served domestic integration and which had been continuously applied in Prussian–German history, had to be so intensified that in the course of time something 'new and revolutionary' resulted —or at least could have done so if the Third Reich had lasted longer. One reason for this intensification can be found in the advanced state of social polarisation between the propertied classes and the proletariat, as became dreadfully evident during the years 1929–32. Another factor was that the 'social enemy' was now embodied in the giant Soviet Union with its entirely different social system. A final reason for the intensification lay in the development of entirely new technical methods of manipulation. It was in the very course of the excessive application of these integration mechanisms that their original aim—preserving the existing social order—eventually got lost from sight. Thus from the continuity in Prussian–German history was born the break of 1933.

To Hitler's way of thinking, in view of his well-known anti-middle-class attitudes and his policy based on power-political and racist axioms, these forces for integration were regarded as the driving forces behind his Programme. But to the retrospective observer it is evident that these forces were so rigorously applied to bind the nation together and preserve the social order that if the Third Reich had continued to exist this very order of bourgeois capitalism would in principle have been smashed. However, Hitler's dictatorship fell in ruins in the war which according to the teleology of his system was its very 'life' pattern.[20] That it did so arose directly from the policy of his Programme which was conducted with such aggression in the field of foreign policy and which in its functional role in the domestic field appeared as a drastic fascist purgative. The ideological, racist factors in Hitler's Programme which he personally regarded as permanently binding dogma and which he thought had to be fulfilled at any price, were clearly necessary for domestic reasons. Yet it was these very factors in the Programme which hindered and indeed destroyed Hitler's power policy which in large part was calculated on shrewd rational lines.

Hence the second thesis: the dominance and ubiquity of the dogma undermined the effectiveness of Hitler's political calculation.

It should have become evident by now that the issue here is not to settle the dispute over the 'primacy of domestic or foreign policy'.[21] If we were to consider each decision in Hitler's policy individually then we would certainly have to talk of the 'primacy of foreign policy'.[22] But if we emphasise also the domestic, functional role of foreign policy at the beginning of the Third Reich and the economic policy of the Nazi system which then gave the war a certain necessity, then we would lean more towards the theory of 'the priority of domestic policy'.[23] But in the context of our examination of foreign policy in the Third Reich what seems far more significant is the fact that Hitler— like the statesmen of Wilhelmine Germany before him—sought to achieve a dialectical unity of domestic and foreign policy.[24] On the domestic front, stable relations in terms of the existing structure were to be the precondition enabling foreign aims to be realised; while these very ideas in foreign policy served the function of consolidating the domestic order. Similarly in the First World War with the question of the alteration or abolition of the Prussian three-class franchise, those who were in favour were almost exclusively those who supported a negotiated peace while those who rejected it were generally those demanding a victorious peace.[25] However, ideologies invented in order to reconcile domestic and foreign policy had always ended by triumphing over the rationally calculated policies they were meant to serve.[26] For Hitler's foreign programme, which also served an integrating function at home, contained of course both political and racist demands. But as we have seen, when the racist dogma shed its cloak of mere propaganda and entered the phase of its implementation, it torpedoed the policy of cunning calculation. Indeed if Adolf Hitler had had his way, his dogma would have destroyed existing society.

For the first time in the history of Prussia–Germany, this phenomenon appeared in such an extreme and destructive form. However, evidence of a power policy interfered with and undermined by dogma can be traced back to as early as Bismarck's day.[27] Just as the existing social order became increasingly problematical judged against the process of developing industrialisation and the social condition which this gave rise to, so the mechanisms in domestic and foreign policy employed to safeguard the status quo had likewise to be applied more intensively. As a result what we have described as a power policy undermined by dogma was produced. In Wilhelmine Germany an irrational system of appointments undermined the effectiveness of a calculated and rational policy. For in the Second Reich, the appointment of men to leading positions was determined not for example by a principle of qualification and competence under parliamentary control but rather by the privilege of birth.[28] It was not Parliament which had power of appointment over the leading political positions but an absolutist Cabinet system whose members clustered round the Crown.[29] It was not the principle of measurable success springing from the bourgeois competitive ethic which held sway but rather the established ideological belief in superior birth and it was this belief which prevented important positions being suitably occupied and which hindered open, parliamentary, discussion and review of political decisions.[30] Traditional dogma always triumphed over political calculation. For reasons which have already been mentioned, the dominance and ubiquity of the *Weltanschauung* which sprang from and served to protect the existing social order finally culminated in Hitler's Programme. This *Weltanschauung* completely undermined the effectiveness of the power policy and moreover sought to create its own élite along the lines of the newly formulated racist dogma—an élite which was intended to replace forever the old ruling classes and bring the course of history to its culmination in a biologically-determined static state. Why was it that a power policy impeded by dogma with roots a long way back in the history of Prussia–Germany came to such a triumph? The third thesis attempts to offer an answer to this question.

Third thesis: The liberal-parliamentarian experiment of Weimar failed because of the resistance to it of the majority of the ruling class in Prussia–Germany.

We would be missing the 'whole' of the development of Prussia–Germany and thus mistake the 'true picture' were we to overlook the

fact that both in Wilhelmine Germany and Hitler's state there were
contemporaries who had already recognised the 'mistake' of a policy
being tainted and hindered by dogma and had tried to put an end to it.
For example the National Liberals in the Wilhelmine Reich, taking
their example from the liberal-parliamentarian societies of Britain and
France, thought of making the principle of 'property and education' a
binding one on the state—including in the appointment of men to
ruling positions. This they intended to do by making the system parliamentarian—but not by democratising the system in the sense of social
equality for the working class. They wanted to do this in order to
increase the power and effectiveness of the German Reich—in foreign
affairs too. But what this meant was to shape it more effectively in the
interest of the propertied bourgeois class. More parliamentarianism at
home as a prerequisite for a powerful imperialistic world policy—that
was the programme of Max Weber, Bassermann and Stresemann.[31]
But in contrast to Britain and France, the preconditions necessary for
the realisation of this idea hardly appertained in Germany. The power
especially of the conservative Prussians, the weight of the Crown, and
the influence of the army determined the character of the State and
German society. For unlike the gentry in Britain, the landowning
nobility in Prussia[32] had not developed into a class of 'entrepreneurs'
thinking in bourgeois categories of a competitive ethic.[33] Nor had they,
as in France, been removed from their ruling political positions by a
revolution of the bourgeoisie. For this failure there are various reasons
of both a domestic and foreign political nature.[34] The 'learning ability'
(K. Deutsch) and adaptability of the Prussian nobility were not sufficient for them to join in the industrial development of the country.
On the other hand, the power of the Junkers who increasingly per-
meated the industrial upper-middle class was great enough for them
to hold out in their traditional inherited positions without adapting
to the 'modern process'. They made powerful and successful efforts to
protect their feudal privileges by means of customs protection, 'charity
gifts', the retention of the system of indirect taxation—in short, through
fiscal laws and the exercise of political influence.[35] In the light of their
experiences in the days of Bismarck and with the prospect of the growing 'threat' from the already powerful working class, the bourgeoisie
adapted themselves to the political decisions and social norms of the
Crown, the army and the Junkers. The parliamentarian alternative,

first seen as one of principle against the existing system of cabinet government, became watered down into an 'alternative'—not against but *within* the system. It was from within the existing political structure that its representatives advocated the indirect path of a policy of peaceful expansionism. For reasons of social and socio-psychological necessity, Bismarck had already introduced such a policy—just as Bethmann Hollweg tried to pursue it in the face of constant hostility.[36] But in pursuing such an 'alternative', the 'moderates' ran into opposition from the right wing as embodied in the Pan-German League, which advocated a direct line of annexation and often found the support of Kaiser Wilhelm II.

There followed the experiment of the Weimar Republic which, particularly in Stresemann's policy, had ties with and continued in the liberal-parliamentary tradition in domestic and foreign policy. In the Third Reich the conservatives and National Socialists shared an identity of interests which lasted up to 1936. It was after this date that Hjalmar Schacht, a representative of the 'liberal conservatives' together with members of the Economics Department of the Foreign Office and representatives from Göring's staff responsible for the Four Year Plan, supported a line in favour of a policy of peaceful expansion. But it was already too late. It was the same now as in Wilhelmine Germany. At that time the greatest power lay with the Crown and thus ultimately with the administration of the day—so when in July 1917 Bethmann Hollweg planned to put through domestic reforms in the face of opposition from these forces, he was deposed. Similarly, after the Weimar experiment, it was once more those of the most radical and active wing of the political Right in Germany who seized power for themselves. Indeed they had already achieved a dictatorial monopoly of power before 1933. As became clearly evident after his death, during the world economic crisis, the 'moderate' alternative represented in Stresemann's policy collapsed in the face of opposition from the majority on the 'conservative' and radical Right. Stresemann's policy had been geared to the ideas of the liberal tradition supporting confederation in 1848 and the example of the National Liberals in the Second Reich.[37] On the domestic front it desired the property-owning bourgeoisie to hold rule in conjunction with the Social Democrats who had after all saved the state and its social structure in 1918. In foreign affairs, Stresemann had pursued a policy geared to revisionism and conducted in a strong manner, even if it was primarily along peaceful, indirect, economic lines. (Thus against Poland the adoption of military measures was contemplated, while against France the economic potential of the Reich was applied.)[38] But once again Stresemann's policy failed in the face of resistance from two broad sources. On the one hand there were the majority of the 'conservative' ruling groups from the landowning classes and those—who were now decisive—on the political Right in industry. On the other hand opposition also came from the petits-bourgeois who were hoping for a charismatic redemption from the 'humiliation of Versailles' and the prevailing economic misery. Spectacular successes on the domestic and foreign fronts—apparent or real—were necessary to simulate changes, when in principle what the majority of the ruling classes in the Reich desired was consolidation or reaction. From the viewpoint of domestic and foreign policy, Hitler seemed to them to be the right servant to carry out their aspirations. Hitler seemed to come at just the right time to establish law and order at home while at the same time creating national glory and bringing about territorial revisions on the foreign front. But this was an outcome which is not unexpected, seen in the light of the development of Prussia–Germany, as the fourth thesis explains.

Fourth thesis: Hitler's dictatorship was the culmination of and surpassed the caesaristic tradition in Prussian–German history.

After the collapse of the parliamentary tradition which had been taken up again in the Weimar Republic, Hitler's dictatorship emerges as the outcome of the most extreme and successful appeal of the day made by the Führer to the German people. The political course which Hitler's distatorship took initially helped towards an apparent and temporary recuperation of the State and German society, in line with the wishes of the ruling social and political classes on the Right wing. Afterwards, however, it aimed at the ruthless destruction of that society. But that this was the case has been explained by the fact, already analysed in detail, that tools of foreign policy had to be used as forces of integration in the domestic field and had to be employed more and more intensively. The Reich, its élite and their followers seemed to resemble a drug addict who never underwent the proper therapy necessary for his condition. Instead the addict simply took

stronger and stronger stimulants, collapsed and was stimulated to a
new 'high' again, until the drug eventually destroyed him. And,
though in the final stages he partly recognised the course of decline
towards ruin, he was unable to prevent his own destruction. What
Hitler offered was a programme of domestic and foreign policy of the
most extremist radical kind, at the centre of which stood the image of
an enemy, in terms of which all the social and political misery and
depression could be completely 'explained'. It was for this reason that
after the Social Democrat and Communist Party organisations had
been smashed, the 'masses' followed Hitler—just as they had listened to
Miquel's nationalist slogans, and had been enthusiastic about Tirpitz's
navy propaganda, just as they had believed Ludendorff's promises of
a victorious peace and had become members of the Deutsche Vaterlandspartei founded in 1917.[39] This Fatherland Party clearly fell outside the legal framework of German constitutionalism and as such can
be considered as a 'mass movement' of the middle class under its
'leaders' Kapp and Tirpitz, and compared with its successor, the
National Socialist Party.

Bismarck had still just been in the fortunate position of not permit-
ting his rationally calculated foreign policy to be destroyed by ideological slogans. Nevertheless, it cannot be overlooked that the beginnings of this process so characteristic of Prussian–German history are
to be found before 1890, too, and that it was the threat of a coup d'état
which provided the *ultima ratio* for Bismarck's government.[40] Afterwards Bismarck's successors managed to prevent the coup d'état plans
of the extreme right, plans of the kind which continued to be entertained by the Pan-Germans.[41] But admittedly to do this Bismarck's
successors had to pay the high price of adopting a policy which Bismarck himself had simply rejected—that of an aggressively pursued
world policy. But Hohenlohe, Bülow, Miquel and Tirpitz were neither
able nor willing to comply with the demand of the liberal bourgeoisie
to create the parliamentary conditions necessary for the successful
pursuit of the world policy now being initiated. On the contrary, in
their measures the German leaders sought to limit the power of
parliament. Besides the determined response of the powers challenged
by Germany, this was an important reason for the failure of the daringly
conceived plans of foreign policy.[42] However, the tribute which had
to be paid for domestic 'unity' was an almost overwhelming exuberant

nationalism, which in its warlike language nevertheless reflected what had in fact been planned for the long-term—that Germany should effect a break-through to attain a position in the world equal to that of the United States, Tsarist Russia and the British Empire.[43] But during the First World War, further ground was won by those on the radical Right with their extremist policy of threatening a coup. The ideas of the Crown Prince, and the policy of Admiral von Tirpitz connected with them, the influence of the Supreme Command under Ludendorff and the formation of the Deutsche Vaterlandspartei all undermined the legitimate basis of the Hohenzollern monarchy. Indeed, with their appeal to the 'masses' they made into reality what Bismarck had implied when he said that in Prussia there could quite easily be royalism without a king.

The caesarist element[44] which had been present in Prussian–German politics since 1862 and the founding of the Reich, together with the appeals for dictatorship[45] which under Bismarck had only been sporadic, now made their appearance in the First World War, incorporating also the 'masses' whom the first Chancellor had always excluded as far as was possible. This 'movement', based on the principle of charismatic leadership and blind obedience, persisted strongly in the 1920s. Indeed it became more powerful than the liberals around Stresemann with their policy which seemed highly rational compared to the plans evolved by a section of the military leadership, who wanted to bring about the re-establishment of Germany's greatness by pursuing a course of cabinet wars.[46] But in principle Hitler's Programme integrated all the political demands, economic requirements and sociopolitical expectations prevailing in German society since the days of Bismarck. His Programme offered an explanation for the misfortunes of the past and the miseries of the present; it projected Hitler's visions of the future[47] but paid twice over in so doing. For in foreign affairs it antagonised the whole of the world and at home the price paid was the radical alteration of society (in the distant future)—that is, it carried on the continuity to its very breach.

The 'answer' the world gave to Hitler's Programme brought about its collapse. With the destruction of the Reich as an autonomous factor in 1945, the collapse of the Programme marks without doubt a deep gulf in the history of Prussia–Germany. And yet it nevertheless leaves open certain possibilities of continuance. For at the very last moment there was one thing which was saved from destruction after all by those who had originally helped the Dictator to power, only then to be subjugated by him: the existing social order (including the industrial plants vital to survival) at least in one part of Germany. At the present time in this part of the defeated Reich, there exists a parliamentarian, democratic order tolerably adapted to the demands of industrial development. Once more within this framework there stand opposing groups and parties which contest the most important questions facing the nation—whether domestic reforms and a realism in foreign policy should determine the policies of the Federal Republic of Germany, or whether domestic reaction and revisionism in foreign policy should prevail. In order to reflect upon these problems and their solutions in a rational, calculated way, rather than answering them dogmatically, we might profit from the historical examination and explanation of the past history of Prussia–Germany. As Margret Boveri has said:[48] 'For how long it will still be possible to pursue the study of past and contemporary history without including the elements of the future implicit in it may perhaps become a touchstone of historical research.'

Selective Bibliography

BERGHAHN, V. R., *Der Tirpitz-Plan. Genesis und Verfall einer inncupolitischen Krisenstrategie unter Wilhelm II*, Düsseldorf, 1971.

BÖHME, H., *Deutschlands Weg zur Grossmacht. Studien zum Verhältnis von Wirtschaft und Staat während der Reichsgründungszeit 1848–1881*, Cologne/Berlin, 1966.

DEHIO, L., *Gleichgewicht oder Hegemonie. Betrachtungen über ein Grundproblem der neueren Staatengeschichte*, Krefeld, 1948.

——, *Deutschland und die Weltpolitik im 20. Jahrhundert*, Frankfurt a.M., 1955.

FISCHER, F., *Griff nach der Weltmacht. Die Kriegszielpolitik des kaiserlichen Deutschlands 1914/18*, Düsseldorf 1961, 3rd ed., 1964.

——, *Krieg der Illusionen. Die deutsche Politik von 1911 bis 1914*, Düsseldorf, 1969.

GRUCHMANN, L., *Der Zweite Weltkrieg*, Munich, 1968.

HILDEBRAND, K., *Vom Reich zum Weltreich. Hitler, NSDAP und koloniale Frage 1919–1945*, Munich, 1969.

HILLGRUBER, A., *Hitlers Strategie. Politik und Kriegführung 1940–41*, Frankfurt a.M., 1965.

——, *Deutschlands Rolle in der Vorgeschichte der beiden Weltkriege*, Göttingen, 1967.

HILLGRUBER, A., *Kontinuität und Diskontinuität in der deutschen Aussenpolitik von Bismarck bis Hitler*, Düsseldorf, 3rd ed., 1971.

—— (ed.), *Probleme des Zweiten Weltkrieges*, Cologne/Berlin, 1967 (NWB).

JACOBSEN, H-J., *Nationalsozialistische Aussenpolitik 1933–1938*, Frankfurt a.M./Berlin, 1968.

KLEIN, F. (ed.), *Der Erste Weltkrieg*, vols 1–3, Berlin, 1968/69.

LINK, W., *Die amerikanische Stabilisierungspolitik in Deutschland 1921–1932*, Düsseldorf, 1970.

MARTIN, B., *Deutschland und Japan im Zweiten Weltkrieg. Von Pearl Harbor bis zur deutschen Kapitulation*, Göttingen/Zürich/Frankfurt a.M., 1969.

MILWARD, A. S., *Die deutsche Kriegswirtschaft 1939–45*, Stuttgart, 1966.

RITTER, G., *Staatskunst und Kriegshandwerk. Das Problem des Militarismus in Deutschland*, vols 1–4, Munich, 1954–68.

RÖHL, J. C. G., *Germany without Bismarck, The Crisis of Government in the Second Reich, 1890–1900*, London, 1967.

ROSENBERG, H., *Grosse Depression und Biscarckzeit. Wirtschaftsablauf, Gesellschaft und Politik in Mitteleuropa*, Berlin, 1967.

SCHIEDER, TH., *Das Deutsche Reich in seinen nationalen und universalen Beziehungen 1871 bis 1945*, in: *Reichsgründung 1870/71. Tatsachen–Kontroversen–Interpretationen*, Stuttgart, 1970, pp. 422–54.

SCHIEDER, W. (ed.), *Erster Weltkrieg. Ursachen, Entstehung und Kriegsziele*, Cologne/Berlin, 1969.

STURMER, M., *Bismarcks konservative Revolution*, in: *Das kaiserliche Deutschland. Politik und Gesellschaft 1870–1918*, ed. M. Stürmer, Düsseldorf, 1970.

WEHLER, H. U., *Bismarcks Imperialismus*, Cologne/Berlin, 1969.

—— (ed.), *Imperialismus*, Cologne/Berlin, 1970 (NWB).

Notes

Abbreviations

ADAP	*Akten zur deutschen auswärtigen Politik*
DBFP	Documents on British Foreign Policy
GWU	*Geschichte in Wissenschaft und Unterricht*
HZ	*Historische Zeitschrift*
IMT	International Military Tribunal (Nuremberg)
NPL	*Neue Politische Literatur*
PVS	*Politische Vierteljahresschrift*
SD	*Sicherheitsdienst* (Secret Service)
SKL	*Seekriegsleitung* (Naval Leadership)
STS	*Staatssekretär* (Secretary of State)
VB	*Völkischer Beobachter*
VfZg	*Vierteljahrshefte für Zeitgeschichte*

INTRODUCTION

1. See H. Heffter, 'Vom Primat der Aussenpolitik', in: *HZ* 171 (1951), p. 1 ff. and also E. O. Czempiel, 'Der Primat der auswärtigen

Politik. Kritische Würdigung einer Staatsmaxime', in: *PVS* 4 (1963), pp. 266 ff. Cf. also K. D. Bracher, 'Kritische Betrachtungen über den Primat der Aussenpolitik', in: *Faktoren der politischen Entscheidung. Festschrift für E. Fraenkel*, Berlin, 1963, pp. 115 ff. and also the *Sonderheft 1. der PVS 1969: Die Anarchische Souveränität. Zum Verhältnis von Innen– und Aussenpolitik.*

2. Despite many works of detailed examination, there is none which seeks to reflect the current state of research and attempts an interpretation. See p. 12 of this work for remarks on the major work by H.-A. Jacobsen, *Nationalsozialistische Aussenpolitik 1933–1938*, Frankfurt/M., 1968. An account of the history of Europe between the years 1918 and 1939 is undertaken by H. Graml in his work *Europa zwischen den Kriegen*, Munich, 1969.

3. A. Mitscherlich, *Die Unfähigkeit zu trauern. Grundlagen kollektiven Verhaltens*, Munich, 1967, 27–40 Tausend, 1968, p. 18 f.

4. See K. Hildebrand, 'Der "Fall Hitler". Bilanz und Wege der Hitler-Forschung', in *NPL* 1969, Heft 3, pp. 375 ff.

5. L. Dehio, *Gleichgewicht oder Hegemonie. Betrachtungen über ein Grundproblem der neueren Staatengeschichte*, Krefeld, n.d.

6. See A. Hillgruber, *Deutschlands Rolle in der Vorgeschichte der beiden Weltkriege*, Göttingen, 1967, and idem, *Kontinuität und Diskontinuität in der deutschen Aussenpolitik von Bismarck bis Hitler*, Düsseldorf, 1969.

7. On the beginnings of the study of social history in Germany see G. Oestreich, 'Die Fachhistorie und die Anfänge der sozialgeschichtlichen Forschung in Deutschland', in: *HZ* 208 (1969), pp. 320 ff.

8. Examples of historical studies based on the idea of 'the primacy of domestic policy' may be found for instance in H. Böhme, *Deutschlands Weg zur Grossmacht. Studien zum Verhältnis von Wirtschaft und Staat während der Reichsgründungszeit*, Cologne/Berlin, 1966, and H. U. Wehler, *Bismarck und der Imperialismus*, Cologne/Berlin, 1968.

9. To conclude a history of German foreign policy with the outbreak of war in 1939 does not seem altogether sensible. For it is precisely in the 1940s that the Führer's conduct of the war and his policy as they converge in his 'strategy' can throw a lot of light on the aims and methods of German foreign politics. Similarly, the British policy of

appeasement by no means ended on 3 September 1939; indeed, it was continued during the period of the 'phoney war'. Cf. the important work by A. Hillgruber, *Hitlers Strategie. Politik und Kriegführung 1940–1941*, Frankfurt/M., 1965. In addition also see K. Hildebrand, 'Der Zweite Weltkrieg: Probleme und Methoden seiner Darstellung', in: *NPL* 1968, Heft 4, pp. 493 ff.

10. The fact that the USA exercised political and economic influence has been demonstrated in the study by H.-J. Schröder, *Deutschland und die Vereinigten Staaten 1933 bis 1939. Wirtschaft und Politik in der Entwicklung des deutsch-amerikanischen Gegensatzes*, Wiesbaden, 1970. Also compare the fundamental work by W. Link, *Die amerikanische Stabilisierungspolitik in Deutschland 1921–1932*, Düsseldorf, 1970; for the USSR see M. Beloff, *The Foreign Policy of Soviet Russia, 1929–1941*, 2 vols, London/New York/Toronto, 1947, pp. x ff.; and Hillgruber in: *Osteuropa-Handbuch, Sowjetunion, Aussenpolitik*, D. Geyer (ed.), Cologne/Vienna, 1972.

11. See R. von Albertini, 'England als Weltmacht und der Strukturwandel des Commonwealth' in: *HZ* 208 (1969), pp. 52 ff., and on social change see the study by A. Calder, *The Peoples' War. Britain 1939–1945*, London, 1969.

12. Albertini, *England als Weltmacht*, loc. cit.

13. Cf. R. von Albertini, *Dekolonisation. Zur Diskussion über Verwaltung und Zukunft der Kolonien 1919–1960*, Cologne/Opladen, 1966.

14. While the élite in the young nation states of Africa and Asia borrowed their educational principles, life-style and competitive ethics from the Etons, Oxfords and Grandes Ecoles of Europe, Europe's intellectual youth gave and continue to give themselves up to the cultures of the Far East and Black Africa in order to find in the contemplative inwardness and primitive naivety of once lightly ridiculed rituals a release from the competitive materialism of the Western world.

15. L. Dehio, *Deutschland und die Weltpolitik im 20. Jahrhundert*, Frankfurt/M./Hamburg, 1961, pp. 110 ff. and 127 ff.

16. See the introduction by G. Ritter, *Staatskunst und Kriegshandwerk. Das Problem des 'Militarismus' in Deutschland*, Munich, 1954; also Hildebrand, *Der Zweite Weltkrieg*, p. 485, and also H.-U. Wehler, ' "Absoluter" und "Totaler" Krieg' in: *PVS* 10 (1969), pp. 220 ff.

17. Böhme, *Deutschlands Weg,* loc. cit. and also O. Pflanze, *Bismarck and the Development of Germany, I: 1815–1871,* Princeton, 1963.
Compare also the economic analysis, of great importance for the research into the Bismarck period, by H. Rosenberg, *Grosse Depression und Bismarck-Zeit,* Berlin, 1967, as well as the first 20 pages of the work by A. Rosenberg, *Die Entstehung der Weimarer Republik,* Frankfurt/M., 1958. For their conciseness these works seem hardly to have been surpassed.

18. Jacobsen, *Nationalsozialistische Aussenpolitik,* loc. cit.

19. Hillgruber, *Vorgeschichte,* loc. cit. and idem. *Kontinuität,* loc. cit. And also F. Meinecke, *Die deutsche Katastrophe,* Wiesbaden, 1946, and H. Rothfels, 'Probleme einer Bismarck-Biographie' in: *Deutsche Beiträge,* 2, Munich 1948, pp. 162 ff. In contrasting comparison see Rothfels' detached view in the preface to *Bismarck, Vorträge und Abhandlungen,* Stuttgart, 1970, particularly pp. 10 ff.

20. For example W. M. McGovern, *From Luther to Hitler,* London, 1961, or W. Steed, 'From Frederick the Great to Hitler. The Consistency of German Aims', in: *Int. Affairs* 17 (1938). For further examples see Hildebrand, *Vom Reich zum Weltreich,* p. 20.

21. From the time of Bismarck to Hitler's Reich, Great Britain appears as the key power, decisive in its 'response' for the success or failure of German 'provocations'. See also K. Hildebrand, *Preussen als Faktor der britischen Weltpolitik (1866–1870). Studien zür Aussenpolitik Grossbritanniens im 19 Jahrhundert.* Habilitation thesis, Mannheim 1972.

22. A. Hillgruber, 'Die "Krieg-in-Sicht"-Krise 1875—Wegscheide der Politik der europäischen Grossmächte in der späten Bismarck-Zeit' in; *Gedenkschrift für M. Göhring,* ed. E. Schulin, Wiesbaden, 1968, pp. 243 ff.

23. See Wehler, *Bismarck,* passim, and W. Sauer, 'Das Problem des deutschen Nationalstaates' in: *Moderne deutsche Sozialgeschichte,* ed. H.-U. Wehler, Cologne, 1966, particularly p. 435.

24. Böhme, *Deutschlands Weg,* esp. pp. 587 ff.

25. See in addition Hildebrand, *Der 'Fall Hitler',* p. 381 f.

26. On this controversy cf. W. Schieder, *Erster Weltkrieg. Ursachen,*

Entstehung und Kriegsziele, Cologne/Berlin, 1969, and the recent book by F. Fischer, *Krieg der Illusionen. Die deutsche Politik von 1911 bis 1914*, Düsseldorf, 1969.

27. See W. Baumgart, *Deutsche Ostpolitik 1918. Von Brest-Litovsk bis zum Ende des Ersten Weltkrieges*, Munich, 1966.

28. Cf. F. Fischer, *Griff nach der Weltmacht. Die Kriegszielpolitik des kaiserlichen Deutschlands 1914–1918*, Düsseldorf, 3rd ed. 1964, pp. 469 ff.

29. J. W. Wheeler-Bennett, *Brest-Litovsk, the Forgotten Peace. March 1918*, London, 1938, 2nd ed. 1956.

30. Hillgruber, *Kontinuität*, p. 13 f.

31. See also the study by K. Schwabe, *Deutsche Revolution und Wilson-Frieden. Die amerikanische und deutsche Friedensstrategie zwischen Ideologie und Machtpolitik 1918/19*, Düsseldorf, 1970.

32. See E. Hölzle, *Die Revolution der zweigeteilten Welt. Eine Geschichte der Mächte 1905–1929*, Hamburg, 1963.

33. For Germany see F. Klein (ed.), *Deutschland im Ersten Weltkrieg 3: November 1917 bis November 1918*, Berlin, 1969, pp. 301 ff.

34. Cf. also K. Hildebrand, 'Stufen der Totalitarismus-Forschung', in: *PVS* 9 (1968), p. 403. On the question of the so-called war-work service laws cf. esp. the principal examination by C. Feldman, *Army, Industry, and Labor in Germany 1914–1918*, Princeton, 1966.

35. B. Guttman, *Schattenriss einer Generation 1888–1918*, Stuttgart, 1950, p. 146. Report dated 20 November 1917 by the former political editor of the *Frankfurter Zeitung* on a talk with Secretary of State von Kühlmann in the Foreign Office in Berlin: 'His (Kühlmann's K.H.) suspicions concerning all of our allies are considerable. The Bulgarians, he claims, are insatiable. If you give them your overcoat and trousers they ask for your shirt and shoes. He reports how the Serbs will be "dealt with" through official channels. They are to be brought to delousing stations for purposes of disinfection and are then eliminated by gas. That, he adds melancholically, is to be the course of wars in future.'

36. See F. Frhr. Hiller von Gaertringen, ' "Dolchstoss"-Diskussion und "Dolchstosslegende" im Wandel von vier Jahrzehnten' in:

Geschichte und Gegenwartsbewusstsein. Festschrift für H. Rothfels, ed. W. Besson und F. Frhr. Hiller von Gaertringen, Göttingen, 1963, pp. 122 ff.

37. Cf. M.-O. Maxelon, 'Stresemann und Frankreich', Diss. Freiburg i. Brsg., 1972.

38. On the policies of Bethmann Hollweg and Rathenau as they were determined by economic motives and methods compare the various works by Fritz Fischer, Egmont Zechlin and Gerhard Ritter. For a summary see K. Hildebrand, *Bethmann Hollweg—der Kanzler ohne Eigenschaften? Urteile der Geschichtsschreibung. Eine kritische Bibliographie,* Düsseldorf, 2nd ed., 1970.

39. The fact that economic consolidation and expansion on a world-wide dimension was a chief motive in German policy from 1920 onwards, through the 'era of Stresemann' to Brüning and Curtius has been demonstrated by Link, *Amerikanische Stabilisierungspolitik.*

40. On the policy and personality of Seeckt see H. Meier-Welcker, *Seeckt,* Frankfurt/M., 1967. On Seeckt's key phrase 'alliance capability' (*Bündnisfähigkeit*) see also M. Stürmer, *Koalition und Opposition in der Weimarer Republik 1924–1928,* Düsseldorf, 1967.

41. On the dubiety of the attempt to give a complete account (the problem of complexity) cf. J. Habermas, *Zur Logik der Sozialwissenschaften,* Tübingen, 1967.

42. For one thing, from 1936/37 onwards, Hitler's régime seems more absolute—that is, more independent of direct influences—than Bismarck's policy probably ever was. Thus a relatively greater importance must be attributed to Hitler's originally power-political programme. Further, to complement the results hitherto achieved, the almost insuperable mass of literature on the 'problem of Bismarck' provides the necessary precondition for a general and comprehensive definition of the phenomenon of Bismarck by means of a methodical re-orientation of questions posed. Such a comprehensive conclusion hardly seems possible for the time being so far as the research on Hitler is concerned. For a critique of Wehler's work compare the very thorough review by W. J. Mommsen in *Welt der Literatur* for 8/10/1969, p. 58 and p. 60 as well as the articles by M. Stürmer and W.-D. Narr, in: *NPL* 1970, pp. 188 ff. and pp. 199 ff. See also Wehler's

introduction to H.-U. Wehler (ed.) *Imperialismus*, Cologne/Berlin, 1970.

43. 'Ideology' is used here not primarily in Marx's sense, nor that of the 'Frankfurt School', but rather as understood by E. Spranger as 'a vision of the future' and as an 'action programme'. Cf. E. Spranger, 'Wesen und Wert politischer Ideologien', in: *VfZg* 2 (1954), pp. 114 ff.

44. See also the reflections on methodology in A. Hillgruber, 'Gedanken zu einer politischen Geschichte moderner Prägung', in: *Freiburger Universitätblätter* 1971.

CHAPTER I

1. P. E. Q. Bradley, *The National Socialist Attack on the Foreign Policies of the German Republic 1919–1933*, Diss. Stanford Univ., 1947.

2. Cf. R. Bollmus, *Das Amt Rosenberg und seine Gegner. Studien zum Machtkampf im nationalsozialistischen Herrschaftssystem*, Stuttgart, 1970, and the book by P. Diehl-Thiele, *Partei und Staat im Dritten Reich, Untersuchungen zum Verhältnis von NSDAP und allgemeiner innerer Staatsverwaltung*, Munich, 1969. Both these works provide convincing proof against this thesis.

3. Cf. W. Petwaidic, *Die autoritäre Anarchie. Streiflichter des deutschen Zusammenbruchs*, Hamburg, 1946.

4. See E. N. Peterson, *The Limits of Hitler's Power*, Princeton Univ. Press, 1970.

5. See W. Horn, *Führerideologie und Parteiorganisation in der NSDAP 1919–1933*, Düsseldorf, 1971.

6. G. Schubert, *Anfänge nationalsozialistischer Aussenpolitik*, Cologne, 1963.

7. On von Epps, see in detail Hildebrand, *Vom Reich zum Weltreich*, esp. pp. 113 ff.

8. Cf. the memoirs of E. von Liebert, *Aus einem bewegten Leben*, Munich, 1925.

9. See the admittedly rather unsatisfactory work by A.-E. Simpson, *Hjalmar Schacht in Perspective*, The Hague/Paris, 1969.

10. For a full account see Hildebrand, *Vom Reich zum Weltreich*, chs 1–5 passim and pp. 189 ff.

11. Above all the studies by G. Schildt, *Die Arbeitsgemeinschaft Nord-West*, Diss. Freiburg, 1965; R. Kühnl, *Die nationalsozialistische Linke 1925–1933*, Meisenheim/Glan, 1966; J. L. Nyomarkay, *Charisma and Factionalism in the Nazi Party*, Minneapolis Press, 1967; and J. Noakes, 'Conflict and Development in the NSDAP 1924–1927' in: *Journal of Contemporary History* 1 (1966), pp. 3 ff.

12. See the remarks of F. Meinecke, *Die deutsche Katastrophe*, Wiesbaden, 1946.

13. O. Spengler, *Preussentum und Sozialismus*, Munich, 1920.

14. For a study of Reventlow see H. Boog, *Graf Ernst zu Reventlow (1869–1943). Eine Studie zur Krise der deutschen Geschichte seit dem Ende des 19. Jahrhunderts*, Diss. Heidelberg, 1965; and also R. Wulff, *Die Deutschvölkische/Freiheitspartei 1922–1928*, Diss. phil. Marburg, 1968.

15. The 'Bamberg or Strasser Programme' of November 1926, for many years regarded as lost, can be found in the Bundesarchiv Koblenz, NS 26896 and has now been published by R. Kühnl in *VfZg* 14 (1966), pp. 317 ff.

16. See H. Pogge-von Strandmann (Oxford), *The Koloniolrat, its significance and influence on German politics, 1880–1906*, Diss. Oxford, 1970, and H. Böhme, 'Katanga in der deutschen Kolonial— und Weltpolitik. Notizen zu einem grösseren Thema', in: K.-H. Manegold (ed.) *Wissenschaft, Wirtschaft und Technik. Studien zur Geschichte. Wilhelm Treue zum 60. Geburtstag*, Munich, 1969, pp. 204 ff. and see further, F. Fischer, *Griff nach der Weltmacht*, passim, particularly pp. 113 ff., 120 ff., 414 ff., 469 ff. and 791 ff.

17. *Der Nationale Sozialist* of 4.7.1930: 'Die Sozialisten verlassen die NSDAP'.

18. See generally in this connection the work by H. Gies, *Richard Walter Darré und die nationalsozialistische Landwirtschaftspolitik*. Diss. Frankfurt/M., 1966.

19. Thus for example E. Jäckel in his interesting examination *Hitlers Weltanschauung. Entwurf einer Herrschaft*, Tübingen, 1969, p. 52.

20. The fact that Hitler was never personally satisfied with the role of 'drummer boy' has been demonstrated by W. Horn, *Führerideologie*. See also E. Deuerlein, *Hitler, Eine politische Biographie*, Munich, 1969, pp. 94 ff.

21. Cf. W. Horn, *Führerideologie,* and also idem. 'Ein unbekannter Aufsatz Hitlers aus dem Jahre 1923', in: *VfZg* 16 (1968), pp. 280 ff.

22. Cf. also the dissertation by A. Kuhn, *Hitlers aussenpolitisches Programm*, which however only takes the 'one' side–expansion in the East—into account. See: A. Kuhn, *Hitlers Programm*, Stuttgart, 1970.

23. A. Hitler, *Mein Kampf*, Munich, 1941, and *Hitlers Zweites Buch. Ein Dokument aus dem Jahre 1928*, introduced with a commentary by G. L. Weinberg, Stuttgart, 1961. On these 'programmatic' documents and other informative sources for Hitler's policy see the essay by A. Hillgruber, 'Quellen und Quellenkritik zur Vorgeschichte des Zweiten Weltkriegs', in: *Wehrwissenschaftliche Rundschau 1964,* pp. 116 ff. Besides the sources listed in that essay, cf. also E. Calic (ed.), *Ohne Maske. Hitler-Breiting. Geheimgespräche 1931*, Frankfurt, 1968, and also 'Hitler's Secret Pamphlet for Industrialists, 1927', ed. and introduced by H. A. Turner, jnr., in: *Journal of Modern History* 40 (1968), pp. 348 ff.

24. Schubert, *Aussen politik*; F. Dickmann, 'Machtwille und Ideologie in Hitlers aussenpolitischen Zielsetzungen vor 1933', in: *Spiegel der Geschichte. Festgabe für M. Braubach*, Münster, 1964, pp. 915 ff., and Kuhn, *Programm*.

25. See particularly K. Lange, 'Der Terminus "Lebensraum" in Hitler's *Mein Kampf*', in: *VfZg* 13 (1965), pp. 426 ff. and generally G. Bakker, *Duitse Geopolitik 1919–1945. Een imperialistische Ideologie,* Assen, 1967. See in addition Horn, *Unbekannter Aufsatz Hitlers*, pp. 280 ff.

26. Jäckel, *Weltanschauung*, loc cit.

27. Hitler's concept of alliances, which was different from the policy of the majority of the Nationalist Right, already finds its expression in the account of his experiences by O. Reimer, *18 Jahre Farmer in Afrika*, Leipzig, 1924, esp. p. 358 f.

28. See A. Hillgruber, *Kontinuität*.

29. The relevant proof for this can be found in Hildebrand, *Vom Reich zum Weltreich*, pp. 77 ff. and passim.

30. See E. Jäckel, *Frankreich in Hitlers Europa. Die deutsche Frankreichpolitik im Zweiten Weltkrieg*, Stuttgart, 1966, pp. 13 ff.

31. On the economic basis of this idea—Hitler reduced the economic problem to the question of food supplies—cf. W. Sauer, in: K. D. Bracher, W. Sauer, G. Schulz, *Die nationalsozialistische Machtergreifung. Studien zur Errichtung des totalitären Herrschaftssystems in Deutschland 1933/34*, 2nd ed., Cologne/Opladen, 1962.

32. W. W. Pese, 'Hitler und Italien 1920–1926', in: *VfZg* 3 (1955), pp. 113 ff.

33. On Hitler's Stufenplan see basically A. Hillgruber, *Hitlers Strategie*, and idem., *'Der Faktor Amerika in Hitlers Strategie 1938–1941.'* Aus Politik und Zeitgeschichte, B 19/66, 11.5.1966, supplement to *Parlament*.

34. Hitler, *Zweites Buch*, p. 163.

35. Idem., *Mein Kampf*, pp. 689 ff.

36. Hitler's statements on the USA can be found in *Zweites Buch*, ch. 9, esp. p. 123 f.

37. *Mein Kampf*, p. 438. See also G. Moltmann, 'Weltherrschaftsideen Hitlers', in: *Europa und Übersee. Festschrift für E. Zechlin*, ed. O. Brunner, D. Gerhard, Hamburg, 1961, pp. 197 ff.; also Hildebrand, *Vom Reich zum Weltreich*, p. 83.

38. Cf. in this connection the characteristic passage in A. Speer, *Erinnerungen*, Berlin, 1969, p. 175.

39. On the vision of the 'new man' as the characteristic feature of totalitarianism cf. K. Hildebrand, 'Stufen der Totalitarismus-Forschung', in: *PVS* 1968, pp. 397 ff.

40. A. Rosenberg, *Zum Zukunftsweg einer deutschen Aussenpolitik,* Munich, 1927.

41. See V. R. Berghahn, 'Zu den Zielen des deutschen Flottenbaus unter Wilhelm II', in: *HZ* 210 (1970), pp. 34 ff.; idem., *Der Tirpitz-Plan. Genesis under Verfall einer inncupolitischen Krisenstrategie unter Wilhelm II*, Düsseldorf, 1971.

42. K. Hildebrand, 'Hitlers *Mein Kampf*; Propaganda oder Pro-

gramm? Zur Frühgeschichte der nationalsozialistischen Bewegung' in: *NPL* 1969, p. 77.

CHAPTER 2

1. Besides the standard work by K. D. Bracher, W. Sauer, G. Schulz, *Die nationalsozialistische Machtergreifung,* Cologne/Opladen, 2nd ed., 1962, see also K. D. Bracher, *Die deutsche Diktatur. Entstehung, Struktur, Folgen des Nationalsozialismus,* Cologne/Berlin, 1969, pp. 125 ff.

2. A. Schweitzer, *Big Business in the Third Reich,* Bloomington, 2nd ed., 1965, inc. pp. 504 ff.

3. E. Nolte, *Der Faschismus in seiner Epoche. Die Action Française. Die Italienische Faschismus. Der Nationalsozialismus,* Munich, 1963, pp. 23 ff. and p. 43.

4. G. W. F. Hallgarten, 'Hitler verwirklicht seinen Grund-Plan, I. Zur Psychologie und Soziologie der nationalsozialistischen Diktatur und Expansion', in: *Blätter für deutsche und internationale Politik,* 10 (1965), pp. 515 ff.

5. See K. Lange, *Hitlers unbeachtete Maximen.* Mein Kampf *und die Öffentlichkeit,* Stuttgart/Berlin/Cologne/Mainz, 1968, pp. 104 ff.

6. On the British view and assessment of National Socialist Germany during this period cf. H. D. Gottlieb, *England and the Nature of the Nazi Régime. A Critical Assessment of British Opinion 1933–1939,* Diss. Oxford, 1953; R. Kieser, *Englands Appeasement-Politik und der Aufstieg des Dritten Reiches im Spiegel der britischen Presse (1933–1939),* Winterthur, 1964; Ph. W. Fabry, *Mutmassungen über Hitler. Urteile von Zeitgenossen,* Düsseldorf, 1969, pp. 199 ff. Generally also H. Illert, *Die deutsche Rechte der Weimarer Republik im Urteil der englischen Presse 1928–1932,* Diss. Cologne, 1966.

7. On Vansittart see I. Colvin, *Vansittart in Office. The Origins of World War II,* London, 1965.

8. *Documents on British Foreign Policy,* 2nd series, vol. 6, pp. 975 ff.

9. J. M. d'Hoop, 'Frankreichs Reaktion auf Hitlers Aussenpolitik 1933–1939', in: *GWU* 15 (1964), pp. 211 ff. and A. Kimmel, *Der*

Aufstieg des Nationalsozialismus im Spiegel der französischen Presse 1930–1933, Diss. Bonn, 1969.

10. See: J. Minart, *Le Drame du Désarmement francais (1918– 1939)*, Paris, 1959, and P. E. Tournoux, 'Les Origines de la ligne Maginot', in: *Revue d'Histoire de la Deuxième Guerre Mondiale* 9 (1959); in addition, M. Baumont, 'Die französische Sicherheitspolitik, ihre Träger und Konsequenzen 1920–1924,' in: H. Rössler (ed.), *Die Folgen von Versailles 1919–1924*, Göttingen/Zürich/Frankfurt, 1968.

11. See W. Link, 'Die Ruhrbesetzung und die wirtschaftspolitischen Interessen der USA', in: *VfZg* 1969, pp. 372 ff.

12. See the habilitation paper by W. Link, *Amerikanische Stabilisierungspolitik.*

13. Cf. the account in H.-A. Jacobsen, *Nationalsozialistische Aussenpolitik 1933–1938,* Frankfurt/Berlin, 1968, pp. 406 ff. and D. Ross, *Hitler und Dollfuss. Die deutsche Österreich-Politik 1933–1934,* Hamburg, 1966.

14. J. Krulis-Randa, *Das deutsch-österreichische Zollunionsprojekt von 1931,* Zürich, 1955. This work places the attempts at an economic rapprochement between Germany and Austria within the continuity and tradition of German–Austrian economic relations since the 19th century.

15. On the American position cf. Schröder, *Deutschland und die Vereinigten Staaten,* loc. cit.

16. K. Niclauss, *Die Sowjetunion und Hitlers Machtergreifung. Eine Studie über die deutsch-russischen Beziehungen der Jahre 1929 bis 1935,* Bonn 1966.

17. See August Thalheimer's theory of fascism in: O. Bauer, H. Marcuse, A. Rosenberg et al. *Faschismus und Kapitalismus. Theorien über die sozialen Ursprünge und die Funktion des Faschismus.* ed. W. Abendorth. Introduced by K. Kliem, J. Kammler, R. Griepenburg, Frankfurt/Vienna, 1967. For a detailed account of Thalheimer's theory of fascism see K. H. Tjaden, *Struktur und Funktion der 'K.P.D.– Opposition' (KPO). Eine organisationsgeschichtliche Untersuchung zur 'Rechts'–Opposition im deutschen Kommunismus zur Zeit der Weimarer Republik,* Meisenheim, 1964, pp. 55 ff.

18. For a full account of the 'fascist' experiment in Germany from the point of view of economic history and in comparison to the 'crisis therapies' of the other industrialised nations, cf. D. S. Landes, *The Unbound Prometheus. Technological Change and Industrial Development in Western Europe from 1750 to the Present*, Cambridge U.P. 1969, esp. pp. 398 ff., and also D. Petzina, 'Germany and the Great Depression' in: *Journal of Contemporary History* 4 (1969), pp. 59 ff. See also generally 'Big Business in German Politics: Four Studies', in: *American Historical Review*, LXXV (1969), pp. 37 ff., esp. ibid., pp. 56 ff.: H. A. Turner, jr. 'Big Business and the Rise of Hitler'.

19. H. Rosenberg, *Grosse Depression und Bismarck-Zeit. Wirtschaftsablauf, Gesellschaft und Politik in Mitteleuropa*, Berlin, 1967.

20. See the study by H. U. Wehler, *Bismarck*, loc. cit.

21. See Hildebrand, *Vom Reich zum Weltreich*, p. 129, on this opinion shared also by contemporaries.

22. As early as 8 February 1933, Hitler told his Cabinet of his intention to 'go all out for the military forces in the next four or five years'. On the 'priority of re-armament' cf. Jacobsen, *Nationalsozialistische Aussenpolitik*, p. 765.

23. See H.-G. Schumann, *Nationalsozialismus und Gewerkschaftsbewegung. Die Vernichtung der deutschen Gewerkschaften und der Aufbau der 'Deutschen Arbeitsfront'*, Frankfurt/M., 1958.

24. Th. Vogelsang, 'Dokumentation zur Geschichte der Reichswehr 1930–1933', in: *VfZg* 2 (1954), p. 434 f.

25. See M. Braubach, *Der Einmarsch deutscher Truppen in die entmilitarisierte Zone am Rhein im März 1936*, Cologne/Opladen, 1956, and A. Hillgruber, *Hitlers Strategie, Politik und Kriegführung 1940–41*, Frankfurt/M., 1969, p. 14 (n. 5).

26. E. Raeder, *Mein Leben, Von 1935 bis Spandau 1955*, Tübingen, 1957, vol. 1, p. 281. Seen in connection with his policy, Hitler's demand of 2 June 1935 ordering that the U-boat constructions be kept a secret, and his order of 16 January 1935 to accelerate the naval build-up, seem to have been directed against his continental enemies, France and Russia. Perhaps, in accordance with the colonial threat, these demands also indicate the possibility of Germany preparing a further tactical weapon to force the British into agreement. Cf. Jost Dülffer, *Weimar*

Hitler und die Marine (1920–1939), Düsseldorf, 1973, who examines the question of whether, as for example P. Zieb, *Logistik-Probleme der Marine,* Neckargemünd, 1961, assumes, the plans for Naval armament from 1933 to 1936 already imply long-term aims of Hitler's expansionist intentions, which—in contradiction to his Programme and own statements—therefore already envisaged Great Britain as a possible enemy.

27. A careful analysis is needed of Hitler's relationship to Japan in the early 1930s. Preparatory to that see J. P. Fox, *The Development of Germany's Far Eastern Policy, 1933–1936.* A study of Nazi Germany's so-called 'balancing' policy towards China, Japan and Manchoukuo in the period between the Manchurian Crisis and the signing of the Anticomintern Pact (London School of Economics, Univ. of London, Diss.).

28. On the problem of the secrecy of Hitler's policy, cf. A. Hillgruber, 'Quellen und Quellenkritik zur Vorgeschichte des Zweiten Weltkrieges', in: *Wehrwissenschaftliche Rundschau 1964,* p. 125.

29. W. W. Schmokel, *Dream of Empire. German Colonialism 1919–1945,* New Haven/London, 1964, p. 88.

30. Besides the talks held with Ward Price on 18 October 1933, 16 Feb. 1934, 5 Aug. 1934, and 17 Mar. 1955, cf. Hitler's other 'British contacts' at this time in Jacobsen, *Nationalsozialistische Aussenpolitik,* pp. 765, 766, 769, 771, 774, 776, 779, 780, 784, 785, 790, 797, 798, 799 and 800.

31. Hildebrand, *Vom Reich zum Weltreich,* pp. 248 ff.

32. Jacobsen, *Nationalsozialistische Aussenpolitik,* esp. pp. 73 ff.

33. See K. O. Frhr. von Aretin, 'Prälat Kaas, Franz von Papen und das Reichskonkordat von 1933', in: *VfZg* 14 (1966), pp. 252 ff. and E. Deuerlein, *Das Reichskonkordat, Beiträge zur Vorgeschichte, Abschluss und Vollzug des Konkordats zwischen dem Heiligen Stuhl und dem Deutschen Reich vom 20. Juli 1933,* Düsseldorf, 1956. See also D. Junker, *Die deutsche Zentrumspartei und Hitler 1932/33,* Stuttgart, 1969.

34. That is, Hitler's Programme is to be understood as the subjective shaping and organised sum of the foreign political aspirations emerging in and articulated in German society. The expansionist demands (for

the continent and overseas) which contradicted one another in their detail, were systematised by Hitler into a programme. But what must not be overlooked is that the primacy of the continental policy corresponded far more to the desires of the strongest partner within the German economy, the heavy industries, than overseas aims would have done to their interests. Colonial demands were more strongly advocated by the manufacturing industries, those in trade and shipping, but for the time being these demands had to take second place. See generally—and particularly for the war years—the DDR publication *Anatomie des Krieges, Neue Dokumente über die Rolle des deutschen Monopolkapitals bei der Vorbereitung und Durchführung des Zweiten Weltkrieges*, edited with an introduction by D. Eichholtz and W. Schumann, Berlin 1969.

35. See J. L. Heinemann, 'Constantin von Neurath and German Policy at the London Economic Conference of 1933: Backgrounds to the Resignation of Alfred Hugenberg', in: *Journal of Modern History*, 41, (1969), pp. 160 ff.

36. See F. Fischer, *Krieg der Illusionen, Die deutsche Politik von 1911 bis 1914*, Düsseldorf, 1969, pp. 117 ff.

37. In both the Reich and Prussia Hugenberg held office in four ministries—in the Economics and the Agricultural and Food Ministries of each.

38. Cf. F. Frhr Hiller von Gaertringen, 'Die Deutschnationale Volkspartei', in: E. Matthias/R. Morsey (eds.), *Das Ende der Parteien*, Düsseldorf, 1960, pp. 543 ff.

39. A. Ritthaler, 'Eine Etappe auf Hitlers Weg zur ungeteilten Macht. Hugenbergs Rücktritt als Reichsminister. Dokumentation,' in: *VfZg* 8 (1960), pp. 193 ff.

40. See the thoughtful account in B.-J. Wendt, Munich, 1938. *England zwischen Hitler und Preussen*, Frankfurt/M., 1965.

41. Jacobsen, *Nationalsozialistische Aussenpolitik*, p. 398 f.

42. See H. Roos, *Polen und Europa. Studien zur polnischen Aussenpolitik 1931–1939*, Tübingen, 1957, and Z. J. Gasiorowski, 'The German–Polish Non-aggression Pact of 1934',: *Journal of Central European Affairs*, 15, (1955), pp. 3 ff.

43. J. Korbel, *Poland between East and West. Soviet and German Diplomacy Toward Poland*, 1919–1933, Princeton, 1963, esp. pp. 68 ff.

44. Among the numerous works on this problem mention may be made of H. Roos, 'Die "Präventivkriegspläne" Pilsudskis von 1933', in: *VfZg* 3 (1955), pp. 344 ff.

45. Memo of the late Field Marshal Frhr von Weichs, written testimony in the Institut für Zeitgeschichte in Munich, No. 182, pp. 8 ff., quoted by Hillgruber, *Quellenkritik*, p. 118.

46. See p. 82 above.

47. The so-called revolutionary methods involved in the tactic of using 'fifth column' support were unknown either to German or European politics in the 19th and 20th centuries. See L. Jedlicka, 'Vom Kaisertum Österreich zur Doppelmonarchie Österreich-Ungarn' in: *Entscheidung 1866. Der Krieg zwischen Österreich und Preussen*, ed. W. v. Groote and U. v. Gersdorff, Stuttgart, 1966, and also E. Zechlin, 'Friedensbestrebungen und Revolutionierungsversuche', in: *Aus Politik und Zeitgeschichte. Beilage zur Wochenzeitung 'Das Parlament'* of 14 June 1961, B 24/61. Neither can the 'novelty 'of this manoeuvre lie in the fact that in 1933 it was supposed to have become an integral method adopted by Hitler. He set far more store on traditional methods (the armed forces and diplomacy).

48. *Documents on British Foreign Policy 1919–1939*, 2nd series, London, 1946 ff., vol. 4, report of 30 Jan. 1934.

49. See K. A. Jarausch, *The Four Power Pact*, Columbia 1964, and Ch. Bloch, *Hitler und die europäischen Mächte 1933/34. Kontinuität oder Bruch*, Frankfurt/M., 1966 and the definitive work on this topic by G. Wollstein, *Die nationalsozialistische Aussenpolitik 1933/34*, Diss. Marburg, 1971.

50. *Documents on German Foreign Policy*, series C, vol. 2, No. 271, pp. 513 ff.

51. Ibid., vol. 3, No. 358, p. 681. He had already reported these plans previously to Raeder on 5.11.1934 and to Lord Allen of Hurtwood on 25.1.1935. For a study of the British Ambassador Sir Eric Phipps, see the work by J. Ott, *Botschafter Sir Eric Phipps und die deutsch-englischen Beziehungen*, Diss. Erlangen, 1968.

52 W. E. Scott, *Alliance against Hitler, The Origins of the Franco–Soviet Pact,* Duke, 1962.

53. From the large amount of literature on this subject cf. the highly informative essay by J. Petersen, 'Deutschland und Italien im Sommer 1935. Der Wechsel des italienischen Botschafters in Berlin', in: *GWU* 20 (1969), pp. 330 ff.

54. With the outcome of the study by M. Funke, *Sanktionen und Kanonen. Hitler, Mussolini und der internationale Abessinienkonflikt,* Düsseldorf, 1970, the thesis is hardly tenable any longer that the foundation-stone for the 'Axis' was laid during the Abyssinian War.

55. See: G. Meinck, *Hitler und die deutsche Aufrüstung 1933–1937,* Wiesbaden, 1959; B. Carroll, *Design for Total War. Arms and Economics in the Third Reich,* The Hague, 1968; G. Thomas, *Geschichte der deutschen Wehr- und Rüstungswirtschaft (1918–1945),* ed. W. Birkenfeld, Boppard/Rh., 1966.

56. *Documents on German Foreign Policy,* series C, vol. 3, No. 555, pp. 1043 ff. For an interpretation see in detail Hildebrand, *Vom Reich zum Weltreich,* pp. 465 ff.

CHAPTER 3

1. Cf. the essay by F. Jacomini, 'La conferenza di Stresa', in: *Rivista studi polit. internat.,* 1952/I.

2. See generally the on the whole somewhat unsatisfactory study by W. Bernhardt, *Die deutsche Aufrüstung 1934–1939,* Frankfurt/M., 1969, and H.-A. Jacobsen, *Nationalsozialistische Aussenpolitik 1933–1938,* Frankfurt/M., 1968, p. 804.

3. On the character and policies of von Ribbentrop, see P. Schwarz, *This man Ribbentrop, His Life and Times,* New York, 1943. F. L'Huillier, 'Joachim von Ribbentrop', in: *Revue d'histoire de la Deuxième Guerre Mondiale,* 1956, pp. 1 ff. and K. Hildebrand, *Vom Reich zum Weltreich,* esp. 357 ff., pp. 491 ff. and pp. 673 ff., which summarises and extends the reflections of A. Hillgruber, in the attempt to make plausible a new interpretation of the policy of von Ribbentrop. See also the thesis in progress by W. Michalka (Mannheim), 'J. von Ribbentrop als deütscher Botschafter in London (1936–1938)'. Three

studies may be mentioned among the extensive literature on the Naval Agreement: W. Malanowski, 'Das deutsch-englische Flottenabkommen vom 18. Juni 1935 als Ausgangspunkt für Hitlers doktrinäre Bundnispolitik', in: *Wehrwissenschaftliche Rundschau 5* (1955), pp. 408 ff.; D. C. Watt, 'The Anglo-German Naval Agreement of 1935: An Interim Judgement', in: *Journal of Modern History* 28 (1956), pp. 155 ff., and Ch. Bloch, 'La Grande Bretagne Face au Réarmement Allemand et l'Accord Naval de 1935', in: *Revue d'histoire de la Deuxième Guerre Mondiale* 16, (1966), pp. 41 ff.

5. Thus runs the title of a book by the journalist R. Ingrim, *Hitlers glücklichster Tag. London, den 18 Juni*, Stuttgart, 1962.

6. On this problem cf. also G. Holzweissig, *Das Deutschlandbild der britischen Presse im Jahre 1935. Ein Beitrag zur Grundlegung der englischen Appeasementpolitik*, Diss., Hamburg, 1967.

7. For details see Hildebrand, *Vom Reich zum Weltreich*, pp. 343 ff.

8. See p. 35 of the present work.

9. *Documents on German Foreign Policy*, series C, vol. IV, No. 463, pp. 917 ff., where there is no mention of the key word 'colonies', while the *New York Times* of 27 December 1935 does report it in the corresponding report.

10. Lord Londonderry, *England blickt auf Deutschland*, Essen, 1938, pp. 101 ff.

11. See also: K. Hildebrand, *Hitlers Kolonialismus. Zum Problem der kolonialen Politik in der preussisch-deutschen Geschichte*, MS, 1969.

12. See also Hillgruber, *Kontinuität*, p. 23, on Schacht's attempts to divert the Third Reich from its war course on to the path of peaceful economic expansionism overseas.

13. R. Fiedler, 'Hitlers aufregendste Stunden. Vor 25 Jahren: Einmarsch in die entmilitarisierte Zone'; in: *Politische Studien* 12 (1961), p. 168.

14. Jacobsen, *Nationalsozialistische Aussenpolitik*, p. 814.

15. On the intervention of German troops into the Rhineland cf. the excellent study by M. Braubach, *Der Einmarsch deutscher Truppen in die entmilitarisierte Zone am Rhein in März 1936*, Cologne/Opladen, 1956.

16. *VB* of 8 March 1936.

17. Ibid. of 12 March 1936.

18. Cf. the interpretation in A. Hillgruber, *Hitlers Strategie. Politik und Kriegführung: 1940–41*, Frankfurt/M., 1965, pp. 242 ff. Hillgruber sees the colonial demands which Hitler made from 1936 on, as strategic long-term aims within the Dictator's *Stufenplan*.

19. *Politisches Archiv des Auswärtigen Amtes Bonn, Flottenverhandlungen 1936–37*, Pol. I M (301), vol. 1, 'Unterredung mit Aussenminister Eden über den Bau der beiden deutschen A-Kreuzer', London, 29 May 1936.

20. As a fundamental work on this problem see F. Neumann, *Behemoth. The Structure and Practice of National Socialism. 1933–1944*, New York, 1963, and Hitler's address in the Düsseldorfer Industrieklub on 27 January 1932: 'if we were not here, there would be no middle-class left in Germany any more today'. See M. Domarus, *Hitler, Reden und Proklamationen 1932 bis 1945. Kommentiert von einem deutschen Zeitgenossen*, Munich, 1965, vol. I, first part, p. 87. See also K. Hildebrand, 'Deutschland, die Westmächte und das Kolonialproblem. Ein Beitrag über Hitlers Aussenpolitik vom Ende der Münchener Konferenz bis zum 'Griff nach Prag' in: *Aus Politik und Zeitgeschichte*. An article in the weekly *Das Parlament*, B 22/69 of 31 May 1969, p. 27.

21. Terminology and classification according to A. Schweitzer, *Big Business in the Third Reich*, Bloomington, 2nd ed., 1965.

22. Jacobsen, *Nationalsozialistische Aussenpolitik*, p. 816 and p. 819.

23. Ibid. p. 819.

24. See E. L. Presseisen, 'Le racisme et les Japonais. (Un dilemme Nazi)', in: *Revue d'histoire de la Deuxième Guerre Mondiale*, 13 (1963), pp. 1 ff.

25. Jacobsen, *Nationalsozialistichte Aussenpolitik*, p. 819, see also p. 113 f.

26. See the study by Th. Sommer, *Deutschland und Japan zwischen den Mächten 1935–40*, Tübingen, 1962, and E. L. Presseisen, *Germany and Japan. A study in totalitarian diplomacy 1933–1941*, The Hague, 1958, and also B. Martin, 'Zur Vorgeschichte des deutsch–japanischen Kriegsbundnisses', in: *GWU* 1970.

27. In detail see Jacobsen, *Nationalsozialistische Aussenpolitik*, pp. 421 ff.

28. Among the great number of works on the subject is M. Merkes' *Die Deutsche Politik gegenüber dem spanischen Bürgerkrieg 1936–1939*, Bonn. 2nd ed. 1969. This book, which first appeared in 1961, has been considerably extended in the second edition, reflecting the latest state of research in the subject.

29. M. Einhorn, *Die ökonomischen Hintergründe der faschistischen deutschen Intervention in Spanien 1936–1939*, Berlin, 1962, stresses this motive particularly.

30. On British policy towards the Spanish Civil War cf. K. W. Watkins, *Britain Divided. The Effect of the Spanish Civil War on British Political Opinion*, London, 1963.

31. Jacobsen, *Nationalsozialistische Aussenpolitik*, p. 820.

32. J. von Ribbentrop, *Zwischen London und Moskau. Erinnerungen und letzte Aufzeichnungen*, Leoni a. Starnberger See, 1954, p. 93.

33. Jacobsen, *Nationalsozialistische Aussenpolitik*, p. 821.

34. Ibid.

35. Published in the *VfZg* 3 (1955), pp. 184 ff. with an introduction by Wilh. Treue.

36. See Hildebrand, *Vom Reich zum Weltreich,* ch. 6, section 1: passim.

37. Cf. the work being prepared by K. Delius (Mannheim) on Lloyd George's view of Germany from 1911 to 1945.

38. See p. 49 of the present work.

39. *Politisches Archiv des Auswärtigen Amtes Bonn*, Pol. II (89), vol. 3: *Deutsches Nachrichten Büro* of 15 January 1937, reprinted in Hildebrand, *Vom Reich zum Weltreich*, Document 56.

40. *Politisches Archiv des Auswärtigen Amtes Bonn*, Po. II, England–Deutschland, vol. 3: *Aussprache mit dem stellvertretenden Aussenminister Lord Halifax. Bericht v. Ribbentrops an den Führer und Reichskanzler und Reichsminister des Auswärtigen persönlich!* London, 14 February 1937. Reprinted in Hildebrand, *Vom Reich zum Weltreich*, document 57.

41. *VB* of 31 January 1937 (special issue).

42. Quoted from J. Benoist-Méchin, *Wetterleuchten in der Weltpolitik 1937. Deutschland und die Weltmächte (Geschichte der deutschen Militärmacht*, vol. 4), Oldenburg/Hamburg, 1966, p. 51.

43. See Hildebrand. *Vom Reich zum Weltreich*, esp. pp. 357 ff. and pp. 491 ff.

44. See p. 96 of the present work.

45. The biography by K. Feiling, the *Life of Neville Chamberlain*, London, 1947, remains the standard work on the personality and politics of Neville Chamberlain. See in addition H. A. Arnold, *Neville Chamberlain und Appeasement*, Diss. Würzburg, 1965.

46. On the personality and politics of Baldwin cf. K. Middlemas/J. Barnes, *Baldwin*, London, 1969, a work which in some of its evidence corrects the view of research hitherto on the predecessor of Neville Chamberlain.

47. On Lord Lothian's political conception see G. Niedhart, *Grossbritannien und die Sowjetunion 1934–1939*, München, 1972.

48. Jacobsen, *Nationalsozialistische Aussenpolitik*, p. 835.

49. Ibid. p. 834.

50. *VB* of 4 October 1937.

51. Jacobsen, *Nationalsozialistische Aussenpolitik*, p. 836: also basically, K. Drechsler, Deutschland–China–Japan 1933–1939, Berlin, 1964.

52. See the (admittedly unsatisfying) book by J. V. Crompton, *Hitler und die USA. Die Amerikapolitik des Dritten Reiches und die Ursprünge des Zweiten Weltkrieges*, Oldenburg/Hamburg, 1968, esp. pp. 65 ff. Compare also the general work on American foreign policy: H.-J. Schröder, 'F. D. Roosevelts Aussenpolitik 1933–1937', in: *NPL* 1970, pp. 213 ff.

CHAPTER 4

1. On the analysis of the policy of the Chamberlain government cf. Niedhart, op. cit. passim, as well as K. Middlemass, *Diplomacy of Illusion*, London, 1972.

2. According to the definition of Arthur Schweitzer, the phase of 'partial fascism' merges into that of 'full fascism', see Schweitzer, *Big Business*, loc. cit.

3. ADAP, D, I, No. 19. Of the extensive literature on the interpretation and sources of the Hossbach Memorandum, mention may be made of the essay by W. Bussmann, 'Zur Entstehung und Überlieferung der "Hossbach Niederschrift" ', in: *VfZg* 16 (1968), pp. 373 ff.

3a. See J. Henke, *Hitler und England 1937–39*, Boppard/Rh., 1973.

4. See Hillgruber, *Hitlers Strategie*, esp. pp. 242 ff., idem, *Kontinuität*, loc. cit., and idem, 'Wollte Hitler deutsche Kolonien in Afrika? Aufschlüsse über die Grossmachtpolitik des nationalsozialistischen Reiches', in *Frankfurter Allgemeine* of 11 November 1969, p. 13.

5. See p. 113 of the present work. On the relationship between the USA and the Third Reich during the 1930s cf. Schröder, *Deutschland und die Vereinigten Staaten*, loc. cit.

6. A special examination of the phenomenon of fatalism in German politics of the 19th and 20th centuries and the 'conservative ruling classes' on the eve of the First World War would certainly prove informative. In connection with this compare the thoughts of Theodor Schieder on the problem of vulgar Darwinism and his (politicised) concept of evolution in Schieder's essay 'Das Problem der Revolution im 19. Jahrhundert' in: *HZ* 170 (1950).

7. An examination by W. Malanowski (*Der Spiegel*, 1969) 'exposes' the alleged strength of the German armed forces as a bluff on Hitler's part at the same time as the Western powers were themselves overestimating Germany's military strength. But it was precisely the potentially hostile Western powers' perception and appraisal of the German armed forces, limited as this perception was by its time, which was the deciding factor for the course of history—not the 'objective findings', which admittedly are still to be examined, which have come to light so sensationally today. See in this connection Hillgruber, *Strategie*, p. 34 f.

8. The study in progress by E. Most (Mannheim) on the British policy on the League of Nations gives useful information on Chamberlain's considerations already dating from 1936, which led him to adopt his 'concept' of appeasement. See also the work by K. Middlemas

mentioned in n. 1 of this chapter, which finds the roots of Chamberlain's policy of appeasement dating back as far as 1934.

9. The question concerning 'conception or improvisation' is a central one handled in the dissertation, still in progress, by K. Gutzmer (Marburg/L.), *Die englische Deutschlandpolitik 1931–1935. Konzeption oder Improvisation*.

10. Hildebrand, *Vom Reich zum Weltreich*, p. 765 f.

11. One aspect of the problem of the interdependence of domestic and foreign policy in England worth investigating would be the question as to whether Chamberlain thought about the possible fundamental social changes within the existing social and economic structure in Britain brought about by war. On the social changes which materialised during the war cf. the book by A. Calder, *People's War*, loc. cit., and the essay by D. Artaud, 'La Grande Bretagne et la lutte contre l'inflation', in: *Revue d'histoire de la Deuxième Guerre Mondiale* 1969, no. 76, pp. 39 ff.

12. On Churchill and his policy cf. the biography in several volumes by M. Gilbert.

13. *ADAP*, D. I, No. 31, App. pp. 46 ff.

14. The Speer memoirs reveal that Hitler was already toying with these thoughts in his calculations rather earlier: A. Speer, *Erinnerungen*, Berlin, 1969, p. 85.

15. On the economic motivations behind the appeasement policy compare B. J. Wendt, *Economic appeasement Handel und Finanz in der britischen Deutschland-Politik von 1933–1939*, Düsseldorf, 1971.

16. Cf. M. Salewski, *Die deutsche Seekriegsleitung 1935–1941*, Frankfurt/M., 1970, passim, on the basic axiom of German–British 'friendship' in the thoughts and considerations of the German Naval Command up to 1938. See also idem, 'Selbstverständnis und historisches Bewusstsein der deutschen Kriegsmarine', in: *Marine–Rundschau 67* (1970), p. 74.

17. *ADAP*, D, I, No. 21, p. 33 f.

18. Compare the concluding remarks of this work as well as Hillgruber, *Kontinuität*, passim, on the different variations of German power politics on the path from Bismarck to Hitler.

19. See p. 42 and p. 45 of the present work.

20. Staatliches Archivlager Göttingen, *Nürnberger Prozessmaterial* L–151, Generaloberst H. Göring: App. Nr. 6 of dispatch No. 1267.

21. Göring's colleague Wohlthat, in a conversation on 16 September, 1966 with Prof. Werner Link (Kassel) in New York, confirmed the thesis of the 'economic alternative conception'. Dr Link informed the author of this in a communication of 30 November 1969.

22. On resistance activities from 1938–39 cf. P. H. Hoffmann, *Widerstand–Staatsstreich–Attentat. Der Kampf der Opposition gegen Hitler,* Munich, 1969, and also K.-J. Müller, *Das Heer und Hitler. Armee und nationalsozialistische Regierung 1933–1944,* Stuttgart, 1969. In addition see H. C. Deutsch, *Verschwörung gegen den Krieg. Der Widerstand in den Jahren 1939–1940,* Munich, 1969. On the role of Göring see among others, F. Wiedemann, *Der Mann, der Feldherr werden wollte,* Velbert/Kettwig, 1964, p. 113 f.

23. *ADAP,* D. I, pp. 132 ff.

24. This could only have been the case if it can be demonstrated that Hitler had already read the original report, of which this is a summary, before 5 November 1937.

25. See p. 102 f. of this work.

26. See M. Messerschmidt, *Die Wehrmacht im NS-Staat. Zeit der Indoktrination,* Hamburg, 1969, pp. 48 ff. and K. J. Müller, *Das Heer und Hitler. Armee und nationalsozialistische Regierung 1933–1944,* Stuttgart, 1969.

27. On Keitel cf. W. Görlitz (ed.), *Generalfeldmarschall Keitel, Verbrecher oder offizier? Erinnerungen, Briefe, Dokumente des Chefs, OKW,* Göttingen/Berlin/Frankfurt, 1961.

28. See Müller, *Hitler und Heer,* pp. 189 ff. and also Messerschmidt, *Wehrmacht,* p. 82.

29. See also J. Dülffer, 'Weisungen an die Wehrmacht 1938/39 als Ausdruck ihrer Gleichschaltung (I)', in: *Wehrwissenschaftliche Rundschau 1969,* pp. 651 ff.

29a. The difference between Eden and Chamberlain consisted as is known in their contrasting estimations of Italy and Mussolini.

30. From all the extensive literature on the question of the 'annexation' cf. the works by U. Eichstädt, *Von Dollfuss zu Hitler, Geschichte des Anschlusses Österreichs 1933–1938*, Wiesbaden, 1955, and J. Gehl, *Germany and the Anschluss*, London/NewYork/Toronto, 1963.

31. Jacobsen, *Nationalsozialistische Aussenpolitik*, pp. 406 ff.

32. J. R. von Salis, *Weltgeschichte der Neuesten Zeit*, vol. 3. Zürich, 2nd ed., 1962, p. 594.

33. Cf. the work by K. Middlemas on the foundations of Chamberlain's foreign policy.

34. See also F. Fischer, *Krieg der Illusionen*, pp. 205 ff. and pp. 289 ff. Admittedly the decisive factor was the British–German collaboration in preserving or bringing about peace and the localisation of conflict.

35. In this connection compare the plans for partition of the Austrian–Hungarian monarchy already entertained by Bismarck, see p. 6 of this work.

36. See U. Eichstädt, *Von Dollfuss zu Hitler*, loc. cit.

37. Jacobsen, *Nationalsozialistische Aussenpolitik*, pp. 439 ff.

38. *ADAP*, D. V, No. 152, p. 172 f.

39. On the German attitude to the Abyssinia problem cf. M. Funke, *Der internationale Abessinienkonflikt*, loc. cit.

40. See particularly the study by B.-J. Wendt, *Economic appeasement. Also B.-J. Wendt, Appeasement 1938. Wirtschaftliche Rezession und Mitteleuropa*, Frankfurt/M., 1966.

41. Bundesarchiv Koblenz, ZSG III 1610: the *Australian Statesman* of 23 February 1938.

42. On Sir Nevile Henderson and his policy cf. the dissertation by R. Strauch, *Sir Nevile Henderson. Britischer Botschafter in Berlin von 1937–1939. Ein Beitrag zur diplomatischen Vorgeschichte des Zweiten Weltkrieges*, Diss. Bonn, 1959.

43. *ADAP*, D. I, No. 131, p. 186 f.

44. See also Hillgruber, *Kontinuität*, p. 23.

45. On all these problems see the introduction of T. Mason's documentation of the social history of the Third Reich, in preparation.

46. On the role of the so-called minorities in prerevolutionary Europe cf. K. Hildebrand, 'Die Suche nach dem "wahren" Preussen', in: *PVS* 1970.

47. Cf. J. K. Hoensch, *Geschichte der Tschechoslowakischen Republik 1918–1965*, Stuttgart, 1966, and J. W. Brügel, *Tschechen und Deutsche 1918 bis 1938*, Munich, 1967.

48. Jacobsen, *Nationalsozialistische Aussenpolitik*, p. 442.

49. Ibid. p. 443.

50. *Politisches Archiv des Auswärtigen Amtes Bonn*, Pol. II, England–Deutschland VII: *Aufzeichnung von Bismarcks*, 10.5.1938.

51. See also M. Mackintosh, *Juggernaut: A History of the Soviet Armed Forces*, New York, 1967.

52. See A. Hillgruber, *Deutschlands Rolle in der Vorgeschichte der beiden Weltkriege*, Göttingen, 1967, p. 78 f.

53. W. Foerster, *Generalstabschef Ludwig Beck*, Munich, 1953, p. 107 f.

54. See Müller, *Heer und Hitler*, pp. 345 ff.

54a. The book by J. Henke, *Hitler und England 1937–1939*, loc. cit., throws light on these possibilities which could have implied a military ousting of Britain from the Continent.

55. See Salewski, *Seekriegsleitung*, loc. cit. and J. Dülffer, Weimar, *Hitler und die Marine*, loc. cit. In this connection cf. particularly the memorandum 'Aufbau der Kriegsmarine 1926–1939' by government adviser Dr Treue, in: *Bundesarchiv/Militärarchiv Freiburg*: Pg.–33965 and also idem, Nachlass Beck HO 8–28: *Nürnberger Documents* Ps 3037 (Wiedemann). The author would wish to thank Dr M. Michaelis (London) for having kindly drawn his attention to these two documents.

56. See p. 50.

57. Cf. Salewski, *Seekriegsleitung*, loc. cit.; Dülffer, Weimar, *Hitler und die Marine*, loc. cit. and C.-A. Gemzell, *Raeder, Hitler und Skandinavien. Der Kampf für einen maritimen Operationsplan*, Lund, 1965, p. 94 f.

58. On the character of Beck cf. Foerster, *Beck*, loc. cit.

59. Müller, *Hitler und Heer*, pp. 345 ff.

60. See p. 57.

61. On the mission of Ewald von Kleist-Schmenzin, for example, see the biography by B. Scheurig, *Ewald von Kleist-Schmenzin, Ein Konservativer gegen Hitler*, Oldenburg–Hamburg, 1968.

62. On this thesis cf. B.-J. Wendt, Munich, 1938; *England zwischen Hitler und Preussen*, Frankfurt/M., 1965.

63. Cf. the corresponding remarks in the 'Hossbach Memorandum', loc. cit.

64. *ADAP*, D. II, No. 279, pp. 363 ff.

65. See also p. 57.

66. Ibid.

67. *VB* of 13 September 1938.

68. Cf. Benesch's talk with Stampfer on 19 October 1939, in: W. Link (compiler), *Mit dem Gesicht nach Deutschland*, Düsseldorf, 1968, Doc. 77.

69. From among the mass of literature on the Munich Conference cf. the works by B. Celovsky, *Das Münchener Abkommen 1938*, Stuttgart, 1958; H. K. G. Rönnefarth, *Die Sudetenkrise in der internationalen Politik. Entstehung–Verlauf–Auswirkung*, Wiesbaden, 1961; K. Eubank, *Munich*, Oklahoma, 1963; B.-J. Wendt, München, 1938, loc. cit.; D. N. Lammers, *Explaining Munich. The Search for Motive in British Policy*, Stanford, 1966, and—as a supplement and corrective—K. Robbins, *Munich 1938*, Gütersloh, 1969.

70. See Hillgruber, *Deutschlands Rolle*, p. 89.

71. Ibid.

72. *ADAP*, D, IV, No. 247, pp. 251 ff.

73. See for details K. Hildebrand, *Deutschland, die Westmächte und das Kolonial problem*, op cit., p. 23 f.

74. On the attitude of the Labour Party towards Nazi Germany see the study still in preparation by S. Wichert (Belfast), *Englands Linke und das Kolonial problem*, op. cit., p. 23 f.

75. On the response of the Churchill circle to Germany cf. the study by D. Aigner, *Das Ringen um England. Das deutsch–britische Ver-*

hältnis. Die öffentliche Meinung 1933–1939. Tragödie zweier Völker,
Munich/Esslingen, 1969, esp. pp. 151 ff.

76. See the essay by D. C. Watt, 'Der Einfluss der Dominions auf
die britische Aussenpolitik von München 1938', in: *VfZg* 8 (1960),
pp. 64 ff., on the influence of the Dominions on British policy; and
also idem, 'South African attempts to Mediate Between Britain and
Germany 1935–1938', in K. Bourne and D. C. Watt (eds.), *Studies in
International History, Essays in Honour of Professor W. N. Medlicott,*
London, 1967, pp. 402 ff., as well as the dissertation in progress by
R. Tamchina (Hamburg) on the relations between Great Britain and
the Dominions during the era of the policy of appeasement.

77. On this attempt, and the German–French agreement of 6 Decem-
ber 1938, cf. E. Scheler, *Die politischen Beziehungen zwischen
Deutschland und Frankreich zur Zeit der aktiven Aussenpolitik
Hitlers, Ende 1937 bis zum Kriegsausbruch,* Diss. Frankfurt/M., 1962.

78. See Schmokel, *Dream,* esp. pp. 121 ff.

79. This concept borrowed from Fraenkel (E. Fraenkel, *The Dual
State. A Contribution to the Theory of Dictatorship,* London/New
York/Toronto, 1941) is used here in the sense defined briefly by Hillgruber: 'Without doubt a complete triumph for Hitler and a consequently total realisation of his Programme, would have amounted to
a "revolution" in the sense of a violent social upheaval. For according
to Hitler's racist ideological principles the total re-shaping of Europe
which he intended would also have involved doing away with the old
ruling class in Germany. But in fact the development got stuck halfway. So it was that "only" a seemingly chaotic "dual state" came about,
in which the old and newly forming ruling groups existed side by side
with only partial interfusion.' Hillgruber, *Kontinuität,* p. 24.

80. *IMT Protocols,* vol. 34, p. 190, Doc. 023/C (introduction).

81. Ibid.

82. See Dülffer, Weimar, *Hitler und Marine,* loc. cit. In this connection compare also the communication of Raeder to Keitel of
7 November 1938, on the 'build-up of the fleet'. Akte M/55/34 of the
Bundesarchiv/Militärarchiv Freiburg. The author's thanks to Dr J.
Dülffer for drawing attention to this document.

83. Bundesarchiv Koblenz, NS 19, Himmler–Reden 15, quoted by: H. Booms, 'Der Ursprung des Zweiten Weltkrieges–Revision oder Expansion', in: *Geschichte in Wissenschaft und Unterricht 16* (1965), p. 353.

84. *VB* of 10 November 1938.

85. See also particularly Moltmann, *Weltherrschaftsideen Hitlers,* loc. cit.

86. See Moltmann, *Weltherrschaftsideen Hitlers.*

87. See Hillgruber, *Kontinuität,* pp. 24 ff.

88. For a fuller account cf. the concluding remarks of this work. Reference may here be made to the studies by E. Kehr, *Der Primat der Innenpolitik,* edited by H.-U. Wehler, Berlin, 2nd ed. 1970, and H. Herzfeld, J. v. Miquel, 2 vols., Detmold, 1938.

89. See J. C. G. Röhl, *Germany without Bismarck, The Crisis of Government in the Second Reich 1890–1900,* London, 1967, esp. pp. 224 ff.

90. Cf. Hildebrand, *Der Fall Hitler,* p. 381 f. on the continuity between Bismarck and Hitler in foreign policy which also served a domestic function.

91. See primarily H. J. Puhle, *Agrarische Interessenpolitik und preussischer Konservatismus im wilhelminischen Reich (1893–1914),* Hannover, 1966, esp. pp. 111 ff.

92. See above all the reflections of A. Hillgruber, 'Die "Endlösung" und das deutsche Ostimperium als Kernstück des rassenideologischen "Programms" des Nationalsozialismus', in *VfZg* 1972, pp. 133 ff.

93. As is well known, the 'breeding' of a 'new' race of men was prepared for in the SS and Hitler-Youth ideology, the 'measures' introduced in the war as part of the 'policy of occupation' (the extermination of Jews and those of 'inferior race'; the 'Germanisation' of 'racial groups' recognised as of high enough worth) should make clear that the vision of the 'biological revolution' which seemed so 'utopian' by no means lay in the distant future. (See H. Höhne, *Der Orden mit dem Totenkopf,* 1967; A. Dallin, *Deutsche Herrschaft in Russland 1941–1945. Eine Studie über Besatzungspolitik,* Düsseldorf, 1958; M. Broszat, *Nationalsozialistische Polenpolitik 1939–1945,* Stuttgart,

1961, and K. Kwiet, *Reichskommissariat Niederlande. Versuch und Scheitern nationalsozialistischer Neuordnung, Stuttgart,* 1968.) The 'man-in-the-street', the lower middle class, was 'promoted' to the rank of 'superman' through the vehicle of ideology. The intoxicating feeling of racial superiority made him forget any thought about rebelling against the class structure. However, in the war, with the race policy moving beyond its function of stabilising the system and now pressing for its own realisation, the common man did contribute to bringing about this goal as a soldier or member of the SS. Now in fact wanting to be promoted to the position of 'master', he turned into a criminal and was condemned as such after the war.

94. Staatliches Archivlager Göttingen, Nürnberger Prozessmaterial, NI–6078: Minutes of the 16th session of the trade committee, 11.11.1938.

95. On the sense and nonsense of the concept of totalitarianism see Hildebrand, 'Stufen der Totalitarismus-Forschung', in: *PVS* 9 (1968), pp. 397 ff.

96. See in this connection the concluding remarks.

97. On the interpretation of this document, which has given rise to much historical controversy, cf. primarily E. Zechlin, 'Deutschland zwischen Kabinettskrieg und Wirtschaftskrieg. Politik und Kriegführung in den ersten Monaten des Weltkrieges 1914', in: *HZ* 199 (1964), pp. 347 ff.

98. See V. R. Berghahn, *Der Tirpitz-Plan,* loc. cit.

99. See p. 7 of this work.

100. See the important works by Böhme, *Deutschlands Weg,* loc. cit. and Wehler, *Bismarck,* loc. cit. on the questions which were already becoming vital under Bismarck, concerning the creation of an area of economic expansion in central Europe and overseas expansion.

101. National Archives Washington, T–77, 642; OKW/Ausl. VII, Bericht 2: Lammers an Epp, RM No. 747/39 A, 9.3.1939, reprinted in: Hildebrand, *Vom Reich zum Weltreich,* Doc. 58a.

102. See Salewski, *Seekriegsleitung,* loc. cit.; idem, *Selbstverständnis der Kriegsmarine,* p. 78, and J. Dülffer, Weimar, *Hitler und die Marine,* loc. cit.

103. Cf. the essay by O. Grochler, 'Kolonialforderungen als Teil der faschistischen Kriegszielplanungen', in: *Zeitschrift für Militärgeschichte* 5 (1965), pp. 547 ff.

104. *ADAP*, D, V, No. 119, pp. 127 ff.

105. See Booms, *Ursprung*, pp. 346 ff.

106. *ADAP*, D, IV, No. 391, p. 438 f.

107. *DBFP*, III series, vol. 4, No. 195, pp. 210 ff.

108. Bundesarchiv Koblenz, ZSG 101/12, p. 84, quoted by Booms, *Ursprung*, p. 353.

109. Text of the speech in: M. Freund, *Geschichte des Zweiten Weltkrieges in Dokumenten*, Freiburg/Munich 1953 ff., vol. 2, No. 9, pp. 16 ff.

110. On the controversy cf. Hildebrand, *Vom Reich zum Weltreich*, p. 607 f.

111. G. Niedhart (Mannheim) is preparing a special examination into this. Generally on German–Polish relations in 1939 see Zagorniak, 'Les préparatifs allemands de l'attaque contre la Pologne', in: *Revue d'Histoire de la Deuxième Guerre Mondiale 1970*, and Jedruzczak, 'La Pologne et la genèse de la 2ème guerre mondiale', in: ibid. Also A. M. Cienciala, *Poland and the Western Powers 1938–1939*, London/Toronto, 1968. For a more complete view on the general problem of the outbreak of the Second World War see: L. Mosley, *On Borrowed Time. How World War II Began*, London, 1969.

112. C. J. Burckhardt, *Meine Danziger Mission 1937–1939*, Munich, 1960, p. 241.

113. On von Ribbentrop's (admittedly failed) conception of forging a German–Japanese alliance as a front against Great Britain, and not, as Tokyo wanted it, against the USSR, cf. A. Hillgruber 'Zum Kriegsbeginn im September 1939', in: *Österreichische Militärische Zeitschrift 1969* (H.5), p. 358 f.

114. See Dülffer, Weimar, *Hitler und Marine*, loc. cit.

115. See generally the study of diplomatic history by A. A. Offner, *American Appeasement: United States Foreign Policy and Germany, 1933–1938*, Cambridge/Mass., 1969.

116. *ADAP*, D, I, 423, p. 535.

117. *VB* of 29 April 1939.

118. See also S. Friedländer, *Auftakt zum Untergang, Hitler und die USA*, Stuttgart/Berlin/Cologne/Mainz, 1965, passim.

119. *ADAP*, D, VI, No. 283, p. 297 f.

120. See Gemzell, Raeder, pp. 180 ff. and Salewski, *Selbstverständnis der Kriegsmarine*, p. 78. What seems particularly noteworthy is that according to the reflection of the 2nd Air Fleet, a war against Britain was regarded as hopeless.

121. *ADAP*, D, VI, No. 433, pp. 477 ff.

121a. See also von Ribbentrop's address of 24 January 1939 to generals and admirals on behalf of the Supreme Command, in: Bundesarchiv/Militärarchiv Freiburg, Case 553 PG 33 613. The author thanks Dr J. Dülffer for drawing his attention to this document.

121. See p. 7 and p. 81 of this work.

123. A. S. Milward, *Die deutsche Kriegswirtschaft 1939–1945*, Stuttgart, 1966, esp. pp. 9 ff. and D. Eichholtz, *Geschichte der deutschen Kriegswirtschaft*, vol. 1: 1939–1941, Berlin, 1969.

124. See Niedhart, *Grossbritannien und die Sowjetunion*, pp. 327 ff.

125. On earlier considerations cf. D. N. Lammers, 'Britain, Russia and the Revival of "Entente Diplomacy": 1934' in: *Journal of British Studies*, 6 (1967), pp. 99 ff.

126. See A. Hillgruber, 'Die sowjetische Aussenpolitik 1939–1945', in: *Osteuropa-Handbuch, Sowjetunion: Aussenpolitik*, loc. cit.

127. See p. 73.

128. *ADAP*, D, VI, No. 521, p. 598 f.

129. See also: H. Metzmacher, 'Deutsch–englische Ausgleichsbemühungen im Sommer 1939', in: *VfZg* 14 (1966), pp. 369 ff.

130. Cf. in detail Hildebrand, *Vom Reich zum Weltreich*, pp. 607 ff.

131. Burckhardt, *Danziger Mission*, p. 348.

131a. On the British estimation of the German naval armaments cf. Public Record Office (London), FO 371/23 054, Harrison to Kirkpatrick on 19 June 1939 apropos Raeder's speech on 9 June 1939 in Stuttgart. The author wishes to thank Dr J. Henke for drawing his attention to this document.

132. *ADAP*, D, VII, No. 192, pp. 167 ff. On the question of sources here, see W. Baumgart, 'Zur Ansprache Hitlers vor den Führern der Wehrmacht am 22 August 1939. Eine quellenkritische Untersuchung', in: *Vierteljahrshefte für Zeitgeschichte* 16 (1968), pp. 120 ff.

133. Ibid. On the general problem see also B. A. Carroll, *Design for Total War. Arms and Economics in the Third Reich*, The Hague/ Paris, 1968, and particularly T. W. Mason, introduction to an edition in preparation of economic historical sources of the Third Reich.

134. See Hillgruber, *Sowjetische Aussenpolitik*, loc. cit.

135. See idem, *Kriegsbeginn*, 1939, p. 359.

136. R. Coulondre, *De Staline à Hitler. Souvenirs de deux ambassades 1936–1939*, Paris, 1950, p. 293.

137. See the study by Zieb, *Logistik*, loc. cit.

138. B. Dahlerus, *Der letzte Versuch. London–Berlin Sommer 1939*, Munich, 1948. On the basis of Cabinet papers, D. C. Watt in 'Enter Dahlerus', in: *The Spectator* of 31 January 1970, p. 142 f., proves that the 'last attempt' was not concluded in the summer of 1939 but was continued up until December 1939. See p. 101 of this work also.

139. A fundamental study has not yet been made of Hitler's system of information and on the level of the actual information which he did in fact have.

CHAPTER 5

1. On Clausewitz cf.: H.-U. Wehler, '"Absoluter" und "Totaler" Krieg. Von Clausewitz zu Ludendorff', in: *PVS* 10 (1969), pp. 220 ff.

2. P. Angel, 'Les responsabilités hitlériennes dans le déclenchement de la Deuxième Guerre Mondiale', in: *Revue d'histoire de la Deuxième Guerre Mondiale* 15 (1965), p. 19.

3. See L. Gruchmann, *Der Zweite Weltkrieg, Kriegführung und Politik*, Munich, 1967, pp. 25 ff.

4. Cf. W. Malanowski, op. cit.

5. See also: J. Kimche, *Kriegsende 1939? Der versäumte Angriff aus dem Westen*, Stuttgart, 1969.

6. See: J. R. M. Butler, 'Grundlagen der Strategie Grossbritanniens und Frankreichs 1939', in: A. Hillgruber (ed.), *Probleme des Zweiten Weltkrieges*, Cologne/Berlin, 1967, pp. 41 ff.

7. Cf. L. Thompson, *1940. Year of Legend, Year of History*, London, 1966 and A. M. Nekric, *Vnesnaja politika Anglii 1939–1941* (The Foreign Policy of Britain 1939–1941), Moscow, 1963.

8. Hillgruber, *Strategie*, passim.

9. Idem, *Deutschlands Rolle*, p. 99. Also F. Friedensburg, 'Die sowjetischen Kriegslieferungen an das Hitlerreich', in: *Vierteljahreshefte für Wirtschaftsforschung*, 1962, pp. 331 ff.

10. F. Halder, *Kriegstagebuch. The Daily Notes made by the Chief of the Army General Staff 1939–1942*. Ed. by H. A. Jacobsen, vol. 1, p. 90.

11. *VB* of 7 October 1939.

12. U. von Hassell, *Vom anderen Deutschland. Aus den nachgelassenen Tagebüchern 1938–1944*, Freiburg i. Br., 2nd ed. 1946, p. 87. Entry for 11 October 1939.

13. Notes on the briefings of the Naval High Command to Hitler, 1939–45 (Film des Arbeitskreises für Wehrforschung, Stuttgart), for September and October 1939 and later, passim.

14. On the different concepts of foreign policy in Bismarck's and Wilhelmine Germany, see Hillgruber, *Kontinuität*, and idem, *Deutschlands Rolle* and idem, *Krieg-in-Sicht Krise*, loc. cit.

15. See the study by V. R. Berghahn, *Der Tirpitz-Plan*, loc. cit.

16. Cf. Friedländer, *Auftakt*, passim.

17. *Der Generalquartiermeister, Briefe und Tagebuchaufzeichnungen des Generalquartiermeisters des Heeres, General der Artillerie Eduard Wagner*, ed. E. Wagner, Munich/Vienna, 1963, p. 144 f.

18. Politisches Archiv des Auswärtigen Amtes Bonn, BüroSTS, England, Berlin, for 7 November 1939. SD communication: 'Die Lage in England'. See also ibid. STS No. 916 and appendix.

19. As a temporary summary see K. Hildebrand, 'Der Zweite Weltkrieg: Probleme und Methoden seiner Darstellung', in: *NPL* 1968, pp. 493 ff. In preparation, B. Martin (Freiburg i. Br.), *Friedensinitiativen während des Zweiten Weltkrieges*.

20. Of course, the question of the 'de facto level of information' (Jacobsen) of the Führer really requires a thorough examination. See also p. 90.

21. *Hitlers Weisungen für die Kriegführung 1939–1945. Dokumente des OKW*, ed W. Hubatsch, Frankfurt/M., 1962, p. 40.

22. See (from the Marxist viewpoint) P. Kircheisen, *Die Deutschlandpolitik der Westmächte während des Komischen Krieges*, Diss. Halle–Wittenberg, 1965.

23. B. Martin, *Deutschland und Japan im 2. Weltkrieg. Von Pearl Harbor bis zur deutschen Kapitulation*, Zürich/Frankfurt, 1969, p. 19 f.

24. Ibid.

25. *ADAP*, D, IX, pp. 1 ff.

26. Mussolini's disapproval of the German–Russian pact is clearly evident in a letter of the Duce to the Führer on 3 January 1940: *ADAP*, D, VIII, No. 504, pp. 474 ff.

27. See Gemzell, *Raeder, Hitler und Skandinavien*, loc. cit.

27a. See. H.-D. Loock, *Quisling, Rosenberg und Terboven, Zur Vorgeschichte und Geschichte der nationalsozialistischen Revolution in Norwegen*, Stuttgart, 1970.

28. With the decision in favour of the Atlantic strategy (Wegener) the navy had drawn the consequences from the misfired policy of risk and deciding struggle (Tirpitz). See Gemzell, op. cit., and Berghahn, *Der Tirpitz-Plan*, loc. cit.

29. Cf. Gruchmann, *Der Zweite Weltkrieg*, pp. 57 ff.

30. Halder, *Kriegstagebuch*, vol. 1, p. 308.

31. Cf. Hildebrand, *Vom Reich zum Weltreich*, pp. 624 ff.

32. Situational briefings by the Naval High Command of 21 May 1940.

33. *ADAP*, D, IX, No. 354, pp. 390 ff.: 'Aufzeichnung des Gesandten und Ministerialdirigenten Clodius' of 30 May 1940; ibid. no. 367, pp. 407 ff.: 'Aufzeichnung des Botschafters Ritter' of 1 June 1940.

34. See in detail Fischer, *Griff*, pp. 469 ff., pp. 627 ff. and pp. 791 ff. who—admittedly one-sidedly—stresses precisely the basic agreement of both imperialist strategies.

35. In this connection see the essay of I. Fetscher, 'Die Industrielle Gesellschaft und die Ideologie der Nationalsozialisten', in: *Gesellschaft, Staat, Erziehung* 7 (1962), pp. 6 ff.

36. For all the contrasts between the old and new élites, the conservative ruling groups and the SS, what cannot be overlooked, of course, is that an inter-penetration on both sides had already taken place. See E. Neusüss-Hunkel, *Die SS*, Hannover/Frankfurt/M., 1956. Cf. also A. Schickel, 'Wehrmacht und SS. Eine Untersuchung über ihre Stellung und Rolle in den Planungen der nationalsozialistischen Führer', in: *Wehrwissenschaftliche Rundschau* 9 (1969), pp. 241 ff.

37. See now R. A. Divine, *Roosevelt and World War II*, Baltimore, 1969, and primarily J. M. Burns, *Roosevelt. The Soldier of Freedom 1940–1945*, New York, 1970.

38. See G. Moltmann, 'Die Genesis der Unconditional-Surrender-Forderung', in: *Probleme des Zweiten Weltkrieges*, ed. A. Hillgruber, Cologne/Berlin 1967, p. 171. On the other hand, it would merit a careful study to throw light on the response of American politicians and representatives of the economy to Hitler's suggestions about dividing up the world (above all in the winter 1939/40). In this connection the mission approved by Roosevelt and undertaken by James D. Mooney (General Motors) seems interesting. See W. Link, who is about to edit Mooney's memoranda and notes.

39. On 'Operation Sea Lion' see: K. Klee, *Das Unternehmen Seelöwe. Die geplante deutsche Landung in England. Ein Beitrag zum Verhältnis zwischen Politik und Kriegführung im Sommer und Herbst des Jahres 1940*, Göttingen, 1958, and also the assessment by Hillgruber of Hitler's invasion 'intentions', *Strategie*, pp. 166 ff. See also Loock, *Quisling*, p. 200, which stresses Hitler's fear that 'Operation Sea Lion' might 'provoke a premature and undesired intervention into the war by the United States'.

40. Nolte, *Faschismus*, p. 436. For a critical view see: G. v. Roon, 'Holland in Not', a review of the book by K. Kwiet, *Reichskommissariat Niederlande. Versuche und Scheitern nationalsozialistischer*

Neuordnung. Stuttgart, 1968, appearing in: *Die Zeit* of 5 December 1969, p. 31.

41. See Hildebrand, *Hitlers Kolonialismus,* loc. cit.

42. See Hillgruber, *Endlösung und Ostimperium,* loc. cit.

43. Cf. Böhme, *Der deutsch-französische Waffenstillstand im Zweiten Weltkrieg* (Part I), Stuttgart, 1966, p. 42 f.

44. See E. Jäckel, *Frankreich in Hitlers Europa,* pp. 32 ff. and passim.

45. 'The Führer's Secretary: The Führer's Diary' (30.1.1934–30.6.1943). Collection of particulars from old notebooks (typescript 1015—Appendix 5, Safe 5.5, in: Library of Congress, Washington, entry on p. 60.

46. Hauptarchiv Berlin–Dahlem, Heinrich-Schnee-Archiv III, 25, Fasc. 97, 'v. Ri. und Rosenberg', pp. 27 ff.

47. On the relationship between the economy–society–state complex and war strategy see the documentation by Eichholtz/Schumann, *Anatomie des Krieges,* and the essay by D. Petzina, 'La politique financière et fiscale de l'Allemagne pendant la seconde guerre mondiale', in: *Revue d'Histoire de la Deuxième Guerre Mondiale* 1969, No. 76, pp. 1 ff.

48. *ADAP,* D, X, No. 101, pp. 92 ff.

49. See Nolte, *Faschismus,* p. 407.

50. See Hillgruber, *Endlösung und Ostimperium,* loc. cit.

51. Situational briefing of the Naval High Command of 1 July 1940. App. 3: Memorandum of the Naval leadership of 6 July 1940.

52. See W. Link, *Amerikanische Stabilisierungspolitik,* p. 9, where he interprets the 'guidelines for German policy towards Britain' of September 1940, which differed sharply from Foreign Minister Simon's.

53. On these ideas see Martin, *Deutschland und Japan,* eg. p. 68.

54. Cf. Hillgruber, *Strategie,* pp. 146 ff. and p. 515.

55. This is explained by B. Martin in the work he is preparing on the peace attempts made during the Second World War.

56. Hillgruber, *Strategie,* pp. 79 ff.

57. Halder, *Kriegstagebuch,* vol. 2, p. 21 (13.7.1940).

58. In Britain in 1940 the possibilities were considered both of supporting Russia against a possible attack by Hitler and also of preventing the possible intensification of the alliance between the two dictators by means of a British intervention in the Soviet Union. See Hillgruber, *Deutschlands Rolle*, p. 112.

59. This is particularly evident in Hitler's considerations on 31 July 1940. Cf. Hillgruber, *Strategie*, pp. 218 ff.

60. If is not possible at this point to discuss the historical dispute over when Hitler finally made the decision to attack Russia. See the comprehensive account in Hillgruber, *Strategie*, passim, esp. pp. 207 ff. and 351 ff.

61. Ibid., pp. 352 ff.

62. Ibid., pp. 205f., 292 ff. and 297 ff.

63. Staatliches Archivlager Göttingen, NG 361: Bormann to Lammer on 2 November 1940.

64. Cf. *ADAP*, D, XI, 1, No. 325, pp. 448 ff.; No. 326, pp. 445 ff.; No. 328, pp. 462 ff.; No. 329, pp. 472 ff.; also No. 309, pp. 428 ff.

65. Hillgruber, *Strategie*, pp. 351 ff.

66. D. Lampe, *The Last Ditch*, London, 1968.

67. On 'Operation Sea Lion' and the Battle of Britain and their significance within the policy and strategy of the Third Reich in 1940 see Hillgruber's account in *Strategie*, esp. pp. 166 ff.

68. Hillgruber, *Strategie*, p. 357.

69. Idem, *Deutschlands Rolle*, p. 111.

70. Ibid.

CHAPTER 6

1. See Hillgruber, *Strategie*, pp. 316 ff. The following thoughts and assessment are fundamentally in line with the results of this habilitation paper.

2. Idem, *Der Faktor Amerika*, loc. cit.

3. Cf. pp. 113 ff.

4. See Hildebrand, *Vom Reich zum Weltreich*, pp. 700 ff. Cf. also the announcement made on 20 November 1941 by von Epp, Colonial Minister designate, who in terms of the priority given to the Russian war drew the attention of those groups in the German economy interested in colonial business to the business possibilities in the USSR. See Document 78 in Hildebrand, *Vom Reich zum Weltreich*.

5. See Martin, *Deutschland und Japan,* loc. cit. In this case it was Hitler himself who drew the attention of those businessmen interested in Far Eastern business to the possibilities offered in Russia, which seemed to him quite inexhaustible. See Martin, op. cit., p. 167.

6. Besides the well-known (mis-) judgment of the Generals and Hitler on the resistance potential of the Soviet Union—a view also shared by the American General Staff up to December 1941—compare in this connection the statement made by Hitler after his Paris visit on 23 June 1940 and recorded in Speer's memoirs: in comparison with the victory over France it seemed to Hitler at the time that 'a campaign against Russia was child's play'. See Speer, *Erinnerungen*, p. 188.

7. Cf. p. 116. For the Reich this was also true of the economic capacity. Only when Speer took over the organisation of the war economy and with the 'liberal' period in economic policy which he initiated, did production figures for commodities necessary for the war increase substantially. See also G. Janssen, *Das Ministerium Speer. Deutschlands Rüstung im Krieg,* Berlin/Frankfurt/M./Vienna, 1968, and: *Deutschlands Rüstung im Zweiten Weltkrieg, Hitler's Konferenzen mit Albert Speer 1942 bis 1945,* ed. and introduced by W. A. Boelcke, Frankfurt/M., 1969.

8. In the politics of the 1930s, the 'Jewish Question' might possibly have served Hitler as a 'pawn' in dealings with the Western powers. Cf. the appraisal of D. C. Watt, 'Pirow's Mission in November 1938, "Free Hand" for Hitler and Relief for the Jews', in : *Wiener Library Bulletin* XII (1958), p. 53. The fact that the Führer apparently never tried using this 'lever' may perhaps indicate the relevance of anti-semitism precisely as an integral component in his Programme.

9. See p. 77 f. above.

10. As an 'exception' in this connection see the book by H. Bley, *Kolonialherrschaft und Sozialstruktur in Deutsch-Südwestafrika*

1894–1914, Hamburg, 1968, who sees in the campaign of extermination waged against the Hereros a link with Hitler's policy of genocide.

11. But it must nevertheless not be overlooked that a relatively large number of members of the 'old' ruling classes were to be found in the SS. See Neusüss-Hunkel, *SS,* loc. cit. The real 'novelty' must lie therefore in the 'biological revolution' which was not just simply propagated, but actually planned for and partially initiated.

12. See the concluding remarks in this work as well as the analysis in Hillgruber, *Kontinuität,* p. 7.

13. On the domestic integrating function of foreign political strategies cf. H.-U. Wehler, *Bismarck,* esp. ch. 6 and also Sauer, *Nationalstaat,* loc. cit.; J. C. G. Röhl, *Germany without Bismarck,* passim; V. R. Berghahn, *Deutsche Rüstungspolitik,* esp. the concluding remarks, and Fischer, *Krieg der Illusionen,* pp. 34 ff. A study of the period of the Weimar Republic from this point of view remains to be done.

14. On this notion see H. Arendt, *Elemente und Ursprünge totaler Herrschaft,* Frankfurt/M., 1955, p. 296.

15. Even the military system of the time of Frederick the Great ought also to be analysed from this point of view. Preparatory work on this has been done by O. Büsch. *Militärsystem und Sozialleben im alten Preussen 1713–1807. Die Anfänge der sozialen Militarisierung der preussisch–deutschen Gesellschaft,* Berlin, 1962. The chief question in such a study would have to be: How far did domestic and socio-political limitations prejudice the development of a rationally calculated power policy, or: How far are domestic and socio-political prerequisites responsible for the creation of an expansionist and aggressive foreign policy?

16. Hildebrand, *Vom Reich zum Weltreich,* p. 701, where Hitler's statements of 9.1.41 are discussed.

17. According to a message reaching Berlin via Madrid it even said that Under Secretary of State Butler fostered a great admiration in his heart for the Führer: *DGFP,* Ser. D, vol. 12, No. 104 (28.2.41).

18. Hitler, *Mein Kampf,* pp. 689 ff.

19. OKW: *Kriegstagebuch des Oberkommandos der Wehrmacht (Wehrmachtführungsstab),* ed. P. E. Schramm in collaboration with

A. Hillgruber, W. Hubatsch, and H.-A. Jacobsen, Frankfurt/M., 1961, vol. 1, p. 328.

20. Hillgruber/Hümmelchen, *Chronik*, p. 27.

21. On the problem of Hitler's Mediterranean strategy see basically A. Hillgruber, 'Politik und Strategie im Mittelmeerraum', in the collection of papers delivered at the International Historians' Colloquium on the war in the Mediterranean 1939–45 held in Paris (8–11 April 1969): (French language), Paris, 1970.

22. Hubatsch, *Weisungen*, No. 32, pp. 129 ff. Cf. also Besymenski, *Barbarossa*, pp. 284 ff. and 287 ff. as well as I. Kircheisen, 'Afghanistan–umkämpftes Vorfeld Indiens', in: J. Glasneck/I. Kircheisen, *Türkei und Afghanistan–Brennpunkte der Orientpolitik im Zweiten Weltkrieg*, Berlin, 1968, pp. 159 ff.

23. K. Klee, 'Der Entwurf zur Führer–Weisung No. 32 vom 11.6.1941. Eine quellenkritische Untersuchung', in: *Wehrwissenschaftliche Rundschau 6* (1956), pp. 127 ff. In particular cases reference was made, moreover, to this directive. So it was regarded as valid.

24. See also J. Leasor, *Botschafter ohne Auftrag. Der Englandflug Rudolf Hess*, Oldenburg, 1962.

25. See H.-A. Jacobsen, *Die Zweite Weltkrieg, Grundzüge der Politik und Strategie in Dokumenten*, Frankfurt/M./Hamburg, 1965, p. 110. See specially idem, 'Kommissarbefehl und Massenexekution sowjetischer Kriegsgefangener', in: H. Buchheim/M. Broszat/H.-A. Jacobsen/H. Krausnick, *Anatomie des SS-Staates*, vol. 2, Freiburg i. Br., 1965, pp. 163 ff.

26. On this agreement of social forces (the armed forces) with Hitler's policy cf. the account by Messerschmidt (*Wehrmacht*, pp. 306 ff.) which is in contrast with Dallin's thesis (*Besatzungspolitik*, loc. cit.), on 'Operation Barbarossa'.

27. In the war plans of the First World War there was already a difference in the envisaged treatment to be applied to the subjugated populations in West and Eastern Europe respectively. See Fischer, *Griff*, p. 55.

28. See the informative Kwiet, *Reichskommissariat Niederlande*, pp. 92 ff. and pp. 152 ff.

29. Hildebrand, *Hitlers Kolonialismus*, loc. cit.

30. In this connection cf. Fetscher, *Industrielle Gesellschaft und Ideologie der Nationalsozialisten*, loc. cit., and W. Sörgel, *Metallindustrie und Nationalsozialismus*, Frankfurt/M., 1966, pp. 5 ff.

30a. Cf. also H. Pfahlmann, *Fremdarbeiter und Kriegsgefangene in der deutschen Kriegswirtschaft 1939–1945*, Darmstadt, 1968.

31. Transcribed and reprinted in A. Hillgruber (ed.), *Staatsmänner und Diplomaten bei Hitler. Vertauliche Aufzeichnungen über die Unterredungen mit Vertretern des Auslandes 1939–1941*, dtv. editn, Munich 1969, p. 301, also appears in: idem, Staatsmänner und Diplomaten, vol. 2; 1942–1944, Frankfurt/M., 1970, pp. 541 ff.

32. See Martin, *Deutschland und Japan*, passim. Also Hillgruber, 'Japan und der "Fall Barbarossa" ', in: *Wehrwissenschaftliche Rundschau 18* (1968), pp. 312 ff.

33. Martin, op. cit. passim.

34. Hitler's assessment of the USA during the years 1928–33, that is from the impression given of a superpower of great economic strength (Dawes and Young Plans) to the collapse during the world economic crisis, ought to be carefully examined—as A. Hillgruber has suggested.

35. Hillgruber, *Staatsmänner*, pp. 304 ff.

36. On Ante Pavelić's state see: L. Hory/M. Broszat, *Der kroatische Ustascha-Staat 1941–1945*, Stuttgart, 1964. But see also the critical review by G. Hering, 'Zur Geschichte des Südslawischen Faschismus', in: *Österreichische Osthefte* 7 (1965), pp. 425 ff.

37. See Hillgruber, *Endlösung und Ostimperium*, loc. cit.

38. Cf. H. Krausnick, in: M. Broszat/H.-A. Jacobsen/H. Krausnick, *Anatomie des Staates*, Olten and Freiburg i. Br., 1965, vol. 2, pp. 391 ff.

39. See: E. Hesse, *Der sowjetrussische Partisanenkrieg 1941 bis 1944 im Spiegel deutscher Kampfanweisungen und Befehle*, Göttingen/Zürich/Frankfurt, 1969.

40. In 1914–18 already the ideological and totalitarian development was decisively responsible for the fact that the war could come to no peace settlement such as had occurred in the (Cabinet) wars of the preceding centuries in European political history.

41. This impression becomes particularly evident when one reads in the memoirs of Marshal Zhukov about the insufficient preparedness of the Red Army and the (rational) miscalculation on the part of Stalin over Hitler's attack on the USSR. See G. Zhukov, *Erinnerungen und Gedanken*, Stuttgart, 1969.

42. Cf. for a historical perspective: F. Fischer, 'Kontinuität des Irrtums. Zum Problem der deutschen Kriegszielpolitik im Ersten Weltkrieg', in: *HZ* 191 (1960), pp. 87 ff.

43. See Hillgruber, *Strategie*, p. 552 f.

44. From among the great number of works mention might be made of: R. Wohlstetter, *Pearl Harbor. Signale und Entscheidungen*, Erlenbach–Zürich/Stuttgart, 1966. See generally also the essay by J. M. d'Hoop, 'Les Etats-Unis et la crise du Pacifique (décembre 1941/ avril-mai 1942)', in: *Revue d'Histoire de la Deuxième Guerre Mondiale*, 1969, No. 74, pp. 67 ff.

45. Martin, *Deutschland und Japan*, p. 35 is able to refute the thesis hitherto regarded as valid concerning the alleged surprise effect which the Japan attack had on the Reich.

46. This explanation seems more appropriate to the way Hitler was thinking in the years 1940–42 than the ingenious idea of Sebastian Haffner (*Der Stern* of 19.10.1969, pp. 103 ff.), that Hitler had consciously drawn America into the war in December 1941 in order to march against the USSR together with the Western Powers. This idea certainly preoccupied Hitler towards the end of the war. But of the present time it can hardly be verified, though bearing in mind Hitler's 'deviousness' it cannot simply be dismissed out of hand.

47. Martin, *Deutschland und Japan*, p. 105.

48. In January 1942—the daring plan of 14 July 1941 of attacking the USA together with Japan had long since been given up—Hitler expressed to the Japanese Ambassador, Oshima, the view that he did not yet know 'how the USA could be beaten': See H.-A. Jacobsen, *1939–45. Der Zweite Weltkrieg in Chronik und Dokumenten*, Darmstadt, 5th ed., 1961, p. 290.

49. Martin, *Deutschland und Japan* passim.

50. On Germany's India policy in the Second World War see G. Selter, *Zur Indienpolitik der faschistischen deutschen Regierung wäh-*

rend des Zweiten Weltkrieges, Phil. Diss., Leipzig, 1965, and the admittedly somewhat unsatisfying work by R. Schnabel, *Tiger und Schakal, Deutsche Indienpolitik 1941–43*, Vienna, 1968. On this theme see the work in preparation by Milan Hauner (Cambridge), *Indien in der Konzeption der Achsenmächte 1940–1942* (working title).

51. Hassel, *Tagebücher*, p. 253. Entry for 22.3.1942.

52. Roosevelt had consistently sought conflict with Japan and Germany. Indeed, even in the 1930s, in view of the policies of Roosevelt and American policy towards Germany, which was determined in no small way by economic interests, there can hardly be any talk of an 'American appeasement' as Offner, *Appeasement*, loc. cit., maintains. Cf. also the study by H.-J. Schröder.

53. On the American policy towards Germany in the Second World War cf. G. Moltmann, *Amerikas Deutschlandpolitik im Zweiten Weltkrieg, Kriegs- und Friedensziele 1941–1945*, Heidelberg, 1958.

54. See K. R. Greenfield, 'Die acht Hauptentscheidungen der amerikanischen Strategie im Zweiten Weltkrieg', in Hillgruber (ed.), *Probleme*, p. 272.

55. Martin, *Deutschland und Japan*, pp. 110 ff.

56. H. Heiber, 'Der Generalplan Ost', in: *VfZg* 6 (1958), pp. 281 ff.; the complete text reprinted in S. Madajcyk, 'Generalplan Ost', in: *Polish Western Affairs*, vol. III/2, 1962, pp. 391 ff. The attempt was made to realise the plan only relatively slowly, so that the resettlement operations proceeded gradually.

56a. See G. Eisenblätter, *Grundlinien der Politik des Reiches gegenüber dem Generalgouvernment 1939–1945*, Diss. phil., Frankfurt/M., 1969, pp. 205 ff., where it is proved that the 'General Plan for the East' had already been presented to Himmler on 15 July 1941. Hence it originated in the month of 'triumph' in the East; see pp. 113 f. of this work.

57. Hildebrand, *Vom Reich zum Weltreich*, p. 720 f.

58. See p. 115 above.

59. Besides Martin, *Friedensinitiativen*, loc. cit., cf. also P. Kleist, *Zwischen Hitler und Stalin. Aufzeichnungen*, Bonn, 1950.

60. A. Hillgruber, *Staatsmänner und Diplomaten*, vol. II, loc. cit., p. 12 f.

61. See Jäckel, *Frankreich in Hitler's Europa*, pp. 234 ff.

62. Hillgruber/Hümmelchen, *Chronik*, p. 81.

63. See above, note 43.

64. D. Bonhoeffer, *Gesammelte Schriften*, vol. 1 (ed. E. Bethge), Munich, 1958, pp. 488 ff.

65. See H.-A. Jacobsen, 'Zur Schlacht von Stalingrad', in: Hillgruber (ed.), *Probleme*, pp. 145 ff.

66. Cf. for example the 'Gedanken zur Friedensordnung'. 'Memorandum to the Secretary of State, Foreign Office, with the request that it be checked as to whether it is suitable to be delivered to the Führer' (November 1941). The probable writer of this memo, Albrecht Haushofer, develops ideas about a negotiated peace—not without scepticism as to the possible success. Bundesarchiv Koblenz, Nachlass Haushofer, HC 833.

CHAPTER 7

1. Cf. Hillgruber, *Kontinuität*, p. 16.

2. This point is emphasised in contrast to Joachim Fest's analysis, which lays the accent primarily on the power political motif: J. Fest, Foreword in: *Adolf Hitler. Gesichter eines Diktators,* ed. J. von Lang, Hamburg, 1968. On this aspect see also K. Hildebrand, 'Hitlers *Mein Kampf:* Propaganda oder Programm des Führers', in: *NPL*, 1969, pp. 79 ff.

3. See p. 105 above.

4. On the problem of 'coalition strategy' in the history of Prussia–Germany and Modern Europe see the essay by A. Hillgruber, 'Formveränderung in der Koalitionskriegführung in der Epoche 1792/1815 —ein Aufriss', in: *Geschichte in Wissenschaft und Unterricht*, 1966, pp. 265 ff., and idem, 'Der Einbau der verbündeten Armeen in die deutsche Ostfront 1941–1944', in: *Wehrwissenschaftliche Rundschau* 1960, pp. 659 ff.

5. Cf. K. Hildebrand, *Vom Reich zum Weltreich*, pp. 713 ff.

6. See generally: K. Dönitz, 'Die Schlacht im Atlantik in der deutschen Strategie', in: Hillgruber (ed.), *Probleme*, pp. 159 ff.

7. Gruchmann, *Der Zweite Weltkrieg*, p. 281.

8. See primarily: Hillgruber, *Sowjetische Aussenpolitik 1939–1945*, loc. cit.

9. See p. 108 f. and pp. 135 ff. above.

10. Only two statements made by Hitler in the years 1932 and 1939 seem to recognise at all the connection between foreign policy and society. Not least of all because of his anti-middle-class resentment, Hitler had certainly never consciously wanted to put foreign policy to the service of the existing social order. That he nevertheless did in fact do this should have become apparent in the course of this present study.

11. On this problem cf. the work still in preparation by Bernd Martin, *Friedensinitiativen*.

12. See p. 98 above.

13. On 27 January 1943, Gauleiter Sauckel, the 'Plenipotentiary-General for Manpower', issued a decree ordering the complete deployment of labour in pursuit of total war. On 18 February 1943, in a speech made at the Berlin Olympic Stadium, Goebbels announced 'total war'. On 11 February 1943 the call-up of schoolchildren of 16 years of age for the German Air Force was begun.

14. See generally A. Hillgruber, *Hitler, König Carol und Marschall Antonescu. Die deutsch-rumänischen Beziehungen 1938–1944*, Wiesbaden, 2nd ed., 1965.

15. Cf. also Martin, *Deutschland und Japan*, p. 177.

16. Gruchmann, *Der Zweite Weltkrieg*, p. 350, and esp. Hillgruber, *Sowjetische Aussenpolitik 1939–1945*, loc. cit.

17. Gruchmann, *Der Zweite Weltkrieg*, p. 346.

18. On the Russian–German peace attempts cf. K.-H. Minuth, 'Sowjetisch-deutsche Friedensfühler 1943', in: *Geschichte in Wissenschaft und Unterricht* 16 (1965), pp. 38 ff.; on von Ribbentrop's peace initiatives which could only begin practically in February 1945, see R. Hansen, 'Ribbentrops Friedensfühler im Frühjahr 1945', in: ibid. 18 (1967), pp. 716 ff.

19. See Gruchmann, *Der Zweite Weltkrieg*, p. 237.

19a. The losses suffered by German industry only became relevant, however, in the latter half of 1944.

20. Cf. Th. Schieder, 'Die Vertreibung der Deutschen aus dem Osten als wissenschaftliches Problem', in: Hillgruber (ed.), *Probleme*, pp. 379 ff.

21. See H. von Krannhals, *Der Warschauer Aufstand 1944*, Frankfurt/M., 1964, 2nd ed.

22. Cf. E. Klink, *Das Gesetz des Handelns. Die Operation 'Zitadelle'*, Stuttgart, 1966.

23. See generally F. W. Deakin, *Die brutale Freundschaft. Hitler, Mussolini und der Untergang des italienischen Faschismus*, Cologne/Berlin, 1964.

24. See Jacobsen, *Der Zweite Weltkrieg*, p. 205.

25. A. Hillgruber/G. Hümmelchen, *Chronik des Zweiten Weltkrieges*, Frankfurt/M., 1966, p. 97.

26. See now A. Speer, *Erinnerungen*, and e.g. J.-J. Jäger, *Die wirtschaftliche Abhängigkeit des Dritten Reiches vom Ausland—dargestellt am Beispiel der Stahlindustrie*, Berlin, 1969.

27. Svetlana Alliluyeva, *Only One Year*, London, 1969. Cf. basically Hillgruber, *Sowjetische Aussenpolitik 1939–1945*, loc. cit.

28. See J. Schröder, *Italiens Kriegsaustritt 1943. Die deutschen Gegenmassnahmen im italienischen Raum*, Göttingen, 1969.

29. Hubatsch, *Weisungen*, pp. 233 ff.

30. See also H. Höhne, *Der Orden unter dem Totenkopf. Die Geschichte der SS*, Gütersloh, 1967, pp. 499 ff.

31. Martin, *Deutschland und Japan*, p. 106.

32. The study in preparation by Martin, *Friedensinitiativen*, will offer some very informative results on this.

33. V. R. Berghahn, 'NSDAP und "Geistige Führung" der Wehrmacht 1939 bis 1943', in: *VfZg* 17 (1969), esp. pp. 51 ff.

34. Messerschmidt, *Wehrmacht*, p. 451.

35. See P. Hoffmann, *Widerstand, Staatsstreich, Attentat*, Munich, 1969, p. 223.

36. Cf. generally M. Mourin, *Le drame des états satellites de l'Axe de 1939 à 1945*, Paris 1957 and specifically E. Schmid-Richberg, *Der Endkampf auf dem Balkan*, Heidelberg, 1955.

37. J. Hilberg, *The Destruction of the European Jews*, Chicago (2nd ed.), 1967.

38. Martin, *Deutschland und Japan*, p. 189.

39. Ibid., p. 191.

40. See generally H. Feis, *Churchill, Roosevelt, Stalin. The War They Waged and the Peace They Sought*, Princeton, 1957, pp. 283 ff.

41. Hillgruber/Hümmelchen, *Chronik*, p. 115.

42. In a certain sense there was already a second front in Italy of course from September 1943.

43. On the partisan war in Russia cf. E. M. Howell, *The Soviet Partisan Movement 1941–1944*, Washington, 1956.

44. Cf. Gruchmann, *Zweiter Weltkrieg*, p. 254 ff.

45. Cf. Martin, *Deutschland und Japan*, p. 196.

46. See Jung, *Die Ardennenoffensive 1944–45*, Göttingen/Frankfurt/Zürich, 1969.

47. See Gruchmann, *Der Zweite Weltkrieg*, p. 417 f. See also Martin, *Friedensinitiativen*, where this initative is analysed more thoroughly than it has been hitherto, on the basis of newly discovered material.

48. On the conference diplomacy of the Allies in the Second World War, see Feis, *Churchill, Roosevelt, Stalin*, loc. cit.

49. Hillgruber, *Sowjetische Aussenpolitik 1939–1945*, loc. cit.

50. Cf. Höhne, *Orden*, p. 485.

51. Hillgruber/Hümmelchen, *Chronik*, p. 148.

52. See Speer, *Erinnerungen*; cf. also W. Boelcke, 'A. Hitlers Befehle zur Zerstörung oder Lähmung des deutschen Industriepotentials 1944/45' in: *Tradition*, Dec. 1968.

53. On this question see Höhne, *Orden*, pp. 528 ff. and Gruchmann, *Der Zweite Weltkrieg*, p. 444.

54. Compton, *Hitler und die USA*, p. 232.

Notes

55 Cf. Höhne, *Orden*, p. 532.

56. See generally the study by R. Hansen, *Das Ende des Dritten Reiches. Die deutsche Kapitulation 1945*, Stuttgart, 1966.

57. Cf. G. Alperovitz, *Atomare Diplomatie—Hiroshima und Potsdam*, Munich, 1966 and F. B. Misse, 'Le rôle des Etats-Unis dans les conférences de Malte et Yalta', in: *Revue d'Histoire de la Deuxieme Guerre Mondiale* 1969, No 75, pp. 41 ff.

58. See also A. Baring, *Aussenpolitik in Adenauers Kanzlerdemokratie*, Munich, 1969.

CONCLUSION

1. This is demonstrated in the study by Jacobsen, *Nationalsozialistische Aussenpolitik*, a work which not only has a complete command over the present state of historical research but also is an excellent documentation of material.

2. See Wehler, *Bismarck*, passim, esp. ch. 6; Sauer, *Nationalstaat*, loc. cit.

3. In contrast to Wehler, we would not regard Bismarck's foreign policy as determined all that exclusively by the 'primacy of domestic policy', for 'first of all after 1871, settling internal conflicts by means of decisions in foreign policy was no longer a way out' (M. Stürmer, 'Bismarcks konservative Revolution', in: idem, *Das kaiserliche Deutschland. Politik und Gesellschaft 1870–1918*, Düsseldorf, 1970). The essentially power political system of confrontation of the Great Powers—always related of course to the internal preconditions in the state—creates its own sphere of play for foreign policy, which can be understood (and represented) as *one* aspect of the historical reality, a balanced explanation of the 'whole reality' then being attempted with the necessary inclusion of factors of domestic politics too. On this methodological procedure cf. Hillgruber, *Kontinuität*, p. 5 f., and idem, *Gedanken zu einer politischen Geschichte*, loc. cit.

4. Wehler, *Bismarck*, passim, esp. ch. 6; and also Stürmer, *Konservative Revolution*, loc. cit., and idem, 'Staatsstreichgedanken im Bismarckreich', in: *HZ* 209 (1969), pp. 566 ff.

5. H. Rothfels, *Bismarck und der Staat*, Darmstadt, 3rd editn, 1958, p. 331.

6. On the role of the land-owning classes in Prussia–Germany see primarily the account by H. Rosenberg,' Die Pseudodemokratisierung der Rittergutsbesitzerklasse', in: *Probleme der deutschen Sozialgeschichte*, Frankfurt/M., 1969, pp. 7 ff.

7. See H. Rosenberg, *Grosse Depression*, loc. cit., on the problem of unequal development.

8. This process of the Crown and the middle classes coming together in the face of presumed or actual threats from the proletarian class is valid for the whole of European social and political history. It was already to be observed in Britain in the 17th century and was repeated in France and Germany in the 18th and 19th centuries. Cf. the remarks by W. Link in 'Die aussenpolitische Rolle des Parlaments und das Konzept der kombinierten auswärtigen Gewalt', a paper read at the Wissenschaftliche Kongress 1969 of the Deutschen Vereinigung für Politische Wissenschaft, on 'Probleme der Demokratie heute', MS, pp. 9 ff.

9. See the habilitation paper in preparation by K. Rohe (Münster) on the efforts made in Britain in the latter half of the 19th century to integrate the working class into the state in pursuit of the new imperialism.

10. See note 3, above, as well as the account in Berghahn, *Flottenbau unter Wilhelm II*, which demonstrates that in devising his risk strategy Tirptiz was apparently intending both aims—the primary goal of foreign policy and the functional one in domestic politics.

11. On the propaganda methods of the Bismarck period, important in this connection, cf. the work by E. Naujoks, *Bismarcks auswärtige Pressepolitik und die Reichsgründung (1865–1871)*, Wiesbaden, 1968.

12. H. Gollwitzer, 'Der Cäsarismus Napoleons III im Widerhall der öffentlichen Meinung Deutschlands', *HZ* 173 (1952), p. 65 f.

13. Berghahn, *Der Tirpitz-Plan*, loc. cit.

14. Afterwards, during the 'Bülow era', the social policy was suspended in the expectation that the now completed fleet would solve the social problem by means of the economic successes confidently

awaited. See Berghahn, *Der Tirpitz-Plan*, loc. cit. on this. The policy of arms build-up and the speculation on future profits which was related to it were supposed to be the answers to social questions—a tendency which was also an integral feature of Hitler's war economy. The difference, however, lay in the fact that the Bülow–Tirpitz imperialism was not so inevitably aimed at war, as was the case for Hitler (personally) and for his régime.

15. Stürmer, *Konservative Revolution*, loc. cit.

16. Cf. the essay, written from the Marxist viewpoint, by W. Gutsche, 'Bethmann Hollweg und die Politik der "Neuorientierung". Zur innenpolitischen Strategie und Taktik der deutschen Reichsregierung während des Ersten Weltkrieges', in: *Zeitschrift für Geschichtswissenschaft* 13 (1965), pp. 209 ff.

17. On the early history of anti-semitism, see the leading work by P. W. Massing, *Vorgeschichte des politischen Antisemitismus*, Frankfurt/M., 1959. In this connection the study by E. Zechlin, *Die deutsche Politik und die Juden im Ersten Weltkrieg* (in collaboration with H. J. Bieber), Göttingen, 1969, is also of interest.

18. Terms such as the 'political Right' and the 'conservatives' have been used—of necessity within the framework of this investigation—in a rather abbreviated and sweeping way. They naturally require more careful definition and differentiation; for the period of the Weimar Republic they have been analysed in detail with reference to the Deutschnationale Volkspartei in the study by M. Stürmer, *Koalition und Opposition in der Weimarer Republik 1924–1928*, Düsseldorf, 1967.

19. This version of the 'stab in the back' legend was already being aired in the First World War: Zechlin, *Juden im Ersten Weltkrieg*.

20. See Hildebrand, *Vom Reich zum Weltreich*, pp. 392 ff.

21. See also the essay by E. Krippendorf, 'Ist Aussenpolitik Aussenpolitik?', in: *PVS* 4 (1963), pp. 243 ff.

22. Cf. in this connection the reflections of H. Heffter, 'Vom Primat der Aussenpolitik', in: *HZ* 171 (1951), pp. 1 ff., and Hildebrand, *Vom Reich zum Weltreich*, p. 266, note 64.

23. See fundamentally E. Kehr, *Der Primat der Innenpolitik*.

Gesammelte Aufsätze zur preussisch-deutschen Sozialgeschichte im 19. und 20. Jahrhundert, ed. and introduced H.-U. Wehler, Berlin, 1965.

24. See Krippendorf, op. cit. The search for a 'unity', an 'identity' in the course of a phased (and violent) solution to the problems first on the home front and then in foreign policy, is reflected for example in the famous quotation made by Wilhelm II in 1905 'under the re-lit Christmas-tree': 'First shoot down the Socialists, de-capitate them and render them harmless—if necessary by a blood-bath—and then war abroad. But not first and not at the same time'. B. v. Bülow, *Denkwürdigkeiten,* ed. F. von Stockhammern, vol. 2, Berlin, 1930, p. 198. From this point of view see the statements made by Hitler on 3 February 1933 to his generals: *Vogelsang, Dokumentation,* p. 434 f.

25. Cf. Fischer, *Griff,* pp. 425 ff.

26. We would reject the central thesis of the work by Ludwig Dehio (*Deutschland und die Weltpolitik im 20. Jahrhundert,* Frankfurt/M., 1961), where he talks of the Wilhelmine power policy in the World War being free of an ideology and therefore ineffectual (!). Rather we would draw attention to the fact that it was precisely the ideology of the German society—obsolete and incongruent to the power policy being practised—that contributed decisively to the fact that the rationally calculated political policy could not come into operation. It was not the lack of an ideology but on the contrary the primacy of dogma which was the decisive factor in the history of Prussia–Germany.

27. See the research discussions on the problem of the annexation of Alsace and Lorraine; clearly it was not merely political deliberation but also the emotional feelings of public opinion which determined the solution to the problems: on the controversy (between Lipgens, Gall, Buchner, Becker, Gall and Kolb) cf. the summary by L. Gall, 'Das Problem Elsass-Lothringen', in: *Reichsgründung 1870/71,* ed. Th. Schieder and E. Deuerlein, Stuttgart, 1970, pp. 366 ff. esp. p. 367, note 4.

28. See J. C. G. Röhl, 'Higher Civil Servants in Germany, 1890–1900', in: *Journal of Contemporary History,* vol. 2, No. 3, July 1967.

29. See Röhl, *Germany without Bismarck,* passim.

30. The saying familiar to the Western democracies that war is far too important a thing to be left to soldiers just did not have any validity

in Prussia–Germany. While in the West the parliamentarian system (and its ideology) influenced war strategy beneficially in effect, in Prussia–Germany the cabinet system (and the ideology belonging to it) hindered the development of political calculation. On the considerable difficulties, even for Bismarck in 1870/71, of safeguarding a 'primacy of policy' over ideology, cf. E. Kolb, 'Kriegführung und Politik 1870/71', in: Schieder/Deuerlein, *Reichsgründung,* pp. 95 ff.

31. Cf. for example the protocols: *Von Bassermann zu Stresemann. Die Sitzungen des nationalliberalen Zentralvorstandes 1912–1917,* ed. K.-P. Reiss, Düsseldorf, 1967.

32. See H. Rosenberg, *Die Pseudodemokratisierung.*

33. On this process see the classic study by R. H. Tawney, 'The Rise of the Gentry 1558–1640', in *Essays in Economic History,* ed. E. M. Carus-Wilson, London, 1966, vol. 1, pp. 173 ff. A bibliography on the 'controversy over the gentry' can be found in J. Hexter, 'Storm over the Gentry' in his *Reappraisals in History,* 1961, pp. 117 ff.

34. Stretching a long way into Prussian history it would be worthwhile to investigate whether the preservation of privileges at home gave rise to measures in foreign policy or whether the Prussian militarism as a system did in fact spring from foreign threats—whether genuine or thought to be so. See K. Hildebrand, 'Die Suche nach dem "wahren" Preussen', in: *PVS* 1970.

35. Impressive examples for this are offered in the study by H.-J. Puhle, *Agrarische Interessenpolitik und preussischer Konservativismus im wilhelminischen Reich (1893–1914). Ein Beitrag zur Analyse des Nationalismus in Deutschland am Beispiel des Bundes der Landwirte und der Deutsch-Konservativen,* Hannover, 1966, and P.-C. Witt, *Die Finanzpolitik des Deutschen Reiches,* 1903–1913, Lübeck/Hamburg, 1970.

36. See K. Hildebrand, *Bethmann Hollweg—der Kanzler ohne Eigenschaften? Urteile des Geschichtsschreibung. Eine kritische Bibliographie.* Düsseldorf, 2nd editn, 1970.

37. See p. 9 above.

38. See on this Stresemann's speech before the 'Arbeitsgemeinschaft deutscher Landsmannschaften' in Greater Berlin on 14 December 1925, in: *Akten zur deutschen auswärtigen Politik 1918–1945,* series B:

1925–1933, vol. 1, 1 December 1925 to July 1926, Göttingen, 1966, pp. 727 ff. Cf. also Hillgruber, *Kontinuität,* p. 18.

39. A thorough study of the Vaterlandspartei still remains to be undertaken. The work by K. Wortmann, *Die Geschichte der Deutschen Vaterlandspartei* 1917/1918, Diss. Halle, 1926, hardly tackles the problems raised here satisfactorily. In this connection cf. the reflections of K. Löwith, Max Weber and Carl Schmitt, in the *Frankfurter Allgemeine Zeitung* of 27.6.1964.

40. See in detail Stürmer, *Staatsstreichgedanken.*

41. See H. Pogge-von Strandmann, 'Staatsstreichpläne, Alldeutsche und Bethmann Hollweg', in: H. Pogge-von Strandmann/I. Geiss, *Die Erforderlichkeit des Unmöglichen. Deutschland am Vorabend des Ersten Weltkrieges,* Frankfurt, 1965.

42. See Barghahn, *Der Tirpitz-Plan,* loc. cit.

43. See also Fischer, *Krieg der Illusionen,* esp. pp. 62 ff.

44. See H.-U. Wehler, 'Sozialökonomie und Geschichtswissenschaft', in: *NPL* 1969, p. 356.

45. Böhme, *Deutschlands Weg,* p. 574. In the summer of 1878 the Liberals from Baden felt Bismarck's domestic course to be 'complete autocracy' and the 'dictatorship of the Reich Chancellor', while in Berlin on the other hand they called for the 'man of iron'... diary entry of the Baroness von Spitzemberg, quoted by Stürmer, *Konservative Revolution,* p. 16.

46. Cf. F. L. Carsten, *Reichswehr und Politik 1918–1933,* Cologne/Berlin, 1964, p. 25, and Meier-Welcker, *Seeckt,* p. 200, and Hillgruber, *Kontinuität,* p. 17.

47. See p. 20 above.

48. M. Boveri in a review of P. Hoffman, *Widerstand, Staatsstreich, Attentat,* Munich, 1969, in: *Der Spiegel* of 20.10.1969, p. 199.

Index

Index

Index